INTELLIGENCE ISN'T ENOUGH

Carice Anderson

Intelligence Isn't Enough

A Black Professional's Guide to Thriving in the Workplace

Jonathan Ball Publishers
Johannesburg • Cape Town • London

All rights reserved.
No part of this publication may be reproduced or transmitted,
in any form or by any means, without prior permission
from the publisher or copyright holder.

© Text Carice Elizabeth Anderson 2021
© Published edition 2021 Jonathan Ball Publishers

Published in South Africa in 2021 by
JONATHAN BALL PUBLISHERS
A division of Media24 (Pty) Ltd
PO Box 33977
Jeppestown
2043

ISBN 978-1-77619-078-2
ebook ISBN 978-1-77619-079-9

*Every effort has been made to trace the copyright holders and to obtain
their permission for the use of copyright material. The publishers apologise
for any errors or omissions and would be grateful to be notified of any corrections
that should be incorporated in future editions of this book.*

www.jonathanball.co.za
www.twitter.com/JonathanBallPub
www.facebook.com/JonathanBallPublishers

Author photograph on cover by Kevin O'Reilly
Cover by Michiel Botha
Design and typesetting by Nazli Jacobs
Set in Nimrod

To my parents, grandparents
and all those who came before them.

To London,
may these lessons make your path
to impact much smoother.

Contents

Preface   9

Chapter 1
A whole new world   15

Chapter 2
Get your mind right   51

Chapter 3
People matter   108

Chapter 4
Developing your cultural intelligence   160

Chapter 5
Building your personal brand   186

Chapter 6
Communication is key   216

Conclusion
Organising you for impact   259

Acknowledgements   273
Sources   276
Index   280

Preface

I graduated from university in 1998 and started my first full-time job only a few months later. After about a year, I came to hate that job so much that I distinctly remember hoping to get into a car accident so that I wouldn't have to go to work. I didn't want to die; I just wanted to break my right arm so that I couldn't write or type.

What I really needed was a break. I just needed my work frustration to stop, and in my desperate 23-year-old mind, this was the best solution. I could have taken a day off but that seemed too temporary. I felt helpless and probably a bit hopeless too. I didn't have the tools to diagnose my situation, let alone to fix it. All I knew was that I was miserable. I felt stuck.

Now, as I look back on 20 years of work experience, there were so many things I could have done differently. The power to change my perspective and my situation was in my hands, but I just didn't know it at the time. My goal in writing this book is to impart to you what I've learnt so that you never have to feel the way I did. If I'm too late and you're already feeling that way, I want to help you identify all the useful items in your toolbox that might help you to see your situation differently and ultimately to turn it around.

I was the first person in my family to major in business and the first to work in a corporate space. I come from a family of educators, social workers and ministers, so nobody in my close circle could advise me on what to expect or how to succeed in this new world. Back then, the internet wasn't what it is now, so I could not lean on the web to fill in the gaps. To be honest, even if I had had access to the internet, I would not have known to use it to navigate this unfamiliar territory. I did not know what I did not know, so I didn't even know what questions to ask. Admittedly, I have made many, many mistakes out of pure ignorance, coupled with a dash of youthful arrogance. Because I had the right undergraduate degree (and eventually the right master's degree), I thought I had everything I needed to succeed.

Fast-forward 13 years: in 2012, I started working at McKinsey & Company, an American management consulting firm. I joined their Johannesburg office as a Professional Development Manager (PDM). McKinsey is the oldest, biggest and most influential management consulting firm in the world, with over $10 billion in annual revenues, 127 offices and 27 000 employees around the world. As a PDM, I was responsible for staffing Black consultants on client engagements, for coaching, for giving feedback to consultants and for organising annual and midterm review meetings with leadership.

For the first time in my career I heard both sides of the story – what consultants thought the expectation was versus what leadership actually expected. I realised that there was a huge gap between the two. I suddenly understood that many Black consultants were just as clueless as I had been in 1998. With the internet and all the other resources now available, I expected the new generation to be savvier and more hip to the game. But they weren't. Many of them had no idea about the world they had stepped into. Like me, they did not know what they did not know.

I do not want the next generation to suffer the way I did. In this book, I want to share with you what I've learnt over the course of my career in the USA and South Africa, across the public and private sectors. I share the insights I gained during my years at Harvard Business School (I was privileged enough to obtain an MBA from Harvard, one of the best universities in the world), as well as what I've learnt while working for some of the best-known brands in the world, which include McKinsey and Deloitte. I impart lessons from my work as a Leadership Development Facilitator for Google, McKinsey, Bain & Company and the Allan Gray Orbis

Preface

Foundation. My network includes some of the brightest Black leaders in the world, who have been educated in, and worked across, North America, Europe and Africa, and I offer their advice, experiences and perspectives as well as my own. Not everyone will have the opportunity to work in these environments, but I believe everyone should be exposed to the valuable lessons we've learnt – and the mistakes we've made – in these spaces. Our world, our organisations, our relationships and ultimately our ability to have an impact on our world will be the better for it.

Historically, Black people have been marginalised in certain parts of the world. 'Marginalised' is defined as the state of being 'excluded from or existing outside the mainstream of society, a group, or a school of thought'. For Black people, this implies that there are things we do not know or have not been exposed to. Even if you grew up in a place where Black people weren't marginalised, it is highly unlikely that you, as a young Black person, are a fourth- or fifth-generation corporate employee.

From a professional development standpoint, the impact of the historical and global marginalisation of Black people has to be acknowledged. As Black people, we have to acknowledge that not every instance of poor performance can be blamed on racism or bias on the part of our colleagues. We need to admit that we might not know certain things and that a lack of knowledge affects our performance and our relationships at work.

I can just imagine how much more prepared I would have been, or how different my family's dinner-table conversations would have been, had my grandfather been an employee or partner at Goldman Sachs. But he wasn't. He worked in a steel mill for 41 years. This lack of exposure definitely contributes to Black people's unfamiliarity with corporate environments. It does not mean that Black people cannot succeed in those areas, but it does mean that we have a lot of catching up to do.

Most universities and colleges do not adequately prepare young people to navigate corporate spaces. Many articles and books have been written about crafting the perfect CV, and many more tell you how to prepare for an interview and what to do if you want to get your dream job. However, very few – if any – have been written for Black professionals who are just starting out in their careers and are the first members of their family to have a white-collar, professional job. Even fewer provide those readers with the essential information they need to know and the important questions they need to ask as they figure out what works best in their environments.

Every organisation is different, so career advice cannot be a one-size-fits-all exercise. However, the sooner you understand the environment upon your arrival, the better you can do and the more fun you can have. If you ask certain key questions, half the battle has been won. In this book, I aim to provide young Black professionals with a number of critical questions to ask and to research. I also offer some commonly shared coaching tips while shining a light on a number of issues that do not garner enough attention.

Many of my Black professional friends sit around and lament the younger generation's lack of readiness. Many Gen Xers or baby boomers are frustrated with millennials, complaining that they are impatient and want opportunities they haven't earned and aren't ready for. We, the older generation, tell you that you have to wait, but we never explain what you should be doing while you wait, how to succeed in your current role or how best to prepare for that next career move.

After having run a leadership development programme at McKinsey and coached millennials on an individual basis, I believe I'm a millennial kindred spirit. Sometimes I even feel like a misplaced millennial, born in the wrong generation. When I look back at the mentality I had in my twenties, I can relate to a lot of millennial angst and frustration, because I felt the same way. (For instance, people often questioned my decision to hop from one job to the next when I didn't feel happy or fulfilled.) I believe I can be a bridge between generations. If we sit down to listen to each other and refrain from labelling, we can have productive conversations and fruitful relationships.

Preface

As a PDM at McKinsey, I coached people on professional and interpersonal challenges in the workplace. I helped them figure out how to get the feedback they needed, how to decode it and how to create an action plan to turn things around. But, because most companies don't have PDMs, you'll have to play this role for yourself.

I want millennials and Generation Z to have a more efficient trajectory in their careers. I want you to make new mistakes – not the same old ones I made more than 20 years ago. I want to help close the gap between the expectations of leaders and those of their employees, and to help educate younger generations. Most of all, I want to see young Black talent rise to the highest positions in corporate America, corporate Africa and corporate Europe. We need talented Black people to be represented, to lead and excel in every sector – in public and corporate spaces, in government and as entrepreneurs. I see many talented young Black people opting out of, or failing in, corporate environments because they're frustrated, not knowing how to succeed. My hope is that I can play a key role in helping you succeed and thrive in the career you've chosen. I will show you that ascending in your career is not just about being intellectually gifted or having the right qualifications and degrees.

While some people are meant to be amazing employees, others might choose a career as an entrepreneur. However, succeeding at work is important, even if you ultimately choose a career outside a corporate environment. Corporate work experience can be very valuable in terms of improving your professionalism, communication and strategic thinking skills. I ran a small business for several years and my experience as a corporate employee definitely helped me create a better customer service experience.

Once you've left a large corporation or started your own business, your former colleagues will be a part of your professional network. This is the group of people that you can lean on to help you solve problems and bounce ideas off. I want you to start off on the right foot. In this book, I'll show you how to use the skills you've learnt in whatever work environment you find yourself – whether you're running a successful business or being a great employee at any other organisation.

Chapter 1
A whole new world

So, let's start with the good news. You successfully completed university or a master's programme and did well enough for you to have been hired as a full-time employee. You skilfully navigated an arduous multiple-round interview process and landed a wonderful role in an amazing company. Getting a job is like qualifying to run a marathon. You have been admitted, your number has just been pinned to your chest but you still have to run the race. You have not done anything yet. The real work starts now.

Here's the bad news: in my experience, only 30 per cent of your success can be attributed to your education and hard skills, which have been influenced and shaped by your intelligence quotient (IQ). You've probably spent the last 20 years focusing on these. The remaining 70 per cent of your success is based on your ability to understand and manage yourself and work well with others – qualities that most of you have probably never worked on. Bestselling author and emotional intelligence expert Daniel Goleman takes this argument one step further. He believes that emotional intelligence accounts for 80 to 90 per cent of the differentiating skills that contribute to success. Your efforts in school, university or college have been focused on mastering certain topics, and you've probably spent most of your academic career working as an individual contributor. You didn't have to play nicely with the other kids in the class, and while you might have been on some challenging (read: horrific) group projects, you only had to spend a finite amount of time with your teammates. You may even have had the luxury of choosing your group. At work, you do not have that luxury. Although you might move from one group to another, you can neither control who you work with nor who your manager will be. To put it bluntly: until you are moved to another team or work for another company, work is one endless group project.

The 70-20-10 guidelines for learning how to be an effective leader were developed by the Center for Creative Leadership after more than 30 years of research. They are especially useful for thinking through your career and performance at work. According to these guidelines, 10 per cent of your learning comes from training, 20 per cent from other people (such as mentors, coaches, sponsors and managers), while a whopping 70 per cent comes from challenging on-the-job assignments and experiences. If you're fresh out of university or college and you've just started out on your career, your learning has come solely from classroom training. You haven't had the opportunity to build relationships with the individuals you will learn from, nor have you had key job experiences and assignments. These two elements, which you lack at this point, will eventually make up the bulk of the learning which you will need to be a leader in your workplace.

Remember, work is not like school. I know this may sound obvious, but it needs to be said. (I wish someone had said it to me when I first started working, or even ten years ago!) Even though I consciously knew I was starting my career, the switch did not flip that I was now in a different environment with different rules and that my approach would also have to change. The system worked, and I worked it, so if it ain't broke, why fix it? As usual, I resolved to put my head down, work hard and put in long hours. I would be disciplined. That was pretty much the extent of my plan.

Let's spell out a few differences between work and university. At university, having a great relationship with a professor is not a requirement for getting good grades. I never built any relationships with my professors and I still graduated with honours in the top 25 per cent of my class. You got the syllabus for the course. The professor told you when the exams were scheduled (unless they got you with the sneaky pop quiz from time to time). You knew what percentage of your final grade was made up of the final exam versus other components of the course. You knew that if you attended lectures, took notes, studied sufficiently and performed well on the test and/or delivered a high-quality paper, you would get a good grade. That was the formula. You knew that if you did your part, you would be successful.

Well, I quickly learnt that that ain't work. In the workplace, you get no credit for showing up. And tests don't come at scheduled times: they come every day, some of them big, some of them small. You are graded and evaluated continuously. Sometimes it's clear what you are being tested on, but sometimes it's not. And, unlike school, university or college, you can't just drop your job like you would a class or lecture. Now you have financial obligations such as rent, car payments, food, insurance and utilities that you have to pay, and those bills keep coming every month. In addition, depending on your manager or the company culture, you may or may not be told what the rules are, what success looks like or how to achieve it.

When you join a corporation, it will be up to you to figure out what questions you need to ask and who to build relationships with. So what will best equip you to build the most effective relationships? What can you do to excel in those challenging job assignments and experiences that will constitute the bulk of your learning? And what do you need to know about your working environment for you to maximise those relationships and experiences?

It stands to reason that some people maximise these relationships, experiences and assignments better than others. What are the factors that make the difference?

Working *in* versus working *on* your career

Entrepreneurs often talk about the difference between working *in* their business and working *on* their business. Working *in* your business is about serving your customers and delivering whatever goods and/or services you sell. Working *on* your business, however, is about taking a step back and thinking strategically about how you spend your time and resources. It entails questioning your strategy and asking yourself whether you are serving the right customers and building important relationships.

Let's use a cupcake company as an example. Working *in* your business is about buying the flour, eggs, sugar and other ingredients to make the cupcakes. It's about making the cupcakes, delivering them and collecting the money. Working *on* your business is asking yourself whether you are selling the right mix of cupcakes to the right people at the right price. It's about questioning whether your marketing efforts are reaching your ideal customers.

As I reflected on these questions over the years, I realised that you can look at your career in the same way. Working *in* your career is about working hard and doing your job well every day, which is critical. Working *on* your career, however, is about thinking through the enablers – relationships, opportunities, feedback, coaching, personal branding – that are critical to your success and advancement at work. It's about examining whether you are spending your time on the most critical activities that will set you up to make an impact in your field.

> "The biggest difficulty is accepting that you can't do everything and that achievement isn't necessarily about how many things you do, but about doing the most strategic things with a lot of impact. You need to be clear about your purpose. What is going to bring you closer to achieving your goals?" – *Obenewa Amponsah, former Executive Director, Africa Office, Harvard University Center for African Studies, and former CEO, Steve Biko Foundation*

Look at the table on the opposite page. The answers to the questions on the left will help you do well in the moment. The answers to the questions on the right will help you advance and build a career.

A whole new world

Working *In* vs Working *On* Your Career

Working *in* your career reflection topics	Working *on* your career reflection topics
What is expected of me on this project?	Am I aware of what is expected of me for my role and tenure? Am I meeting those expectations?
How am I performing on my current project?	Am I progressing at the expected pace?
How technically strong am I?	Am I getting exposure to the right kinds of opportunities that will help me build my skills and advance?
Do I have the right resources to perform these tasks? If not, what else do I need?	Am I focused on building the right skills that will take me to the next level?
When is the deadline for this project?	What are the themes I've identified from my feedback?
What feedback am I getting/have I received on this project?	Do I have a mentor? How should I engage this person(s)?
What roadblocks am I running into?	Do I have a sponsor? How should I engage this person(s)?
What are my areas of strength?	What is the quality of my relationships?
What are my areas of development?	Am I building relationships with the right people?
How can I leverage my strengths to address my areas of development?	What is the gap between my desired and actual brand? What can I do to close the gap?
	How do I communicate about myself in this environment?
	What could I learn from the journeys of other successful people in the organisation?
	Whart are the situations that best leverage my strengths?
	How often will my manager and I meet to discuss my career goals, progress and next steps to close gaps between current and desired state?

We all know that we must put in the time, but I want to encourage you to ask yourself: how am I spending my time? Am I clear about all the areas that are most important and am I spending enough time on each one? Am I sacrificing the important for the urgent? Am I saying 'no' to the wrong activities and 'yes' to the right activities? Am I forming the right relationships at the right levels at the right time?

The Pareto Principle says that 80 per cent of your impact at work comes from 20 per cent of your efforts. Your job as a junior employee is to figure out what that 20 per cent is. Most of us have spent more time working *in* our careers than working *on* our careers because we didn't understand our working environments and what it takes to be successful in those spaces. There are many elements of our work environments that we cannot control. Focusing on these reinforces a victim mindset and makes us feel powerless. However, focusing on what you *can* control is empowering and reinforces the idea that you do have significant opportunities to shape your experience.

Victim vs Victor mindset

VICTIM	VICTOR
Why is this happening to me?	Why is this happening for me? What lessons can I learn from this situation?
I have no control. There is nothing I can do.	I can't control everything but I will focus on what I can control and influence.
I am here because others sabotaged me.	I will reflect on the role I played in getting here and what I could have done differently. I will make the necessary changes going forward.
My destiny was predetermined.	I can make choices that shape the direction of my life.
It's not my fault.	I take responsibility and ownership.
I focus on the past.	I focus on the future.
I make excuses.	I explore options and I make a way.

Making important choices

When I started university, a lot of people told me what I should study. I got talked out of studying psychology and voice, and everyone urged me to major in business so that I could make a decent living with an undergraduate degree. So I decided to major in business, and around my second year, I had to pick a specific major in business. I remember looking at a piece of paper that listed all the major options for the undergraduate business school. *Accounting?* No. *Finance?* No. *Economics?* No. *Health Care Management?* No. *Management?* Sounded too generic – no. *Marketing?* That sounded cool. As long as it took me to read the options was as much time as I spent picking my major. I did not research any of them nor the possible careers I could pursue with each major.

During my third year, I took a sales class and on one occasion the professor said: 'If you're a marketing major, 90 per cent of you will have to go into sales.' I had a very negative connotation around the term 'sales', and in an instant I was discouraged from exploring the work opportunities linked to my major. I took the word of this professor at face value because I respected his authority as an adult. That was a mistake. When I was growing up, I was taught to respect authority. I believed that adults were all-knowing, so I trusted their advice, usually without question. Adults don't always know what they're talking about. When it comes to your career, always question what they tell you. Do the research yourself. Get multiple opinions and compare them to your own personal goals and values. Don't depend on misinformed, albeit well-meaning, adults to give you guidance about your life and career, because they often operate from what they know, which might be (and probably is) less than what you would think.

Your life and your career are not like picking the wrong class. As a working professional, your choices matter. Also, keep in mind that your next employer will ask you about your career choices to this point. Be prepared to answer questions such as: 'Why did you choose this job?' 'Why did you choose to leave?' 'What skills or knowledge did you gain?' 'What did you learn about yourself and others?' 'And why do you want to go from that job to this one?' 'What is the connection between the two?' 'What is your path going forward?'

Besides having to answer these questions, sometimes your decisions can pigeonhole you. When I left my first full-time job, I was only approached for similar jobs. It was frustrating, because that job was not what I wanted to do but it was on my CV, so recruiters were drawn to it. Unlike me, you now have social media and the internet, which was only in its infancy when I was at university. Today, young people have a lot more ways to learn about what is available and how to go about getting there. Question your assumptions and the options you *think* are in front of you. Ask yourself: am I missing anything? Am I limiting myself? Am I basing my list of options on what people around me have said or done? What else could there be?

I spent several years running away from jobs that I did not enjoy and that didn't energise me. Every time, my next job would be pretty much the same. I finally realised that if you decide to run *away* from something, make sure you also run *towards* something. If not, you'll end up right back in the same position.

What work is really about

As you begin your career, it's important to understand what work is about and the expansive purpose of this experience. If you don't understand the entirety of the experience, you will most likely be frustrated and blindsided by your lack of awareness. We're often told that work is all about working hard and delivering excellent results, but it is also about so much more. Work is *really* about learning and managing who you are and what is important to you, building and maintaining relationships with others despite the many differences that exist, and figuring out and navigating the organisational culture – all while working hard and delivering excellent results.

As you can see, there is much more involved than what you were told or taught. So the better you know yourself, the better you can try to position yourself for success through your choices about what to do, where to do it and who to do it with. And the better you understand others, the better your relationships and teams will be, and the more fun and impact you will ultimately have at work. When you start out, work can be very challenging because there is a lot to juggle, much of which you have not been prepared for. While you are figuring out yourself and others, you are also still expected to deliver high-quality work. This explains why you need to be thoughtful, strategic and deliberate about how you spend your time and energy.

Balance out your training

We have all been to the gym and seen that guy who has tremendous muscle mass in his arms, chest, back and shoulders but, sadly, toothpicks for legs. This is because he chose to only focus on his upper body. When parts of your body are underdeveloped, those parts are weak, which puts you at risk of injury. Your body will never reach its full potential unless you address the weaker, underdeveloped areas. If you have just started out on your career, you are like that guy at the gym. You have certain parts that are underdeveloped and you are out of balance, which puts you at risk. You could easily weaken your career and fail to reach your full potential in the corporate space.

Just like there are major muscle groups in the body (such as arms, legs and core), there are major muscle groups in your corporate career that you want to assess, exercise and build. They are *knowing yourself, knowing others* and *knowing your environment*.

Just like you prepare your mind and body before you start exercising, you need to do the same with this journey. Chapter 1 lays the foundation and provides important truths and perspectives to cultivate the right conditions for maximum impact. *Knowing yourself* involves investigating your mindset and understanding your emotions (discussed in Chapter 2). *Knowing others* focuses on how you build and sustain important relationships in the workplace (discussed in Chapter 3), based on your emotional intelligence (emotional quotient, or EQ). *Knowing your environment* delves deeply into analysing your organisation's culture (discussed in Chapter 4). The next step is for you to combine the knowledge from Chapters 1–4 to craft an authentic personal brand (discussed in Chapter 5) and communication style (discussed in Chapter 6) that help you maximise your impact.

Maximising Your Impact

Knowing your Environment
Understand organisational culture, client/customer and brand

Knowing Others
Understand others' responsibilities, working styles, strengths and areas for development

Maximum impact

Knowing Self
Understand one's mindset, strengths, triggers, and brand

People matter

> "Everything that you're going to accomplish is going to be in collaboration with others." – *Timothy Maurice Webster, author and host of* The Brain & Brand Show *podcast and CNBCAfrica's* Inside her C-Suite

People probably told you that you were going to do great things once you graduated and started your career. They probably said that the world would lay down for you and that you should work hard. What they probably didn't tell you was that you would have to work hard and be excellent *with*, *through* and *for* other people. Excellence does not happen in isolation. Every business is a people business: you work with and for people to provide a service to other people. If you can look at your work through that lens, you'll notice that your focus, approach and priorities will change.

It's important to remember that people have feelings and emotions; they are irrational, illogical, insecure and fragile. Often, people make decisions based on instinct, not data. People are wounded, they can get hurt and they have unexamined triggers that set them off unexpectedly and prompt them to behave badly. People can also be lazy thinkers. They have unconscious biases and can make snap decisions based on those. People bring all their insecurities to work with them. To achieve excellent results, you must work through these insecurities.

But here's the other side: you are exactly the same. You are not a robot, and you too have feelings and triggers, and can be irrational. So you have to navigate other people's craziness as well as your own while trying to deliver great results at work. Even though it's not easy, you will need to learn how to successfully navigate all these realities so that you can operate at an optimum level.

When I started my first job, I saw my manager as I would a professor at university or college. I thought that my manager was going to grade my work and that I didn't need to have a relationship with her, because I didn't have a relationship with my teachers or professors. But imagine the following scenario: a friend of yours, Thandi, is working for you. One day, she turns in a substandard document; you notice that her work is below average. Would you judge her solely on the quality of her work? Of course not. Instead, you would say to yourself: *I know Thandi. I'm sure she tried her best even though it is not what I expected. I like her so much that I'm going to invest time to coach her on this work. I'm going to give her feedback so she can know exactly how to make it better.* If, however, you did not know Thandi as a person, you could only judge her by her work. The truth is, you'll probably judge her more harshly than someone you know well. You may also not have the desire to coach and mentor her, because you have no personal connection with her.

If your manager is not invested in you as a person, she will be less likely to invest in your growth and development. She may be less thoughtful about how she delivers feedback to you, perhaps even telling you that your work needs to improve and that you need to figure it out for yourself. Consequently, you might not do as well because your manager is not fully supporting and coaching you with constructive feedback. Thandi is the same person in each scenario, with the same level of intelligence, but the difference is in the amount and quality of investment from her manager. Remember that a key factor affecting a manager's investment in you, and ultimately how well you do at work, is the quality of your relationship.

Your *why*

Your *why* is your big-picture reason for choosing to work in a certain role at a specific company. There is a reason you chose to work for a particular company in a particular role at a particular time

A whole new world

in your career. Perhaps you wanted to have a certain experience, wanted to be exposed to a new place, product or business, work with certain leaders or develop a specific skill set. And later, once you've started working, your *why* might even be achieving a certain performance rating. Your *why* is therefore not just the reason you chose a specific company, but also what you want to accomplish during your tenure in a specific role.

Understanding your *why* is critical if you want to make peace with the sacrifices you will eventually have to make to achieve your goals. If you know what your *why* is, you can understand why you may need to work long nights – and sometimes weekends – to reread that report or work out the kinks in your presentation or Excel document so that it is ready for your manager on Monday. It might mean attending a team dinner to get to know your colleagues and bond with leadership when you really want to relax at home. When you sacrifice some of your free time, your time with friends and family or your time pursuing hobbies, you are moving closer to your goals.

Looking at your sacrifices through the lens of your *why* gives them meaning and purpose. Throughout my career, I have often seen how people without a *why* become resentful, angry and bitter because they don't understand why they are making sacrifices. Their sacrifices feel empty, serving no clear purpose. They feel as if they are forced to give up what matters to them. Contrast this to someone who freely makes hard decisions: she knows that short-term sacrifices will benefit her in the long run.

A few years ago, I was coaching a young female entrepreneur who wanted to increase her brand visibility. She was extremely knowledgeable about her products, as she had been intimately involved in their research and development. However, she made it clear that she had no desire to be the face of the brand in the marketing efforts. I was baffled. After some probing, she told me that she had been sexually assaulted multiple times as a young person and felt that being the face of this brand would make her vulnerable and a target. She wasn't sure if she could survive another trauma.

I asked her to take a step back and tell me *why* she started her business. She said she grew up seeing many women who were stuck in abusive relationships because they did not have the economic means to leave. She wanted to create an opportunity that could empower women, giving them the means to be financially independent. I asked her how important this mission was to her. She said it was very important. 'Is it important enough to put aside your fears and be the face of this business?' I asked her. She paused for a moment. 'Yes,' she said. Her fear did not disappear right away but she kept coming back to her *why* when the fear crept back up.

Your *why* helps you put aside your fears and deal with the minor (and major) annoyances that you will face in any job. You won't let those fears, inconveniences or annoyances get in the way of your larger mission. Without a bigger purpose, it's very easy to let those negative factors make you abandon your job or business.

> I have vision and I think long-term. It doesn't matter how long it takes me to reach it. I don't care. I'll spend the rest of my life working, learning, making mistakes, failing. I am a visionary. I can see where my life's going and I'm patient. Fierce focus on one thing will get you very far." – *Zimasa Qolohle Mabuse, head of Legal and Compliance, Yalu SA, and founder of The Corporate Canvas*

The idea of following your passion or purpose can be daunting, especially if you don't know what yours is. If you're unsure, follow the topics, challenges, problems or opportunities that you are most curious about, or that get you the most riled up. Spend time visualising *what* you want your life to be, and don't worry too much about the *how*. You'll get there. Some of you may have made an off-the-beaten-path choice, so be prepared that some of the people who love you might not understand or support your decision. For Phuti Mahanyele, the CEO of Naspers South Africa and former CEO of Shanduka Group, her decision to join an unknown company called Shanduka Group – instead of accepting an offer from Standard Bank – was something that her family didn't understand. Her father thought she was crazy. 'Sometimes you will make decisions that only make sense to you,' she says. As much as the people around us want the best for us, the vision that you have for your life is yours, placed inside you. Others may not get it, and that's okay. If it doesn't work out, then you at least you know you're living your life on your terms.

Something to keep in mind as you identify your *why* is whether you are serving a bigger purpose. This is what anchors and guides you. When we read about leaders who abuse their power, misappropriate funds or fall into corruption, it's clear that the purpose of their leadership is to serve themselves or those close to them and not others outside their immediate circle. Is there an issue or group of people that you want to stand up for? Once you figure that out, go and do it. You can begin by making a choice or a move now that will eventually allow you to achieve that goal. Can you imagine what the world would be like if we all stood up for something we believed in? Something that energised us and made the world a better place?

When it comes to your career, spend time reflecting and determining what your *why* is, and be open to the idea that it may change over time as you evolve. What is important to you now may not be important to you once you are married, have children, are a caregiver for your elderly parents or have other priorities. Revisit your *why* on a monthly or quarterly basis to remind yourself of your ultimate goal for now, and update it as you gain more clarity on what really matters to you. Make sure to align your daily tasks, assignments and interactions with your goals. From my experience, success is not only found in those big, important, life-changing moments or achievements. Success is the culmination of the daily, hourly and even minute-by-minute choices we make. Those choices are how we close the gap between where we are now and where we want to be.

If you struggle to identify your *why* because you have such varied interests, you're not alone. I struggled at first because I was passionate about leadership development and natural hair care for Black women and girls. I could not figure out how these two areas were even remotely connected. My friend Donna Rachelson, a personal branding expert, put the pieces together and helped me understand that my *why* is empowerment, which is all about helping others be stronger and more confident in who they are. My *why* might manifest in different forms, but empowerment is the overarching theme, and it's the reason why I wrote this book.

> You have to seize opportunities. I don't like change but I'm willing to do things that make sense even if they are really different. I can imagine people don't understand why you would leave a certain job or decide to move to a new city. But you do it because you think that's where the opportunity is. Being one of the people who is willing to follow through on an opportunity is a powerful thing." – *Dr Jennifer Madden, Dean, Linfield University School of Business, Oregon, USA*

Working on your master plan

> What differentiates good performance from great performance is always wanting and getting more out of yourself, and not getting complacent when things are going well. You cannot settle for 'good enough'." – *Ronald Tamale, former Managing Director, head of Africa Private Equity, Standard Chartered Bank*

A whole new world

So what is your plan? Who do you want to be at work? Imagine it is your first day on the job. You've come through onboarding and now it's time to start working. What is your goal? Do you want to do just enough to not get fired? Do you want to be average? Above average? Or distinctive? When I started my first corporate job, unfortunately I had no plan. I had no goal and no professional expectations. I expected to do well. But here is the difference between expectations and goals: an expectation is something you are anticipating will happen, and it involves feeling assured that that event will occur, while a goal is the end towards which your efforts are directed. If you have a goal, you have an action plan to make that goal happen.

As a junior employee, I had expectations but no goals. I made assumptions, not plans. My personal goal was to make enough money so that I could be independent and come and go as I pleased. (In short, not living with my parents. I love you, Mom and Dad!) I was focused on myself and what I was expecting to get out of the deal. I didn't know that I needed to fit my goals into the company's goals – not the other way around. I showed up and assumed that I would do well, because I had always done well at school and university. I didn't see being average, below average or even a complete failure as options because I had never been any of those things before.

What it takes to be successful at work is very different from what it takes to be successful at school. In a corporate environment, you have to be intentional about your performance because success does not just happen. While there are general principles for professional success, you have to understand how those principles apply to your specific environment. This requires investigating, listening, analysing, planning, acting, reflecting and adjusting.

> "I get upset or irritated when young people say to me, 'Yeah, I wanted this interview but it was not that interesting.' It's not about how interesting it is to you. You are here to bring value. You should always think about what value you can bring to a company, not what they can do for you." – *Jocelyne Muhutu-Remy, Strategic Media Partnerships Manager, Facebook, Africa*

Your definition of success

It's important to know what success looks like for you. Your own definition of success will serve as a personal, internal metric that, in turn, will help you decide what you are working towards. Just like your *why*, re-evaluate your definition of success on a quarterly or semi-annual basis (or whatever interval suits you). Is success a financial goal? Is success being able to provide a certain lifestyle for yourself and/or your family? Is it a certain amount of freedom? Is it having a family and a successful relationship? Is it achieving a certain title or level of responsibility at work? Is it working in a certain type or size of company? Is it working in a certain industry? Or is it a combination of these? What are your values and how best can you honour these while being successful?

When it comes to your definition of success, also be prepared for it to evolve over time. What success means to one person is not the same for another. Success is not a one-size-fits-all. And what matters to you now may not matter as much in five or ten years. The more specific you can be about what success looks like to you, the easier it is to eliminate options or explore alternatives that give you more of what is important to you. This clarity also helps you figure out the path to that success. People may not always agree with your definition. They may have a different dream for you, but what is most important is that you achieve the dream you have for yourself.

A whole new world

> "It is about being really clear about what you're looking for in that space. Be clear about goals and objectives; be clear about what success is for you. Have two or three critical make-or-break things that you really feel will be the hallmark of your time at a company. But it's also important to be open and to see what happens." – *Obenewa Amponsah*

As soon as you've identified what your idea of success is, it will be easier for you to make sacrifices. Throughout your life, there will be trade-offs in every decision you make, no matter how good it may seem. The question is not whether there will be a trade-off, but rather what the trade-off will be and whether you will be comfortable making it. There is always a price to pay to achieve your goals. That sacrifice can be time, money or even the positive opinions of others. I've seen many people who don't ever want to have to make trade-offs and it creates a tremendous amount of frustration.

Once, when I was still at Harvard Business School, a prominent CEO came to speak during one of my classes. One thing that really stood out for me was when she said, 'I have three priorities: my husband, my child and my job.' She went on: 'When I look at my calendar and there is an activity that doesn't line up with one of those priorities, I don't do it. My house is not the cleanest and I don't cook. If friends come over, I ask them what kind of takeaways they want. I don't cook because it takes away time from my three biggest priorities.'

In my life, attending Harvard Business School and moving to South Africa were two of the best decisions I have ever made. Both experiences opened up whole new worlds to me, allowing me to meet people I never would have met (including my husband) and to find passions that I never even knew I had. However, I sacrificed two years of salary and spent years paying off student loans, which had major financial implications. Over the last nine years living in South Africa, I have also missed many special moments and events in the lives of my family and friends back home in the United States.

While these are tough trade-offs, I am comfortable making them. I went into both situations with my eyes wide open and understood the trade-offs. And, despite the challenges, I would do it all over again, because I believe the benefits far outweigh the sacrifices. Sometimes new trade-offs only present themselves later. Your circumstances might change and you might have to reconsider whether the trade-offs are still worth it.

> Recognise that pursuing your passion has trade-offs. Pursuing your passion comes at a price. What are your boundaries? What price are you willing to pay? What are the trade-offs that you're willing or not willing to make? How do you better understand the trade-offs and be aware of them so you can make an informed choice?"
> – Acha Leke, Senior Partner and Chairman Africa, McKinsey & Company

Once you figure out what success looks like to you and what kind of sacrifices you'll have to make, it's time to figure out what the purpose of that success is. Which group(s) of people and larger challenge(s) will be served by your success and your leadership?

Taking ownership

One of the most important concepts that I was introduced to at McKinsey was *ownership*. It's the idea that when you are given a task, you should resolve it as if it is *your* problem – not your client's, customer's or manager's. If left unresolved, the problem will directly affect you, so your sense of urgency and level of commitment in solving the problem will naturally be greater. In the consulting space, ownership focuses on three areas: *ownership of the problem, ownership of professional and personal development* and *ownership of the culture and community in the office*. I explain each of these below.

Ownership of the problem

Let's say your manager asks you to conduct research for a particular project. Conducting the research as requested would be doing your work. If you do it as requested, but also anticipate issues that might be raised and research them as well, you would be taking ownership of the situation. You would evaluate both sets of research, consider which information is most relevant (and why), and formulate an opinion on why the remaining information is not useful. Ownership is thinking about the options that have emerged from your research, prioritising them and explaining why you ranked the options in that order. Ownership is being able to clearly and concisely articulate your research and your thoughts on the way forward.

But ownership is also about overcoming challenges. You don't crumble and back down at the first obstacle. You make a way if there isn't one and approach it with a can-do spirit. You want to be known as the person who goes above and beyond, instead of just doing the bare minimum. You need to have exhausted every option before giving up. Try to think about everything that could go wrong and develop contingency and backup plans. Don't just bring problems: bring solutions, as well as your opinion on each possible option. Instead of dumping the problem in someone else's lap, make it your problem too.

> Resolving someone else's issue is central and not emphasised enough. You can have all the skills in the world and the greatest personality, but if you're not resolving my specific problem, you're not being helpful." – *Jocelyne Muhutu-Remy*

Taking ownership means creating 'client/customer-ready' reports and documents. Always approach a document with the idea that it is going straight to the final client, end customer or the most senior person in the company. Don't depend on your manager or someone more senior to you to fix your spelling, content or numerical mistakes. And if you're dealing with numbers, don't just assume that your calculations are right and that your manager will catch any errors. Finally, it means 'sense checking' your work. Take a step back: consider everything you know about the project and its context and ask yourself whether everything (for example, final numbers, outputs, insights) seems reasonable. If it doesn't, ask yourself where you went wrong.

Solving these problems also means taking ownership of how you will get your work done. Think about how to break down big projects into smaller tasks and when you need to hit key milestones along the way to achieve the overall goal. As much as ownership is about you, it is also about involving the right people at the right time if you need help, have questions or are facing roadblocks that might jeopardise your timeline or the quality of what you will deliver. In general, ownership is about going above and beyond what you were asked to do, thinking about new ways to add value and about applying your mind to solve a problem. Taking ownership is a way to distinguish yourself from your peers. Most people only do what they are told, and very few will go above and beyond. When you do that, people will take notice.

> Good performance is delivering on what is expected of you. Distinctive performance is going above and beyond what is expected. Be curious and ask yourself what could make a difference. It's a mindset of ownership. It's not my boss' problem that I'm helping him or her solve. I own this problem and it's my job to solve it."
> – Acha Leke

Ownership of your professional and personal development

Ownership is not just about taking responsibility for your work. It is also about owning your career. If you are lucky, you will work for a company that provides resources that can help you navigate your career. If you're not so lucky, you will work for a company that doesn't provide those resources. Nevertheless, very few companies – if any – are going to hold your hand and tell you how to get to where you want to be. You must do this yourself.

When you start at a new organisation or get into a new position, one of your biggest jobs will be to understand what is expected of you. This may be clearly laid out at your company or it may not; either way, it is your responsibility to understand what is expected of you. You have to speak to senior people that you think are doing interesting work and find out exactly what they do and how they got there. Don't be shy to ask for coaching and feedback so that you become aware of your strengths and how to use them. This will help you to focus on the right developmental areas for your role and tenure and help you understand what the performance expectations are. Ownership implies that you keep asking questions until you have clarity on what you need to do to perform better.

Ownership is taking responsibility for your mistakes and acknowledging the role you might have played in them. Be accountable for poor performance and don't make excuses; accept and learn from negative feedback. When you take this approach, you'll learn something in the process, which means you will be better off in the long run. If you don't understand your feedback, consider sharing it with multiple mentors and seniors in your company and ask them to help you interpret it. Ownership is creating an action plan to address development areas and leverage strengths to improve your performance. Be prepared to work on those areas consistently, to communicate your progress to all relevant stakeholders, to ask for help along the way and to make adjustments based on continuous feedback. Importantly, it is about making sure that you get the opportunities you need to develop the necessary skills.

> I'd go back to that African proverb – 'If you want to go fast, go alone. If you want to go far, go together.' Can you rush and get things done quickly? Absolutely. Are you going to do it right and go the long mile? Maybe, maybe not. So why chance it when there are so many people around who you can ask to be your mentor? We don't ask a lot of questions because we think that we know everything, especially when we have gotten good grades. But good grades do not make you a top performer in a corporate; that's only how you get a foot in the door. A performance review had less to do with my performance and everything to do with how people felt working with me." – *Tina Taylor, former Chief Information Officer and Chief Quality Officer for GE Lighting Global*

As you advance in your career and start to focus on different areas, you need to understand how performance expectations shift. From a personal development standpoint, it's about intentionally growing yourself as a person. Spend time learning about what you need to develop and what your triggers are, and then deliberately work on growing in those areas. (Useful ways of doing this are, for example, reflection, journaling, therapy, meditation and prayer.) It is not enough to only improve your technical skills. We all know people who are super-smart but who make poor choices or have behavioural patterns that derail their careers. These individuals serve as a cautionary tale, because you don't want to become one yourself.

Taking ownership of your development also implies not immediately blaming poor feedback on racism on the part of your colleagues. Your response should be to evaluate and interrogate the substance of the feedback. Ask yourself: is the quality of my work the best that it can be? Am I really giving my all? Am I aware of what is expected of me? Have I spoken to people to understand what the expectations are? Do I know what the differences are between average, above-average and distinctive work? What am I expected to know for my role and tenure? Have I spoken to people who are advancing at an unusually fast pace to understand what they are doing to differentiate themselves? Have I spoken to the high-flyers in my company to understand what they are doing to differentiate themselves?

> Don't try to hide behind claims of racism if your performance is poor." – *Stefano Niavas, Partner and Managing Director, Boston Consulting Group*

Remember that there are other successful people in your organisation who have advanced, been promoted and assumed different leadership roles, so you are not breaking new ground. Understand what the next level up for you would be. Find people in the organisation who are in roles that interest you and doing the work that you want to do. Ask them how they got there. What hard and soft skills did they have to develop? Which experiences best prepared them for each role? Which qualities best served them in each role to this point?

Ownership of the organisation

In the various consulting firms I've worked for over the years, it was always an unspoken, unwritten rule that you should participate in extracurricular office activities to grow the culture and community in the office. Partners expected you to take ownership of the office and participate in activities that helped people connect.

You were seen as a leader in the office, even if you were still a junior. Remember that you are not a bystander or a voyeur in your organisation: you are an active participant and might be evaluated on your participation or lack thereof.

When you take ownership of your working environment, you will also, inevitably, see problems in the organisation. But you want to be known as someone who brings solutions, not just problems. Importantly, know that the way in which you take ownership might differ from department to department or from company to company What might be considered taking ownership in one environment might be seen as overstepping a boundary or being a slacker in another.

> My gift is that I am a solution finder and that I bring ideas to fruition. If you think you want to do something, you tell me what it is and I can figure out how to make it happen." – *Dr Jennifer Madden*

Racism and bias in the workplace

Let me be clear: taking ownership of your organisation and career does not imply placing any responsibility for fixing a toxic, racist and sexist environment on the shoulders of marginalised individuals. If you work in a company where victimisation takes place, I advise you to report what is happening to human resources (HR) or other leaders in the firm. If nothing changes, then the next step should be to leave that team, department or organisation. In no way should we absolve corporate leaders of their obligation, as good corporate citizens, to transform their cultures into inclusive environments where everyone – regardless of race, socio-economic status, physical ability, gender, religion, sexual orientation – feels like they belong and has an equal shot at success.

When we speak about taking ownership in the workplace, we

also do not discount the existence of racism, stereotyping and unconscious bias in corporate environments. Unconscious bias can be described as stereotypes that people subconsciously hold about other groups of people. It can affect how companies recruit, onboard, develop, compensate, promote and retain employees. This concept really helped me make sense of some of the stereotypes and discrimination I've experienced and witnessed in the workplace. I would be lying if I told you that we live in a post-racial, post-gender world. And while some people are not aware that they hold unconscious biases, we have to admit that everyone has beliefs about various social and identity groups. These biases often stem from the human tendency to organise social worlds by category. If you are working in an institution where there are not many people of colour or women, especially in leadership, and/or not many of them have been successful historically, there is a high probability that you will face bias. If you work in a culture where people see age as a proxy for knowledge and credibility, you might face bias because of your age.

Historically speaking, if you're working for a company that was founded in a country with a history of racial segregation, the chances are slight that the face of success at your workplace will be a person of colour. The chances are even slighter that it will be a woman of colour. Because you may not represent the success profile physically, people may unconsciously place you in the box of unsuccessful people. They may be less likely to forgive poor performance from you than they would be from a person of another race. During my career, I've seen how poor performance by white people is often interpreted as a blip on the screen or a wobble. However, when a Black person performs poorly, people can quickly ask whether that person has what it takes to be successful. If you're working in a male-dominated field, the same snap judgements might be levelled against you if you are a woman.

Fundamentally, people of colour are questioned and doubted more than white people. If the leaders of a company have been at that company for many years and have seen very few successful people of colour or women and have had limited exposure to people of colour and/or women, some of them may believe, subconsciously, that those people don't have what it takes. Unconscious bias is very real, and although you cannot control it, you can control how you respond to it.

Here is a situation that taught me about figuring out how to manage myself and my energy in the face of unconscious bias. Once, during a team meeting, I held a very firm boundary with my manager regarding my holiday dates. When she and I met one-on-one, she imitated how I had behaved in the team meeting, complete with pointed finger and rolling neck. After she finished, I just sat back in my chair. I was stunned and shocked. I knew I had not behaved in that manner. I told my manager that her imitation of me was not only inaccurate but also highly racially offensive. She really struggled to understand why I was so offended. In the blink of an eye, she depicted me as a one-dimensional, angry Black woman in a Tyler Perry movie, a stereotype that many of us work tirelessly to avoid. I am not a neck-roller. I am not a finger-pointer. I was raised by a woman – my mother – who merely had to give you a look (no neck or fingers included) to let you know that you needed to stop whatever you were doing. That was the same look I gave my manager during the team meeting. No raised voice. No finger-pointing. No neck-rolling. But that was how my manager experienced me. Afterwards, I even went to a team member to ask her if I had done that and she said, 'No, you didn't. But you made it clear that the topic [my vacation dates] was not up for discussion.' This was exactly how I remembered it too.

I had two big takeaways from the above situation: First, some people, whether they know or admit it or not, hold certain stereotypes about you as a person of colour or a person of intersectionality (for me, it's that I'm Black and a woman). Sometimes people don't realise how their perceptions of a group of people have been influenced by the few people from that group that they have seen in the media, news, movies and newspapers. Their bias is especially strong if they have never had an opportunity to interact with people that look like that group. They've had nothing to counter those narrow perspectives.

Second, I learnt that I should never work for nine months straight and only take one vacation day. Remember that one of the purposes of work is to better understand yourself and to learn the conditions under which you can show up in the best way. I should not have let myself get to that point of frustration. I should have taken other days off during that period, even if I just took a mental-health day to vegetate on the couch. It was unhealthy and borderline irresponsible of me not to recharge, because it made me irritable, impatient, intolerant and reduced my ability to be as thoughtful as I should have been about what I say and how I say it.

When you're facing racism, sexism or any other type of bias, also remember that the 'say the first thought that comes into your head' approach does not always work well in a professional setting. Try to stay in touch with yourself and check how you are feeling. Are you feeling unusually tired? Are you losing your temper more quickly than usual? Are you more easily irritated? Those are the signs for me, but you have to figure out what the signs are for you. After that incident during the team meeting, I monitored how frequently I took days off and made sure I took an annual midyear break.

> It's important to be conscious about managing yourself. You should be on the lookout for relationships that are toxic and unproductive, affecting your productivity and even your health. You need to love yourself enough and be confident enough that you can find a different work environment. Remove yourself immediately as soon as a relationship becomes toxic. People don't always remember how talented they are. This is not the last job on earth. If you find just one person with influence in

> the organisation and explain to him or her the negative situation, you will be supported. People are inherently good. Don't suffer in silence. And if the formal channels, like HR, don't work, or if the problem is HR, look elsewhere. Remove yourself in an elegant way. Don't ruffle feathers because you never know when you might see that person again." – *Thokozile Lewanika Mpupuni, Group Head of Leadership, Learning and Talent, Absa*

I also want to acknowledge the high price of Black tax. Black tax can be understood in various ways, but I'm referring to the notion that Black people have to work and perform regular tasks twice as well as white people. For many of us, Black tax is real. It's unfair, and unfortunately it affects us in ways that other people will never understand. While we cannot control others' expectations of us, we can be empowered enough to maximise our time, relationships, learning and impact at an organisation. Remember that every situation is an opportunity to learn something about yourself and other people. No matter how bad it is, no matter the outcome, no matter how badly you or the other person(s) might have behaved, you will always have to dissect it to see what you learnt and what your role in the situation was so that you can grow from it. That way, the situation isn't a waste.

Having said that, two things can be true at the same time. Black tax, systemic racism and unconscious bias can exist in an organisation *and* there can still be some areas where we Black folks need to learn more and do better. A Black South African senior leader at a former employer told me: 'I sometimes find that young Black people come in with their qualifications and they think they've arrived. They walk in with an *"I deserve"* mindset. But that is just the basic milestone. You still have to do more. Just because you passed the interview doesn't mean that everyone was 100 per cent behind you. You are still being judged and people are still looking at you with suspicion. Will she fit in? Did we make the right call?

Is this a mis-hire? You need to be open to learning and step up and show up in a big way. Focus. Listen to what the unspoken language is. And know that you're going to have to work hard to earn the stripes to be there.'

I strongly believe there is a shared responsibility in a healthy professional relationship: the organisation has its part to play and you have yours. While organisational change is absolutely necessary, it takes *time, determination and effort.* In the meantime, work on bringing your best self to the relationship.

Making an impact

We can understand our impact at work as the positive difference between what our organisation or team was like before and after our arrival. In the workplace, your impact is the difference or improvement that you make and the value that you add to your teams, organisation, clients and customers. This is done through your performance, contribution, outputs, outcomes, deliverables and/or efforts every day. You want everyone you work with to see and feel the difference that your contributions have made to the team and/or company. Your clients and customers – both internal and external – should be better off for having you as part of the team and organisation. When you were in school, you got some credit merely for showing up. Well, those days are over. Instead of the grade, the distinction, the honour roll, the dean's list, what matters now is impact.

If your goal is to have the maximum impact in your job, you need to ask yourself these questions: how can I best equip and position myself to do this? What do I need to know and do to maximise my impact? Whose help do I need? And how can I continue to improve and grow my skills? The illustration below shows the difference between what you might be thinking and what the real answer is.

What you think you need to have impact vs what you actually need

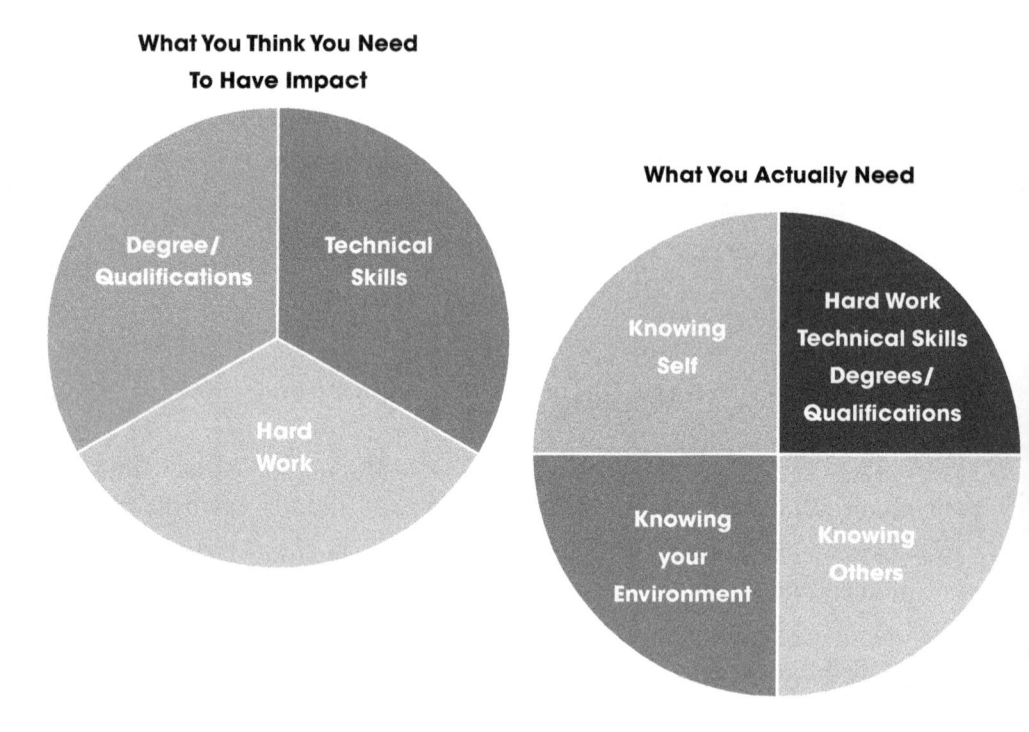

What You Think You Need To Have Impact
- Degree/Qualifications
- Technical Skills
- Hard Work

What You Actually Need
- Knowing Self
- Hard Work, Technical Skills, Degrees/Qualifications
- Knowing your Environment
- Knowing Others

It is important to view your career and your daily, weekly and monthly choices through the lens of impact. You need to ask yourself every day: is what I'm saying, doing, delivering and how I'm presenting myself helping me build or destroy the support that I will eventually need? And how are my organisation, my clients, customers and manager better off as a result of my contribution?

> I'd love to have the most highly qualified engineers, but you know what? I'm quite happy to also train them up. Can I have the right people with the right attitude and mindset? Give me those people. In this way, you build up a team and a culture of people who want to be there, who want to grow." – *Ipeleng Mkhari, Chief Executive Officer, Motseng Investment Holdings*

Becoming a leader

> "If your actions inspire others to dream more, learn more, do more and become more, you are a leader."
> – *John Quincy Adams, sixth President of the United States, 1825–1829*

In *The Five Levels of Leadership* John Maxwell argues that the first level of leadership is when people follow and respect you because of your title. They will do just enough not to get fired. The second level is when people start to respect you so they choose to follow you. The third level is when people follow you because of the impact that you've had on the organisation. The fourth level is when people respect you because you develop other leaders, and the fifth is when people respect you because of who you are and what you represent. You should strive to be a level 4 or 5 leader. They are the ones who will change the world, solve the world's biggest problems and grow other leaders in the process.

You'll soon realise that true leadership has nothing to do with a title. It is about having a vision, inspiring others to help you realise that vision and role modelling what you want to see in others. The type of leader you will become starts with who you are right now, the awareness that you develop, the concepts you focus on and the strategies you employ early on in your career. You've probably heard the saying, 'It's hard to teach an old dog new tricks.' It's true: the older you become, the harder it is to think and behave differently. So start with good habits now and build a teachable mindset that helps you embrace new ideas and ways of doing things while you're still young.

I worked in public education for three years before I moved to South Africa. My colleagues and I used to say, 'Kids want to know you care before they care about what you know.' Adults are the same. They want to see that you value, hear, understand, recognise and appreciate the people that you lead, work with and work for.

If you want to win people's hearts, if you want them to go the extra mile for you and give you their disposable time, you have to know their strengths and weaknesses, what keeps them up at night and what might be going on with them outside work.

Once your colleagues know that you genuinely care about them as people and that you want to add value to their lives, there is no limit to what they'll do to help you achieve your vision. In this way, your vision becomes their vision and mission. Begin to practise and sharpen this skill right now as a junior employee. For many years, I thought that saying the right words was all that mattered. But I quickly learnt that people sense your energy. If your mouth is saying something that your heart doesn't believe, people can sense it. They may not say anything about it, but when you're unable to connect with them and you wonder why, check your heart. Check your intentions and work on aligning your heart, mind and words.

At high-performing companies, performance standards are always high, but I want to remind you about the high bar for leadership and character. This bar is just as important, if not more so, as the one for solving problems. Around the world, many of the problems we face today stem from a lack of values and authentic and inspiring people-driven leadership. You have to be clear on what your values are, the moral code that you live by and the boundaries that you set for yourself.

A situation early in my career made me examine my values and boundaries. I was working at Arthur Andersen when it imploded in 2002. Andersen was part of what was formerly known as the Big Five accounting firms, along with KPMG, Ernst & Young, Deloitte and PriceWaterhouseCoopers. Today, Arthur Andersen no longer exists because a client team falsified financial statements on behalf of the notorious, now defunct energy trading company, Enron. During the implosion, it was revealed that a junior auditor had shredded documents that incriminated the two companies. I'm sure that the order to shred those documents came from a

A whole new world

senior leader on the team. The actions of a few people in the Houston office of Andersen thus brought down the entire firm globally. People lost their jobs and others lost their retirement funds after decades of hard work.

When I learnt about the incident, I asked myself: would I have had the courage to disobey an order from a senior partner? I'm not sure I would have. I grew up in a very hierarchical, religious family, and on top of that I went to Catholic school for 13 years. I grew up following the rules and doing what my elders told me to do. But at Andersen I finally realised that I wasn't a child anymore and that I could not blindly follow the instructions of my superiors or any other adult. I decided that if I was ever asked to do something that went against my values and my beliefs, I wouldn't do it.

I define a moment of truth as a situation when you have to choose between following the path of least resistance or following your conscience, or what you know needs to be done. Learning about the incident during my tenure at Andersen was just such a moment of truth for me. You want to be able to look yourself in the mirror and sleep well. Since then, I have had many more moments of truth and I will continue to have them. Don't allow the world to chip away at who you are and what you believe. So take a deep breath, centre yourself, reflect on who you are and stand firm in what you believe.

You can have the greatest ideas and the highest IQ in the world, but if you don't have the character to see it through, it will never come to fruition. And if it does, you won't be able to sustain it. Leadership is therefore not just about building followers but building other leaders. It is a privilege to serve the people you work with and for. It is about building relationships. Even as a junior, try to be a leader in your field so that when the opportunity arises for you to lead and develop others officially, you are ready.

The world is calling out for true leaders. For now, the only person you can change is you. And although systems need to be changed, you will have to build some credibility before you can start doing that. Take ownership, perform well, get to know your organisation's culture and build relationships with decision-makers and influencers. This will give you the licence, the credibility and the space to raise issues and present the solutions to the problems you see in your work environment. You are early enough in your career to make the necessary adjustments, rewire your brain to understand and manage work and your relationships differently and, ultimately, to have a greater impact in your organisation. Let the real work begin now.

Chapter 2
Get your mind right

Throughout your career, despite your best efforts and intentions, you will undoubtedly experience setbacks. They will come in the form of disappointments, negative feedback, a failed project or a poor performance review. It's not a matter of *if*, but *when*. At no point in your career will you stop being human, which implies that you will never be exempt from making mistakes. When you enter a new corporate environment, you are placed in unfamiliar situations with no blueprint to tell you how to act in them. So, on a daily basis, you learn by trial and error and deal with different personalities, figuring out how best to work with them. Sometimes these new experiences at work will make you feel badly about yourself, thus forcing you to rebuild your self-confidence.

Regardless of how a setback transpires or what it entails, you can never allow it to take you permanently out of the game. Setbacks are hard for everyone, and in my experience, high-achieving folks take these experiences exceptionally hard, exactly because they're not used to them. It is therefore important for you to realise that you can always decide how you see a given situation. There will always be different strategies within your sphere of influence or control that can help you bounce back. Also, remember that you will be better off learning a difficult lesson – it will help you to never make the same mistake twice. Sometimes you can't fix situations, but at the very least you can always change your perspective on them. In other cases, you can turn the situation around, create new alternatives to explore, or you can even completely restore what was lost. No matter what happens, push forward and don't ever give up on yourself completely.

The extent to which you are able to deal with setbacks speaks to your resilience in the workplace. Resilience can be defined as a person's ability to bounce back from unanticipated changes, setbacks, disappointments or failures. And this is where mindset comes in. Your resilience in bouncing back from setbacks completely depends on your perspective.

Mindset can be defined as *your beliefs, thought patterns, perspectives and perceptions on situations in your life.* Your mindset affects how you handle adversity, challenges, success and failure.

> I've made a lot of mistakes along the way, but I've *had* to make them. I would never change my path and all the things I've experienced. Every single mistake has been necessary. Maybe one shouldn't even call them mistakes. They're learning opportunities." – *Ipeleng Mkhari*

During my time at McKinsey, a consultant once asked to meet with me. She told me that she had been rated 'Issues' in her most recent performance review. (At the company, this was the below-average rating and it was not a good sign.) She started off our conversation by saying that no one really cared about her, nobody was willing to help her improve and nobody was invested in her success. Since I was on the Professional Development team, I knew the particular client project she was on and knew some of her team members.

'Well, what about so-and-so, the partner on the study? How is he?' I asked her.

'Oh, he's great,' she said. 'He's always willing to help me and answer my questions. He definitely thinks that I can turn it around.'

'And what about so-and-so, the Engagement Manager?' I asked. 'Oh, she's cool. She's always very willing to coach me and we get along well.'

'When you started this conversation, you said no one cared about you or your performance,' I said. 'You said that no one was invested in your success. But we've just talked about two key leaders on your team that are always willing to coach you so you can turn your performance around.'

She looked at me with an expression of defeat and surprise. 'Yeah, you're right.'

From that point, we started talking about how to turn her performance around. We discussed what she needed to do and how she needed to engage her supporters in and outside the project. Nothing about her actual situation – the client project, the leaders on the team, her performance rating – had changed during the course of our conversation. The only thing that was different was her mindset, the way she looked at her situation. She came into our meeting as a victim and left feeling more like a victor. She felt much more empowered because she now had a concrete plan of action.

How this young person moved from the mindset of a victim to that of a victor is a classic example of how important perspective is in a situation. Two people can have two different experiences and outcomes of the same situation depending on how they look at it. Victims blame others, make excuses and deny the role they played in getting themselves into the situation. Victors, however, own their part, take responsibility for what is in their control, and they have a can-do spirit. Victims ask, 'Why is this happening *to* me?', while victors ask, 'Why is this happening *for* me? What is the lesson?'

Before I started writing this book, I was in a pretty despondent place in my life. I was feeling powerless and sorry for myself. Then it occurred to me that I'm passionate about, and have many ideas on, helping young people in their careers. Couldn't I channel that energy into putting those ideas on paper? So that's what I did . . . and that's why you're reading this book right now.

Maybe there are people who never fall into the trap of feeling like a victim. If you're one of those people, that is awesome. However, the rest of us occasionally slip into the mindset of a victim. The real goal for us is to see how quickly we can talk ourselves out of it. And once we've done that, we can start focusing on what we can control or what we can influence.

Control can be defined as the ability to exercise direct influence or power over something, while influence is the power or capacity to affect an outcome in an indirect or intangible manner. Control says, 'I make the decision', and influence says, 'I can persuade the person who makes the decision' or 'I can influence the outcome in some way.' I recently co-facilitated a training event for women with high potential in the workplace. For one of the exercises, we asked the participants to write down everything that was getting in the way of their achieving their professional goals. We asked them to categorise what they'd written into three categories: areas that they had *no* control over; areas that they *had* control over; and areas that they had *influence* over. When the participants in the workshop categorised their challenges, 60 to 70 per cent of their obstacles were either areas that they had control over, or areas that they could influence. Many of the participants had an 'aha' moment when they realised that they had a lot more power than they originally thought.

> Your mindset allows you to change, learn and improve."
> – *Stefano Niavas*

Your mindset is one of those things that you can control. Remember that your mind is your most powerful asset, one that you should guard, manage, grow and challenge on a daily, even hourly, basis. Your behaviour always starts with a thought, so learning how to manage your thought processes about situations and people is critical to your success. This is often where we get tripped up in our careers. We look at situations and people through a particular lens, without challenging ourselves or working on our perspectives. We don't push ourselves to see other possibilities or entertain the idea that we have blind spots.

> "Yesterday I was clever, so I wanted to change the world. Today I am wise, so I am changing myself." – *Rumi, 13th-century Persian poet, Islamic theologian and scholar*

As you start to examine your mindset and process your experiences at work, your first step will be to identify some of your own problematic thought patterns. Personally and professionally, I've experienced – and seen in others – a wide range of unhelpful mindsets. Some of the most common are a lack of self-awareness, not owning your career and doubting your internal net worth (with its counterpart, perfectionism). Then there are also those 'F' words that hold us back (failure and fear), what I call 'checked baggage', the go-it-alone mentality and the growth vs fixed mindset. We also judge ourselves too harshly when we do not take the long view, and when we measure ourselves by 'the bubble' standards and unrealistic timelines. At the same time, we have to contend with our own limiting beliefs and negative self-talk. Many of us suffer from impostor syndrome and we're paralysed when we don't know every step. We compare ourselves against others and we forget to bring what isn't there. Also, as underrepresented minorities, there are certain mindsets that we sometimes struggle with – stereotype threat and learnt helplessness are prime examples – that keep us from showing up at our best. In this chapter, I'll delve more deeply into each of these topics.

> Mindset is very important. How do I unlearn the fact that I was taught that I was *less than* growing up? Can I unlearn that idea or am I rather evolving, gaining new insight? People are set up to fail if they're told to get certain ideas out of their mind, to unlearn ideas such as *my hair is nappy or kinky* or *I'm not beautiful*. You want to give people new patterns to think about. Instead: *You are beautiful and this is why. Your hair is this way because your ancestors grew up in the southern hemisphere and*

the curls and texture protected their scalps from the sun. It was a powerful force that enabled them to survive. Other people had straight hair because they were in the northern hemisphere." – Timothy Maurice Webster

A lack of self-awareness

The cornerstone of a house is the brick around which other foundational bricks of the house are laid. In your career, your cornerstone is self-awareness. This entails having a balanced perspective on (ie not overestimating or underestimating) yourself, knowing what your strengths are and knowing that you can still develop. The first step in Bill Wilson's famous 12-step programme is to admit that you have a problem. How can you work on a problem that you haven't acknowledged? You can't. Self-awareness is therefore the foundation of your development as a professional and as a person. Without it, you cannot leverage your strengths or address your areas of development.

Lacking self-awareness is similar to driving your car to a destination without knowing your starting point. If you don't have a balanced, realistic view of yourself, you cannot know how far you have to go or the best path to get there, because you do not know where you're starting from. I once worked with someone who was famously known to be horrible at execution. Everything she did started late, ended late and was a total chaotic mess. We took a personality assessment as a team and she scored very low in execution. She was surprised. 'My job is 90 per cent about execution,' she said to me. 'How can I be in this job and score so low?' It took everything in me not to say that I could have told her that for free several years ago. I was shocked that she didn't know this about herself. It made me wonder: what had she been telling herself all those years about her chaotic projects and meetings? Had she been blaming the environment? The team? Her manager? Had she been honest with herself, she could have addressed those issues much earlier.

We unconsciously tell ourselves stories that aren't entirely true, both to protect our own egos and to avoid the truth. But we need to grow up, take responsibility and work intentionally on the areas we have not been so great at. When you're unaware or in denial, you cannot make progress. When I give feedback on one of my company's self-assessments, the first result I always look at is self-awareness, because it gives me a sense of how much the person will challenge or accept the results. Usually, those with low self-awareness will challenge the results, even though the results are based on their answers about themselves.

Your ability to address the other mindsets that I discuss below is dependent on what you are able to admit to yourself. Our minds are powerful, so we should be truthful about ourselves and continue to grow as people and professionals. The only way to change is if you unpack and connect the dots of your story – the traumas, the triumphs, the defining moments and the key people. Learn to identify the elements of your character that will propel you forward, as well as the ones that could hold you back or overshadow other parts of you. This is the first step in building self-awareness, which is a critical element. It does not happen magically or unconsciously: you have to make a concerted effort.

> You should be able to admit if you're not good at something and work on being good at it. I had to face myself in the mirror and admit that I wasn't a great communicator." – *Dr Puleng Makhoalibe, founder, Alchemy Inspiration, and Adjunct Faculty member, Henley Business School*

Not owning your career and managing your performance

When you start working, you have to understand that nobody – not even your manager – is going to care as much about your career as you. You are now the CEO of You Inc, and a CEO doesn't wait to be given the answers. She proactively seeks what she needs to be successful. You cannot wait for your manager to tell you what you need to do to be successful in the organisation. The onus is on you to understand what is expected of you, get the feedback you need and determine what you need to do to improve your performance.

Determine what you are being evaluated on and how your current role or task is preparing you for the next opportunity. This means finding out what kind of developmental and learning opportunities are available and determining whether you should take advantage of them. In an ideal world, your manager would proactively provide this information to you, but nine times out of ten this will not be the case. Take ownership of your career and your development and get what you need to be successful.

Doubting your internal net worth

The concept of 'net worth' traditionally refers to the amount by which assets exceed liabilities. Within the context of your career, think of your internal net worth as what you are worth as a person when you strip away your qualifications, achievements and labels. These things are not liabilities, but they are, however, external to you. Much like any asset or liability, your qualifications, achievements and labels may have value today but tomorrow they may be worthless. At the core of you, how much are *you* worth to *you*? If you strip away all of these external attachments, how would you describe yourself? Who would you be without those?

Get your mind right

During my first job I questioned my internal net worth. I had always been labelled as the one with the good grades. In high school, I was in all the honours and advanced-placement classes and was selected as 'Most Likely to Succeed'. I received a full scholarship plus room and board for university and graduated *cum laude* from the university honours programme. I had always done well in school, with a few notable exceptions (honours chemistry and honours pre-calculus might have been the death of me). I felt that doing well was the only option for my destiny. Doing well wasn't just something I did – it was who I am. It was in my DNA.

The only reason I accepted my first job offer was because the company offered me an annual salary of $32 000 (or R560 000, which seemed like a lot of money in 1998), free parking, free benefits, free breakfast and lunch and free dinner if I worked late. I wasn't certain about what my job entailed, but it was a reputable company that paid well enough for me to live on my own. That was all I cared about at the time. It turned out that my role was to be a systems tester for the company's proprietary benefits administration system. It's no surprise that I didn't like the job, but the bigger surprise for me was that I was not the best at it. On top of that I also walked around *looking* like I didn't like my job.

One day, my manager called me into her office. 'Your performance is not what we would expect,' she said. 'If you don't straighten up, I'm going to have to put you on a PDP (Professional Development Plan – a list of performance expectations) and you'll have 30 days to turn your performance around. Otherwise we'll have to let you go.' This was the ultimate wake-up call. How could this be? If I wasn't doing well, what was I worth? If I wasn't top of the class, what value was I adding to the world? But the deeper question for me was this: if my identity was achievement, who was I if I wasn't doing well? Who would I be without my achievements and my labels?

This was my first big lesson in the importance of managing how I was perceived at work. I don't remember my work being that poor, but I realised that when people saw me looking unhappy, they put me under a microscope and they questioned my work. I had a come-to-Jesus moment when I realised that no matter how much I hated my job, I had bills to pay and I needed to keep my job until I could find something better. I decided to follow the age-old adage 'fake it till you make it'. I started walking around with a smile (albeit fake) and my manager never had that conversation with me again. I also had to start answering my deeper questions about my self-worth. Around this time I started attending a new church and came to understand my worth in God's eyes and from a spiritual perspective. This helped me place my worth and value in something other than achievement. While this approach worked for me, you have to determine what works best for you. It is imperative that you find something – besides achievements – in which to root your value.

This experience showed me that I have value and self-worth even if I never achieve another thing. I realised that I don't have to be doing, achieving, adding more qualifications and living up to labels in order to feel worthy. The very fact that I take up space on Earth means that I have value; I add value by merely being. This is not to say that achievements and qualifications aren't great: we salute others and ourselves when we accomplish milestones. But our worth is not dependent on them. They merely add to the magic, light and beauty that is already there.

A friend of mine in South Africa runs a modelling agency, for which I teach a confidence class. During my classes, I demonstrate an exercise that I saw somewhere on YouTube. It goes like this: I take out a 'R20' note and ask the participants how much it is worth. They say 'R20'. Next, I crumple up the money in my hand and ask them again. Again, they answer R20. Then I drop the money on the floor and step on it. I ask them how much it is worth and they repeat, 'R20'. Even if I say that the money in my hand is worth R10, we know that the money is still worth R20.

The R20 in the exercise I just described represents your self-worth. No matter what you do or don't do, no matter what anyone says or does to you, you still retain your value. It is important for you to have a high internal net worth because when your identity is attached to achievements or labels, your emotions and self-worth fluctuate with every piece of positive or negative feedback. This type of mental volatility makes you an ineffective individual contributor, an unpredictable team player and, eventually, a very insecure leader. It doesn't mean that you cannot get upset about feedback that you do not agree with. What it means, however, is that you do not doubt your value as a person, together with your ability to learn, to do well and to add value to the people around you. I also believe that when you have a low internal net worth, other people pick up on it and treat you according to the value you have placed on yourself. Another gauge of your self-worth is your relationships. If you are someone who allows others to misuse, abuse, disrespect or dishonour you, you have to ask yourself: 'How much do I value myself if I allow people to treat me this way?'

> "I'm not tied to what people think of me – to the titles, the money. I'm not tied to that because I have a higher purpose." – *Tina Taylor*

Interestingly enough, Sharon Martin, a US-based psychotherapist and author, believes that perfectionism can be rooted in the idea that one's self-worth is based on achievement. Martin espouses the idea that perfectionism can be said to have its roots in households where, either intentionally or unintentionally, perfection is set as the standard. I grew up in a household where, in my mind, there wasn't much room for error. I remember the first time I accidentally broke a dish as a child. It wasn't a fancy dish – just a run-of-the-mill, everyday cereal bowl. I thought my life was over and that the earth was going to open up and swallow me whole.

The more I reflect on the role of perfectionism in my own life, the more I realise how debilitating it has been. It has kept me from taking risks and sometimes even from moving forward. Mistakes I had made caused me to beat myself up for days or weeks. When others would make what I deemed 'silly' mistakes, I would comfort them, tell them that it was okay and that they would do better next time. But if I made the same mistake, I would criticise myself no end. Why was it okay for others to make mistakes but not me? Part of me thought that I was too good to make mistakes. Boy, was I wrong!

I once had an e-commerce business and it took me months to make the website public, because I was worried there might be mistakes on it. I checked, double-checked and triple-checked everything, and when I finally launched it I still found more mistakes. I realised that the site would never be perfect, because I was never going to be perfect. I had to accept that I'm not superhuman but the same brand as everyone else: the flawed kind. I saw mistakes as catastrophic, as opposed to what they really are: an opportunity to learn and grow. All I could do was apologise for the mistakes, try to make them right and make sure that I put processes in place so that they never happened again.

Many of us are perfectionists. Perfectionism may have helped us to be successful in school, but it may not serve us well in a corporate environment where time constraints and quick turnarounds are the order of the day. From a more practical standpoint, the idea that you can go off into a corner and emerge victorious three hours later with the answer is a fallacy. You become a risk-averse perfectionist who is afraid to make any type of mistake. This fear keeps you from speaking up – out of fear of saying the wrong thing – and makes you miss or almost miss deadlines because you're always afraid that your work isn't good enough. And from what I've seen, the pressure becomes too great; instead of propelling us forward to greater heights, it crushes us into silence and sometimes even disengagement. Because we feel as though we have no room for error, in our minds it is better to be silent than to be wrong.

Remember that when you are a new employee, you don't know enough to do it on your own. You need the guidance and input of others. The perfectionist in us doesn't want to show anyone anything that isn't perfect, but you might need to work hard to remove your ego from the situation. This is not about looking perfect. This is about getting to the answer as quickly, efficiently and accurately as possible so that you deliver great results for your client or customer.

Avoiding perfectionism doesn't mean your work should be sloppy or that you don't have to double-check your work. However, it does mean that after you've checked it twice, you should ask yourself whether you should check it a third, fourth or fifth time. How much value are you adding with those additional checks? Is the additional value worth the time you spent on those checks? Did you sacrifice time you could have spent on other projects?

> A leader who has not worked out their self-worth is dangerous to society. They put on a mask of excessive confidence when beneath the surface they are deeply insecure. They see everyone as a threat. They see everything as being in their way. Put together a collective of such leaders who have not worked out their self-worth and you have set up a society for failure and irreparable damage. These kinds of leaders create a system in which it is impossible for followers to emerge in their own self-worth. The leader's greatest work is not to point out what is wrong in the world and how only they can fix it. It is to fix themselves. We all suffer when leaders do not do their greatest work. The greatest work is internal." – *Rachel Nyaradzo Adams, founder and Managing Director, Narachi Leadership*

The 'F' words

> Understand where your fear comes from, so when you dig deeper you can start understanding the history or the circumstances of your fear. And then you break that down and say, okay, so this is why I'm behaving like this. It's okay to have a bit of fear, but you can't operate from that place because it's not healthy. You need to remove those blinkers and you'll see the world in a different way.' – *Kagiso Molotsi, People Development Manager, Primedia*

Infants only have two innate fears: the fear of being dropped and the fear of loud sounds. All of our other fears are learnt fears, which means that we can unlearn them or, at the very least, overwrite them. At the root of much of our bad behaviour and poor choices is fear. You have to determine what your particular brand of fear is. There are various things we can be fearful of, for example failure, success, rejection and the unknown. It's important to understand the root of your fear, how it manifests in your life and what your fear(s) gets in the way of. My number-one fear is failure. My fear of failure got in the way of my launching the website for my e-commerce business and learning the lessons I could only learn once I started it. I was also depriving myself of the lesson that I am still worthy, even if I am not perfect. I delayed learning that imperfections are not fatal.

> I would have allowed my younger self to have a lot more fun in life. My life was so structured; I didn't want to mess up. I felt that I needed to conduct myself in a way that was always appropriate. It's not as if I missed out on a whole lot of things, but I could've enjoyed the moment more, knowing that even if something didn't work out, it does not mean that I failed." – *Tina Taylor*

Many of us have spent our whole lives trying to avoid failure. We were never given permission or room to fail. Failure was not an option. From a young age, we've been told that the bar is high for those of us who have the opportunity to be in certain spaces. We were told that we must not mess up this chance because it will be another hundred years before someone who looks like us will get another chance. Often we only want to go into situations where we know what we're doing and what exactly we need to do to be successful. We carry a tremendous burden in thinking that we have to be right all the time and that there is no room for failure. But when we do not take risks and embrace the idea that we might fail, we hinder our chances to grow, innovate, push the boundaries, take risks and learn valuable lessons.

Some of the most successful people have endured great failures. Oprah Winfrey was fired from her newscaster job when she was 24; JK Rowling sent her Harry Potter manuscripts to 12 publishers before getting published. Part of the human contract is that we are fallible. It is a certainty that you will experience failure at some point. But it's all a question of how you look at it, because failure and risk go together. If you never take a risk, you won't be able to push the boundary, test a new idea or experience the growth that only comes from stepping outside your comfort zone. However, with every risk there is a chance of success and failure. In every venture, there are degrees of risk that you can take. You could start small by speaking up in a team meeting or asking a tough question. Or let's look at it another way: let's say you and your team are trying to solve a problem for a customer. In your mind, the path to the answer is a straight line and you fear your 'dumb' suggestion will derail the team. But what if the path to the solution isn't a straight line? What if it is a complicated series of lines and curves that move forwards and backwards, ultimately leading to the answer? What if your suggestion helps the team get closer to the answer by eliminating a certain option? What if your suggestion helps the team feel more confident about the chosen direction?

Then your suggestion, even though it wasn't the 'right' one, helped the team arrive at the ultimate goal. Isn't *that* the whole point?

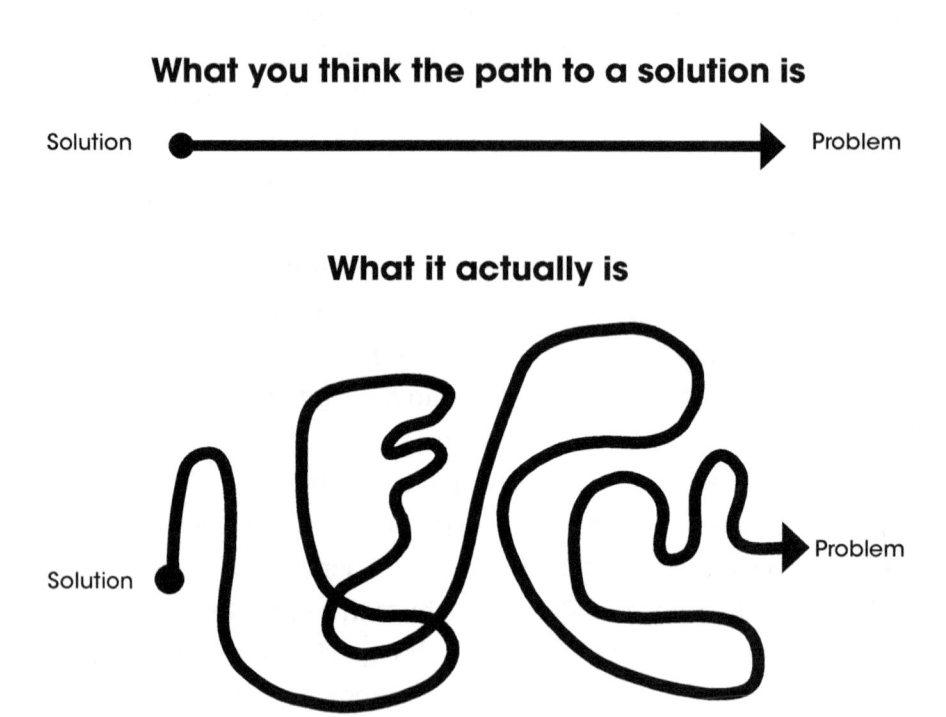

What you think the path to a solution is

Solution ●────────────────────▶ Problem

What it actually is

Solution ●⟿⟿⟿⟿⟿▶ Problem

Failure is never final unless you allow it to be. Failure is not who you are, but an event: 'I failed', not 'I am a failure.' During a talk that Oprah Winfrey gave at Stanford Business School in 2014, she said that failure is just a data point that leads you to your ultimate destiny, which the Creator has designed for you. You are not so powerful that you can interfere with the plan, so relax and focus on the next right step. When I started my online business, I learnt to think in this way. I never knew exactly if my strategies or business decisions would be successful, or how people would react, so I usually started off by trying certain things, learning the lessons, making adjustments and repeating the process. If you have disappointed someone, apologise, make the necessary changes to avoid it happening again, and move forward. Sometimes the lesson you learn is obvious, and other times you have to dig a bit deeper to find it – but it's always there. Always remember that if you are putting yourself out there, if you are taking risks, and if you are being open and vulnerable, you will make mistakes. But wouldn't you rather be a person who took a risk and failed than someone who stood on the sideline, wondering 'what if'?

> We like people who have failed because they're resilient. They've learnt how to put themselves back together, becoming a better version of themselves." – *Stefano Niavas*

Most of us fear ending up in an 'ultimate failure' situation. To help consultants explore their worst-case scenarios step by step, I often conducted the 'what if' exercise at McKinsey. Here is an example of a typical conversation we would have:

> Me: 'Why aren't you speaking up in the team problem-solving discussions?'
> Fellow: 'I'm afraid I'm going to say something stupid.'
> Me: 'And what will happen if you do?'
> Fellow: 'I might get a bad rating on the client study.'
> Me: 'And what will happen if you do?'
> Fellow: 'I might get rated "Issues".'
> Me: 'And what will happen if you do?'
> Fellow: 'I might get counselled to leave [a fancy phrase for fired].'
> Me: 'And then what will happen if you do?'
> Fellow: 'I will be devastated.'
> Me: 'And then what will you do?'
> Fellow: 'I will be depressed.'
> Me: 'And then what will you do?'
> Fellow: 'Eventually I will start looking for another job.'
> Me: 'And then what will you do?'
> Fellow: 'I will start my new job.'
> Me: 'And life goes on.'

When we don't face our worst-case scenarios, we become paralysed by fear. We think it will be the end of the world, but when we look at it closely, we realise that the earth will not open up and swallow us whole. Life goes on and so will you. If one opportunity does not work out, another one will. And who knows? It might be better than the one you were holding on to so tightly.

> Too many people blame others. You need to ask yourself, what role did I play in the failure? What will I do differently next time? Failure happens and it will happen again. You will fail but how do you recover from it? But if you have a plan in place and you know how to deal with it and grow from it, you will become more resilient over time." – *Acha Leke*

Checked baggage

When I talk about baggage, I'm not talking about suitcases and carry-on bags. Baggage refers to pain or strong negative emotions due to unresolved issues, experiences or traumas from the past. This baggage hinders your ability to live in the present and build healthy relationships. When it comes to your job, you may doubt that you have baggage, especially when you've never had a full-time, professional job. But your baggage may have been created by the experiences and advice of others. The more cautionary the advice, the more it shapes how you feel about the corporate world or employment in general.

For example, many people are told that they shouldn't divulge details about their personal lives at work. They're taught that they should maintain a barrier between the professional and personal versions of themselves. While the people who gave you that advice may have had the best of intentions, it may not be relevant for the space you've stepped into. In addition, if a family member or friend went through a tough or unfair experience at work, we may take on some of his or her residual bitterness, anger or stereotypes about corporate culture, based on how we saw that person being treated. I'm not saying we shouldn't take any advice from those around us, but we also can't take every piece of advice at face value. We need to examine the source and relevance of the information.

Long ago, a Black friend of mine started working at a company I had previously worked for. We kept in touch after I resigned, and one day we were having lunch. I asked her how things were going, and the subject of where she was living came up. She said she was in the process of moving and looking at new homes, but she didn't want to tell anyone at work because she was afraid they would use it against her. They might think she should have sorted that out prior to starting, she said. She had moved in with her father-in-law after the sudden death of her husband's mother; after some time, she and her husband had decided to get their own place again. She said that she was always told to keep her private life separate from her work life.

I was surprised to hear my friend's story because I was familiar with the company. I knew if she gave them the context, they would be willing to give her the time off she needed to go and look at places. It made me wonder why she felt uncomfortable about sharing something so innocuous. Would she be able to share anything deeper? Would she be able to form trust-based relationships at work if she couldn't even trust her team with this situation? Could her colleagues trust her if she couldn't even trust them?

Few of our parents ever worked in the type of environments (such as management consulting, investment banks, law firms) that we are working in. The world in which they lived was very different from the one we are in now. For them, it was probably easier to keep the wall up between their private and professional lives. Today, however, many of us are working 12- to 14-hour days in collaborative environments where trust is fundamental to sharing ideas, building relationships and achieving business outcomes.

Examine the advice you've been given and see if it applies to your current work environment. If it doesn't, how can you bring your full self – your personality, strengths, interests and areas of development – to work in an authentic way? This will help you to foster mutual understanding between you and your team, and build those relationships through which you may learn the culture, get the necessary sponsorship and advance in the company. Figure out what you're comfortable sharing to build trust and start there.

When I started at Arthur Andersen, I worked in the human capital consulting practice, and was the only Black consultant on the entire floor. This was quite a contrast from my previous company, so I was in shock. The environment was much more hierarchical and sober-minded, and I felt the gravity of the company and its history in a way that I had not before. At this stage in my career, I still counted the number of Black people in every meeting or conference room. Because of the company's storied history and because of the demographics of the floor, I felt a tremendous amount of pressure to prove that I (and any other Black person, for that matter) deserved to be there. I felt I needed to represent all Black people and that my failure would reflect poorly on all Black people. If I made a mistake, I thought it might call into question their decision about whether Black people should be in that space at all. My failures were all Black people's failures; my successes, all Black people's success. I thought every utterance that came from my mouth had to be profound and insightful. Eventually, this approach backfired: sometimes I didn't speak up at all. I questioned if my contribution met the very high bar I had set for myself.

My particular brand of baggage was the imagery I had grown up with as a Black kid in post-civil rights Birmingham, Alabama. Those images of police dogs and firehoses being released against protesters; of Governor George Wallace physically barring entry to prevent the integration of the University of Alabama, my alma mater. I remembered the stories of my parents and others who had gone to schools outside their communities due to the racist segregation laws in force at the time. These images were burned into my brain and for some reason were triggered when I started working in a lily-white environment. None of my feelings about this space came from anything anyone had said to me recently. It was all purely me. Eventually, the weight of carrying one billion Black people on my proverbial professional back became too much for me and I realised that the only person I could truly and fully represent was myself.

Interestingly, I realised that my white counterparts didn't seem to feel the same burden. Not that they weren't afraid to say something stupid; I'm sure they were. However, they were not fearful of poorly representing – and thus further stereotyping – their entire race. Why should I carry such a burden just because I was born Black? I decided that day that I would always offer my thoughts. Some of them would be good and some of them bad, but at least I knew they were mine. If people wanted to judge all Black people based on what I said, then that would reflect badly on them, not me. I decided that the only way I would be happy, successful and not stressed out was if I took a risk every day to speak my mind, be myself and show up as my most authentic self.

> I was acutely aware of the fact that I'm Black, I'm African, I'm a woman. I walked in with an attitude that was determined to undo any assumptions they had about what any of those three things were. I was going to be that bitchy girl in the office. And it really gave me that confidence. It was not just the confidence to speak up, but eventually also the confidence to relax into my skills and not having to put up that persona. So, my initial space in the first few months was of being a high-walled, inaccessible, angry Black woman. And then I suddenly became this warm, amazing person to work with, a team player who could take any joke. That was a lot of fun. And suddenly I had great relationships with colleagues

in other countries across the company" – *Refilwe Moloto, strategic and investment adviser and host of Cape Talk's Breakfast with Refilwe*

The go-it-alone mentality

Many of us are taught to put our heads down, work hard and wait to be tapped on the shoulder and knighted as the chosen one. Our well-meaning parents, aunts, uncles, cousins and family friends give us this advice. We are told that our work will speak for itself and that we will be rewarded for our efforts.

Working in corporate environments for a number of years, I've realised that many of us were not taught to collaborate with each other (*or anyone else*). I know I wasn't and neither were many people I know. But let me tell you now: every successful person has had a 'hand-up' in his or her career. No one has been successful all on their own. The hand-up doesn't necessarily have to be financial. You might be introduced to someone – perhaps a person you would never have met otherwise – or receive great advice. A hand-up might be someone allowing you to sleep on her couch for free while you fleshed out your business idea. You could even be mentored or sponsored in a corporate space. Remember that we need other people in order to be successful. Let me say it more forcefully: we can't be successful without other people. This is an absolute truth, especially in a professional environment. I once had a South African senior executive tell me: 'Build a network and take people up on their offer to help. You think you need to do it alone or you feel that you're imposing. You can either put your head down, work hard and hope that someone will appreciate you, or you can look up, look around and see who can help you.'

> I've never been the person who wants to do it alone because I've never seen the point of that. It's slow. You just get things done quicker with other people. Even

in my team, when I'm developing a strategy, I'll meet with my team and ask them their opinion. So although I'm driven, I'm driven in the sense that I work through and with other people rather than for myself." – *Thokozile Lewanika Mpupuni*

Asking for help doesn't mean that you don't have to apply your mind and think about how you should approach your work. You still need to do this because that's why the organisation hired you. Rather, your manager wants to know how you would solve problems. You need to start with the end in mind and figure out the necessary steps to achieve that end in a timely fashion. Maybe your team has time for you to go off and try to solve the problem yourself, but if they don't, then understand how you can work faster and more efficiently in that environment, especially if time is a metric by which you are being judged. You have to figure out how to strike the balance between asking for help at the right time and applying your mind to the problem. You don't want to appear to be a lazy thinker who just immediately asks for help, but you also don't want to waste time spinning your wheels trying to solve a problem on your own if you can't.

In order to understand the idea of receiving a hand-up and how it relates to collaboration, let's unpack the fallacies implied in the idea of 'putting your head down, working hard and letting your work speak for itself'.

The idea of 'putting your head down' implies that you are not aware of what is going on in the company, that you are not building relationships and that you are not assessing the dynamics of power and influence in your workplace. When your head is down, literally, you are unable to assess the non-verbal cues of your colleagues; figuratively, it might mean that you are unaware of any corporate landmines. Even in a corporation you are working with people, so it is important for you to always be aware of what is going on with them.

Although Africa is made up of 54 countries, all with different cultures, languages and customs, the ideas of community and relationships connect them all. But when it comes to our professional lives, we are unfortunately not taught about the importance of connection and relationships. We are taught to put our heads down, to work hard and to be excellent. Where is the connection and relationship-building? Once you pass the interviews and actually get the job, corporate is *all* about relationships! How did we not incorporate one of our most basic principles? Going at it alone is very un-African!

> Keep my head down. Work, work, work, work. If I just do that, I'm neither thinking of my business strategy nor my brand strategy. If you're not focused on those things, hard work won't necessarily get you where you need to go." – Artis Brown, *Fuels Executive, ExxonMobil*

We should also unpack the idea of merely working hard. There is no substitute for hard work, of course; it is true that successful people work very hard. However, successful people also work smart. They figure out what is the most efficient use of their time. They ask: 'How can I achieve maximum impact? How can I put in the hours on the areas that matter most?' Successful people don't just put in the hours; they also figure out what great results look like and they focus their attention there. Working smart implies that you know what you should be doing, how you should be doing it and what great results look like.

When you've just been hired, it is almost impossible to know what to work hard on and what 'great' looks like in your company. You can learn and develop your skills through e-learning, but remember that most of what you learn will come from your on-the-job experiences and interactions with people.

Someone once told me: 'Your work does not speak.' And it's true: when was the last time you heard a PowerPoint presentation, an

Excel spreadsheet or a Microsoft Word document utter one word? I'll answer that for you: never. Your work cannot speak for itself. In a corporate setting, you have to make sure that your actual voice is heard speaking about what you have done or achieved. When I worked at McKinsey, associates were expected to participate in office extracurricular activities. Those activities could be client-, associate- or culture-building activities. The company sees its associates as office leaders who should take ownership of the office, which means they need to contribute to its growth and development. An associate's participation (or lack thereof) can count negatively against him or her. During one particular review, the committee was discussing a specific associate, questioning her office contribution. They were under the impression that she had not participated in any of the activities. Luckily, the person who presented her case to the committee had a laundry list of activities that she had not only participated in but also conceptualised and led. Had he not presented those, the committee would have left the room with the perception that she had not contributed to the office's growth and development. It was clear that this associate had gone over and above what was expected of her, but no one (except her case presenter) knew it. This is a perfect example of why we cannot assume that our work speaks for itself. The higher the pressure at your work and the higher the performance standards, the harder you have to work to differentiate yourself. Part of that differentiation process is being able to toot your own horn, talk about your work and create and manage a personal brand that aligns with your work.

Growth vs fixed mindset

The premise of Carol Dweck's best-selling book *Mindset: The New Psychology of Success* is the introduction of two commonly held mindsets: a fixed mindset and a growth mindset. A fixed mindset is focused on outcomes, not processes, and people with this type of mindset believe that intelligence and talent are fixed at birth. They are often afraid of, and avoid, challenges because they see them as threatening. They are concerned that they will fail and their intelligence will be called into question. When they receive negative feedback, they take it personally and can become defensive.

People with a growth mindset, on the other hand, believe that intelligence and talent can increase throughout their lives. Growth-mindset people are focused on effort, process and progress, not outcome. They are not afraid of challenges and see them as opportunities to be embraced; they are not focused on how they will look or what the outcome will be. They are focused on the learning, growth and development that will occur as a result of trying. When people with a growth mindset get negative feedback, they are appreciative of the helpful information and use it to grow.

Growth Mindset ...	**Fixed Mindset ...**
Inquires	Advocates
Focuses on big picture and then self within that context	Focuses on self
Seeks and actions feedback	Does not seek or receive feedback
Takes ownership of learning and development, seeks or creates opportunities to improve	Does not take advantage of or develop opportunities to perform better
Solution-oriented	Problem-oriented
Empowered/Victor mindset	Victim mentality

Get your mind right

As a PDM, I often saw individuals who were rated poorly in their annual review. They were then given a certain amount of time to turn their performance around and improve. I know of one individual who managed to lift herself out of the slump by the next review cycle; another person spiralled into another poor rating and ultimately left the firm. They were equal in intelligence and ability, but their mindsets differed. Person A did not see the feedback as fatal. She saw it as a singular event and not an indictment of her ability to be successful at the company. First, she analysed and internalised the feedback she had received, then she took responsibility for the part she played in her rating and met with her mentors to get their interpretation of the feedback. She created an action plan of what she needed to demonstrate to improve her rating, rallying her supporters around her and keeping them abreast of her progress. She had a laser-like focus on the areas she needed to improvement and she worked on them every day. She frequently asked for feedback so she could understand her progress and what she still needed to do to close the gap.

Person B was the opposite. He took the rating as an indictment of his ability to be successful at the company. Going into victim mode, he started to blame others for his poor performance. He was never clear on the essence of the feedback and never took ownership of his role in the poor rating. He did not rally his supporters, nor did he ask his mentors for perspective. He saw every piece of feedback as another nail in the coffin, as opposed to seeing them as data points to help him determine where he should spend his efforts and energy.

When the next review came around, Person A received a totally different outcome from Person B. I believe that Person A had a growth mindset and Person B had a fixed mindset. I'm not saying that Person B did not have some valid points in his outrage or in his desire to blame others, but his mindset didn't help his case. It's okay to be upset, but at some point you need to move on and focus your cognitive capacity on turning your situation around.

How a Growth Mindset Approaches a Poor Review

What did I do to lead to this outcome?	I will take the feedback as part of my learning.	I will get an accountability partner to help me stay on track.
If I put in the effort, I can be better.	I focus on the process, not the outcome.	I will proactively seek feedback.
I plan how to address the feedback.	I will continue to proactively seek feedback as I develop.	

How a Fixed Mindset Approaches a Poor Review

No one here understands me.	This job is not a good fit.	My manager never liked me anyway.
I'm just going to ignore this feedback.	My manager did a bad job on my review.	I've never been good at Excel.
I can't get any better at this.	My weak areas don't matter to me.	The customer gave me such a hard time.

These two approaches show us that one's mindset is everything. I'm not saying that your mindset will guarantee good ratings, but, when your time at a company comes to an end, at least you would be able to walk away with no regrets, knowing that you gave it all you had. If you have to leave the company because your performance didn't improve, at least you know that you'll be leaving with the respect and admiration of your colleagues. You definitely do not want to say goodbye leaving everyone with a bitter taste in their mouths because of your attitude. Failure or not doing well in the short term is never a waste if you can learn from it. When you learn a lesson, you grow as a person. If you don't grow, you will continue to experience the same situations – even in different contexts – until you learn that lesson. Always challenge yourself and never get comfortable with the status quo. If you are the smartest person in the room, you're in the wrong room. It can be scary to continue putting yourself in these situations.

> If you want to excel, you're going to need someone older than you to help you. You need a mentor. No one can just figure everything out by themselves. I wish I'd had a mentor. I think my life would have been remarkably easier. Now I mentor people who have just entered the corporate world and I see how much easier I'm making their lives." – *Zimasa Qolohle Mabuse*

The trouble with the bubble

Sometimes we think our work environments are all that matters. It's always good to remember that your work is just one type of environment, and that what matters there may not matter anywhere else. The expectations of that environment might not be realistic, so maintaining perspective on where you work and what matters in the bigger scheme of things is key. When I arrived at

Harvard, I knew that I wanted to work in the non-profit space but I was not sure in which area I wanted to specialise. I discovered that people with business backgrounds were bringing their skills to work full-time in public primary- and high-school education. Soon, I was fortunate enough to land a summer internship at Chicago Public Schools, the third-largest public school district in the United States.

While I had a great experience in Chicago, unfortunately Chicago Public Schools was not extending full-time offers for the following year, unlike many of the investment banks or consulting firms that my classmates interned for. I remember how my classmates casually mentioned that they already had offers to start after graduation. I felt depressed. I felt like a loser because I did not have the same level of certainty. But then I reflected more on the situation: in what world do people know where they will be working 10 to 12 months ahead of time? Only in business school, I realised, and business school was not the real world. Business school was a bubble and I remembered not to judge myself by 'bubble standards'. I had clearly chosen a less traditional route out of business school, so it could take me longer to find a job. But that was okay. It was not catastrophic. I was on my own path.

I also saw the bubble mentality at work at McKinsey. McKinsey is very specific about what matters in its culture – problem-solving, analytics, top-down communication. It was also very important for employees to be familiar with the tools of the trade – it was critical to be able to use PowerPoint and Excel effortlessly. I remember bright consultants coming into the organisation and beating themselves up because they were not as skilful as they thought they were or were expected to be. It was devastating for them. The rules and what mattered at McKinsey became their whole world. To succeed in this environment with these skills, using these specific tools was the only mark of intelligence and success. Nothing else mattered. Consultants felt like failures if they couldn't be great in this environment.

One day it hit me: the things that mattered so much in this world did not matter in every world. Everyone in the office revered one particular senior partner – let's call him Mason – because of his influencing prowess and his problem-solving ability. It dawned on me that, unlike Mason, Oprah probably can't even open Excel; she probably doesn't know how to create a waterfall graph in Power-Point. By that environment's skills and standards, Oprah is not considered successful. But outside that space, she is one of the most accomplished, inspiring, impactful and well-respected people in the world. This is why we have to work hard to maintain a broader perspective on skills that matter and how we define success. This helps us maintain our self-esteem and make peace with the outcome if we are not successful by the organisation's standards.

Just because you are not good at something in one space doesn't mean that you're useless everywhere else. A job fit is like a relationship: sometimes it is just not a good fit even between two awesome people. When you spend all week in the bubble with other bubble people, and socialise with bubble people on the weekend, you end up talking, complaining and thinking about the bubble and its rules all the time. This type of insular existence causes you to lose all perspective, and you begin to believe that the bubble is *the* world, not *a* world.

One of the best ways to maintain a healthy perspective is to have frequent contact with people outside your bubble. Non-bubble friends are people who don't work in your field or industry at all – whatever it may be. You'll see that they couldn't care less about your bubble; they are probably completely oblivious to your bubble and its rules. Contact with non-bubble people reminds us that there are other worlds out there. They remind you that not being the best in a particular space is not the end of the world. Make time to engage with the larger world outside to maintain perspective and to keep a healthy view on your company and your job.

Take the long view

Fast-forward and imagine yourself at your 80th birthday: what kind of celebration would you like to have? Who would you like to be there? What would you like to have achieved by then? What do you want people to be saying to and about you? Imagining this helps me to take a long-term view of my career and encourages me to be more vision-oriented. During our careers, we are often presented with many good options and we focus on what is right in front of us. Instead of questioning the options in front of us, we should rather consider whether they will get us closer to what we want to achieve by the end of our lives. Will your choices help you realise your vision? While several options may be good, there is usually one that stands above the rest in that it helps us to achieve our vision for our lives.

This exercise can also help you think about whether there is a disconnect between your life choices and your vision for yourself. In my experience, people often say they want one thing when their actions show the opposite. If you envision having your spouse, children, grandchildren and great-grandchildren at your 80th birthday party, are you at least mindful of the choices and sacrifices that you have to make to realise your vision? Does your current attitude and lifestyle line up with what you say you want? The Japanese concept of *ikigai* is another lens through which you can view your career. *Ikigai* translates as 'a reason to live', and people use the word to refer to the intersection of what you love doing, what you're good at, what the world needs and what the world is willing to pay for. Ideally, you want to have overlap between these four elements, so start thinking about the challenges you see in the world and how you can bring your unique set of gifts and motivations to solve this problem – one that the world is willing to pay you to solve.

If you're missing a certain element, it eliminates the possibility of your achieving the sweet spot between all four elements. Spend time figuring out what problem you can solve with something that really energises you and then spend time getting really good at those skills.

> We hired a millennial on our team, all the right pedigrees in terms of school, everything else. Two months into the job he thought he knew everything and he ended up having an issue with one of the guys on my team. [He talked about] how badly he was being treated. After I broke it down, it was his expectations. I would advise millennials to get a long-term view on their lives. You may not be in the best position today. But don't look at today's situation: think and plan long-term and be strategic in what you're doing. I'm very worried about millennials because many of them are just jumping around from job to job. They go where the grass is always greener."
> – *Ronald Tamale*

The timeline keeper

When we are in our teens, we often create a timeline of how we think our lives will progress, highlighting the particular milestones we want to reach by certain ages. Maybe you had a timeline for your professional or personal life, or maybe it was a combination of the two. According to my timeline, I had to be married by 25, have my first baby by 27 and my second baby by 29. I was 100 per cent unsuccessful at hitting any of these milestones by the expected ages. On the eve of my 30th birthday, I was single (with no decent prospect in sight) and had no children. I remember feeling particularly down about the fact that my life was not where I expected it to be.

Despite this, I had just graduated from the world's most prestigious business school. After two very cold years in Boston, I had just started a well-paid job with Deloitte Consulting and I had bought a townhouse in Atlanta four years earlier. My life was great and I was happy about those achievements, but it was tainted by my disappointment at not having ticked those personal-achievement boxes by the ages I had set for myself. Then, one day, I realised that I had made that timeline when I was a 13-year-old who knew nothing about the world, nothing about how my life would unfold and nothing about the challenges I would face. So why was I holding myself hostage to a timeline created by someone who didn't know *anything* about anything? Why are you allowing that well-meaning but totally uninformed former version of yourself to drive you to self-pity, angst and anxiety?

I'm not suggesting that you dilly-dally; I'm saying that the idea that you should have accomplished everything by 30 is a myth. Have a plan and work at it, but be open to life. Be open to the unexpected, because some of life's greatest lessons happen during those unexpected twists and turns. You are still figuring out who you are and what you want to do, and in the midst of it you are likely to make mistakes. A strict timeline leaves no room for mistakes or unexpected adventures. If someone had told me 20 years ago that I would go to Harvard Business School, meet and marry a first-generation Zimbabwean-American HBS alum and live in South Africa for almost a decade, I would have laughed in that person's face.

The three scariest decisions I have made in my life resulted from events that I couldn't have predicted, but they are also in the top four decisions I've ever made. Years ago, I would have seen these as interruptions that did not factor into my timeline, but today I'm eternally grateful that I did not let that timeline dictate my life choices. My timeline could easily have kept me from some of the greatest adventures and love that I've ever experienced.

Are you trying to live up to a timeline that someone else has created for you? Sometimes it might not even be you but the people around you that push you to achieve certain milestones. Family, friends, colleagues and/or members of your religious community might not only push you into a certain career, they can also pressure you in every aspect of your life if you allow them. If you're not dating anyone, people will ask, 'When are you going to start dating someone?' Once you start dating someone, people will ask, 'When are you going to get engaged?' Once you get engaged, people will ask, 'When are you getting married?' Once you get married, people will ask, 'When are you going to have a baby?' Once you have one baby, people will ask, 'When are you going to have another one?'

While most people are well-meaning, some of them are just nosy and would rather focus on your life than on their own. They are not going to help you pay for a wedding, nappies, childcare or university fees, so why should you let them push you into decisions when *you* will have to live with the consequences? A critical part of adulting is tapping into what you want and not what society tells you that you should want. It's figuring out what your dream for your life is, finding the voice to articulate it and having the courage to live it.

When you close your eyes, what do you see yourself doing in 10, 20, 30 or 40 years? Do you see yourself in a high-powered corporate job? Running your own business? At a desk in a fancy office or out on the road talking to customers? Do you see yourself on a stage speaking? Or maybe writing books? I firmly believe that we all know what our dreams are, but to realise them we have to get quiet, spend time alone and drown out the noise of others, as well as our own limiting beliefs, to actually hear what we've known all along. Life is not a dress rehearsal, so make sure the life and the career you are living is your own and not someone else's.

The timeline mentality pushes us to do things personally and professionally outside of when we would naturally do them. Sometimes, out of frustration at not getting *what* we want *when* we want it, we jump from job to job and role to role, letting our disappointment turn to anger. Our anger and anxiety then make us say and do things that alienate us from others, which defeats our long-term goals.

I'm not saying that you should wait forever for that promotion or developmental assignment, but in the grand scheme of your life, what is the big deal in waiting another six months or a year? When you look back at your career in 15 to 20 years, will you really regret waiting a couple of months, especially if you know that the performance or development concerns that your manager has are valid? When you have to make an important decision in your personal life or career, fast-forward 20 to 30 years down the line and envision whether you will regret that decision. This approach may not work for every scenario in life, but for those decisions that are time-based, it can be very helpful.

Limiting beliefs

A limiting belief is a false constraint that a person places on herself or others. Examples of limiting beliefs could be: 'I'm too old to go back to school', 'I'm too young to be in management' or 'These people don't want to help me.' When I was younger, I used to have an either/or mindset. I felt I could have either *this* or *that*, but not *both*. From a very early age, I was steeped in logical, rational, practical thinking. I was not a dreamer: I cared about the here and now and what was directly in front of me. If I only had $5, my thought process was: what can I afford with $5? I didn't think about what I wanted or needed and how could I make more money to purchase something more expensive. This mentality focused on what I had... but that was then.

I believe that my experience at Harvard Business School awakened the dreamer within me. There, we read many case studies about businesspeople who were not bound by their own resources or even the state of the world. For example, Henry Ford (1863–1947), founder of the Ford Motor Company, developed techniques of mass production of automobiles at a time when there were very few paved roads in America and very few people could even afford cars. Apple co-founder Steve Jobs made us believe in and buy a smartphone that we didn't even know we wanted, and now we can't live without it. These dreamers were not bound by what was. They dreamed of a world beyond what was in front of them and set out to create it.

Today, I focus on *what* I want; the *how* will come later. When I get to the *how*, I think about how I can get everything that I want, even if those things seem mutually exclusive. Instead of filtering your ideas through all your rational constraints, just say it. You can figure out the rest later. You never know, your idea could be the next iPhone; it could be an idea that revolutionises your life and the lives of others. You'll never know the impact your ideas might have if you limit yourself based on what you currently have, what you think you can do or what the world currently looks like.

> Something that really holds people back is self-limiting beliefs. There's a scholarship programme that I encouraged a really brilliant woman to apply for. She said she was going to apply and at the end of the day she didn't apply. There's nothing to say that she would have gotten the scholarship had she applied. But when I looked at the pool of candidates, and then I looked at what I know she'd done, she would have been highly competitive. But what guaranteed her failure was her inability or unwillingness to even step out. And when I asked her later on, 'What made you decide not to apply?' she just said, 'I felt like I wasn't good enough'... It's really about developing your sense of self and the ability to bet on yourself and your achievements." – *Obenewa Amponsah*

In my second year of high school, I took the PSAT (a pre-college/university entrance exam that matric students in the USA can take) and I did really well on the test. Unbeknown to me, colleges and universities were able to get the PSAT scores of high-scoring students. Soon, I started receiving letters from Princeton, Yale and other top universities congratulating me on my marks and encouraging me to apply. Regardless of what those letters said, I did not believe that I was good enough to get in. In my mind, they were just reaching out to me out of courtesy; there was no way they could seriously want me to apply. I didn't know anyone who had gone to those types of schools. I just thought people like me didn't go to those universities. People like me went to local colleges and universities in the city or state, and if you were really stretching it, you went to a neighbouring state, but that was about as far as I thought I could go. I remember putting the letters on my bedside table and thinking, 'I'll show these letters to my kids someday.' It never dawned on me to actually apply. That's how powerful our minds are. Even when I had physical, hard evidence to contradict my belief about what people like me can accomplish, I went with what my mind told me and not the physical evidence. I didn't know anyone who had attended that calibre of school, so it seemed out of reach, even though the evidence to the contrary was in my hand in the form of those interest letters.

Throughout our lives, we put many limitations on ourselves, so it's important to understand and question yourself, your assumptions and the stories you tell yourself about what you can or cannot do. Because I know how my mind sometimes limits me, I always try to take a step back: am I looking at a situation in a limiting way? What assumptions am I making about myself, others, the situation and the possibilities available to me? How can I have it all? How can I make this work? If I don't have the skills, whose help can I ask for to make this happen? By the time I had to apply for graduate degrees, I had learnt from my limiting beliefs. This time, I decided to go the opposite of safe and apply to business schools that were, I thought, totally out of reach for me. And, thankfully, I was accepted to Harvard. Rather let someone else tell you 'no' before you tell yourself 'no'.

> If you think you're a three and you come into a meeting as a three, guess what? You'll get exactly the results that confirm you're a three! What stops you from thinking that you're a ten?" – *Penny Moumakwa, founder and CEO of Mohau Equity Partners, and former Chief People Officer, Discovery Group Limited*

Negative self-talk

Self-talk is talk or thoughts that you direct at yourself. You spend more time with yourself than with anyone else, so it's important to assess if what you're saying to yourself is positive or negative. If someone were to record your self-talk for a week, what would they hear? Would they hear you encouraging or belittling yourself? How you speak to yourself informs how you feel about yourself, which, in turn, informs how you show up in the world. I believe we come to the Earth with perfect confidence and the world slowly chips away at it. We grow up with the opinions of others – things said to us frequently as small children – and we begin to repeat them as if they were our own. As we grow older and unpack those opinions, however, we realise that we are merely regurgitating what was said to us.

I grew up in a household where I received a lot of criticism. Unfortunately, I took on that mindset and directed it towards myself, but in my later years, I have really tried to give myself a break. When it comes to managing your self-talk, sometimes you just have to tell yourself to shut up. You may even need to say it out loud. Interrupt your thought patterns, pause and begin to focus on what is going well, the strengths that you bring and the compassion that you need to extend to yourself as you would to a friend. Remember, if you want to have compassion for others, it starts with having compassion for yourself.

> "Confidence is key. I was raised by two parents who affirmed us as children, and who, by the grace of God, had the ability to send us to decent schools at that time in South Africa. The two things they developed in me are confidence and a sense of self. I want to say to millennials: you are brilliant beyond measure. You are worthy. Be patient, but make sure that you know who you are." – *Ipeleng Mkhari*

Self-talk is not about lying to yourself. It's about maintaining perspective and having a balanced view of yourself and your situation. It's about focusing on what is within your control and what you can influence. It's about remembering that the more effort you put in, the more you can improve and increase your likelihood of success. Self-talk is especially about reminding yourself of your strengths and how you can more fully leverage them. It's about reflecting on all that you've learnt in the past and remembering that if you could learn those things, you can learn new things. It's about remembering how you were able to bounce back from setbacks, disappointments and failures. It's about learning from mistakes and focusing on what you can do differently next time.

> "Most people think I have achieved a lot, but I think I would have achieved more if I didn't have that small voice that kept on telling me, 'You are not enough. You don't speak the best English. You come from a rural background. You come from a poor environment. You didn't go to a private school. You didn't go to an Ivy League school.' I think if I had stopped listening to that voice of doubt sooner, and recognised and appreciated

my own strengths and achievements, I would have gone further in my career." – *Nomfanelo Magwentshu, Partner, McKinsey & Company, COO for 2010 FIFA World Cup Organising Committee*

Impostor syndrome

'Impostor syndrome' is a term coined by psychologists Pauline Clance and Suzanne Imes, and describes the belief that you do not belong in, or have not earned the right to be in, certain spaces. People with impostor syndrome fear that others will discover that they are frauds. I often saw this with the fellows in the leadership development programme I managed at McKinsey. I'm not sure if people felt this way because of the mystique around the company brand. Perhaps they could not believe how far they'd come and questioned if they deserved to be there. Maybe they felt intimidated by the environment – one that had been elusive to people who looked like them and came from similar backgrounds.

At Harvard Business School, it took me a while to believe that I had actually gotten in. Their alumni included the who's who of the business world; it was a place that people like me didn't attend. I kept waiting for someone to knock on my dorm room door or, worse yet, to come to a class to tell me that I was an admissions mistake and that I needed to pack my bags and get out. This is what impostor syndrome feels like.

Let me tell you: from the many admission interviews I attended for my leadership programme, we never accepted someone that we didn't think could be successful. Speaking from a purely practical perspective, it would be a waste of everyone's time and energy to admit someone that we didn't think could make it in that environment. No one who recruits is there for charity. They are there to employ the best candidates – people who will fit well into the organisation. If a hiring manager is part of the selection process, why would they knowingly hire someone who is not right for the job? It would be completely counterintuitive and self-sabotaging.

Erase from your mind the idea that you are a hiring mistake. Your ingoing hypothesis should be: 'I am here for a reason. The company selected me because they want me to be successful and they believe I can be successful. I have to put in the work to fully realise the belief they have in me.'

In my experience, one of the reasons people suffer from impostor syndrome is because they compare themselves to their seniors. We compare ourselves to those who have had more time, exposure and experience. As a PDM at McKinsey, I used to conduct onboarding for new hires. I always told new employees that every successful person was in his or her position at some point in their lives. They had a first day too; they weren't the polished professionals they later became. Just like you, they knew nothing about how the company operates, but after the right experiences, coaching, feedback and effort, they were successful.

Comparing ourselves to our peers can also trip us up. Maybe your colleague is an Excel guru and you aren't. You might feel inferior or think that you don't belong there. But keep in mind that you probably have a skill that that person lacks. Remember that no one person possesses every skill needed to be successful at every level in an organisation. Different roles require different skills, and no one usually has everything. The person who is great at Excel is probably horrible at building relationships or presenting ideas. Instead of being intimidated, ask that person to coach you, and then, when the opportunity presents itself, you can coach him or her in your area of strength.

Another fact to keep in mind is that university teaches you the theoretical aspects of your field, but their application can only be learnt at work. In addition, each environment is different, with people doing things differently. For example, PowerPoint might be a widely used tool at your company, used in a very specific way. University will not teach you this: you will have to learn it on the job. The big takeaway is that you need to give yourself a break. Being new sucks, but don't let it make you doubt your abilities or your drive. Think about all the new things you've done up to this point, how you persevered and how you succeeded.

The good news is that being new doesn't last forever; the bad news is that it rears its ugly head with every new stage in your life. Every new level will expect a new skill set from you. No one would be paying you more money to do the same thing you were doing in your last role. You need to embrace or, at the very least, learn to live with the discomfort of being new. Don't compare yourself to others, make sure you get what you need and put in the effort to improve. The great thing about barrelling through discomfort is that it builds your confidence.

> What has really helped me overcome impostor syndrome are a few things. One, recognising that this voice of doubt is just the accumulation what you've heard about yourself as a Black person and a woman over the years. But that doesn't mean that you need to pay attention to that voice. The other thing that has really helped me to overcome it is just to be okay with failure. I could give the worst speech of my life and no one will die. The stakes are not that high. To add to that, sometimes you need those people who will push you when you can't push yourself. The last thing is, I prepare. I probably over-prepare. That over-preparedness allows me to engage with people in a different way." – *Obenewa Amponsah*

Not knowing every step

Many successful people are planners. Planning and executing our plans are what has helped us to be successful. I am a planner by nature. I like to know where things are headed, how I will get there and exactly what the outcome will be. If I were to guess, I would say that many of the people reading this book are control freaks. That is part of the reason that we have been successful. We've had our lives planned out from a young age and we often write pro and con lists to make decisions. However, as we've gotten older, we've also realised that life doesn't always go according to plan. Remember that every strength has a drawback.

I strongly encourage you to trust your gut, even when the pros and cons don't add up. The most life-changing events in my life occurred when I had plenty of questions and none of the answers, but something in me said: *Do it anyway*. I have grown the most from experiences where I didn't have the next 27 steps planned out.

I remember that my whole village of friends and family prayed for me to be admitted to Harvard Business School. Once I was accepted, I had no idea if I would be able to keep up and graduate. Even though Harvard is in the same country I am from, for me it seemed like an entire galaxy away. I would have to give up many of the things I loved – my house, a salary, my church, a short and pleasant winter – to go to a place where I knew not a living soul and where the winter was 16 long months (okay, it's nine months but that's still *too long*). I had no idea what to expect. Would I be able to do well? Would I graduate and get that *very* expensive piece of paper? As a Black woman, the most pressing question for me was: *who will do my hair?* But I trusted my gut and went anyway, and it turned out to be one of the most transformational experiences of my life.

In my MBA class, I met so many interesting people (including my husband), travelled to Asia, Europe and Africa, and had some of the most stimulating debates and conversations I've ever had. I discovered new passions buried deep within me. And, yes, I even got the piece of paper. I would have missed out on all of this if I had allowed my fear of the unknown or my lack of control to keep me from taking that leap.

I decided to move to South Africa after Fungayi and I got married. It made no sense for us to be married and living on separate continents. I figured I would look back with regret if I didn't take the opportunity to live in another country. This decision presented me with yet another set of unanswered questions. I had been supporting myself since I was 21. And now I was going to a foreign country, without a job, to be with a man I hardly knew. Yes, I was being *a bit dramatic*, but that's how freaked out I was. How was this going to work? Could I find a job? Would I have to ask him every day for R50 (the equivalent of $3) to buy a sandwich? Who was going to do my hair, my eyebrows? I didn't have all the answers, but I moved anyway. Moving to and living in South Africa has been one of the greatest decisions I ever made. I ended up working for McKinsey and discovered another passion, which is working in the leadership development space. I had the opportunity to be part of the journeys of some of South Africa's brightest young minds. I also took the opportunity to start my own business, bringing my entrepreneurial spark to full flame. Had I needed to know every step, I might have missed out on some of the greatest adventures of my life.

The comparison game

When I was growing up, the only people I could compare myself to were my circle of friends and acquaintances. I thought I was doing okay based on what my circle was doing. Unfortunately, today, with the advent of social media and the internet, you can now compare yourself to the whole freakin' world. The comparison game can be a two-edged sword. On the one hand, you can be inspired to do more and raise the bar for your own life. On the other hand, you can become depressed because you feel you haven't achieved as much as others.

Comparing yourself to others distracts you from your purpose and your path. The time that you spend feeling bad or jealous is time you could use to sharpen your vision, master your craft and hone your skills. I always remind myself of Theodore Roosevelt's famous words: 'Comparison is the thief of joy.' Comparing yourself to others literally steals your joy, as you shift your focus away from your unique value proposition. Remember that there are multiple paths and timelines to achieving your goals, so everyone doesn't have to do everything at the same speed or age in life. We all have different gifts, talents and challenges that will impact our journey.

I've also found that people can be short-term in their thinking – another thing that fuels the comparison game. Today, there are myriad lists of achievers, such as 'the 25 under 25' or 'the 30 under 30'. But you don't just want to get on a list: instead, rather focus on longevity and having true impact in your industry. I would rather be on the '50 under 50' or the '60 under 60' list.

Bring what isn't there

As a young (and maybe even as an older) professional, I often wondered (read: complained) about what I saw as the deficiencies of others. *Why can't this person do X? Why does this person do Y so much?* As I've matured, I've realised that I could take another perspective. I could see work as a never-ending search to find an environment with like-skilled and like-minded individuals, or I could view it as an environment in which I brought unique skills, perspectives, gifts and talents. The Myers-Briggs Type Indicator (MBTI) is a tool often used in the workplace to identify employees' personalities. One particular section of this test speaks to your preference to be more structured (or 'J' – 'Judging') versus your ability to be more flexible and adaptable (or 'P' – 'Perceiving').

A consultant once came to me and said that she was really frustrated with her day-to-day project manager and her team. She said that she was a very strong J and they were very strong P's. In her mind, problem-solving in her team was not structured and the execution thereafter was even worse. It was driving her crazy. I asked her a few questions about the team dynamics and her thoughts on what could improve. After hearing her responses, my advice to her was the following: instead of judging everyone for not being a 'J' like you, why don't you bring the 'J-ness' to the team? As soon as you feel that the team is getting distracted, why don't you step up and summarise the discussion? You could even go to the whiteboard and structure what they've discussed. If you are a structured person working with an unstructured team, bring the structure instead of complaining about the lack of it. You might see something that others won't, and you probably have a skill that others don't. Transform those moments of frustration into opportunities to add value to the team.

Stereotype threat

Stereotype threat is a concept developed by psychologists Claude Steele and Joshua Aronson. It describes a certain demographic's preoccupation with, and fear of, living up to certain stereotypes. This influences them to behave in line with, and ultimately to reinforce, those stereotypes. Examples of these stereotypes can be: 'Black people aren't smart' or 'Women can't do math.' Steele and Aronson's studies in the USA have shown that the fear of falling into stereotypes has negatively affected the standardised test scores of Black, Latino and female students. The biggest issue with stereotype threat is that people are expending their brain space focusing on the stereotype instead of using their cognitive ability to perform. Although this research was conducted in the United States, I believe many people who've grown up and/or worked in historically segregated and/or sexist environments struggle with the same thoughts.

Another offshoot of stereotype threat is when talented Black professionals worry that they only got their jobs because they're Black. They are concerned about how this perception will impact them. I reminded consultants that other groups of people often get jobs because of their networks, or for other reasons. I told them: 'Do you think those people question how they got their jobs for one second? Absolutely not. So why should you? For whatever reason you're here, take full advantage of the opportunity and make the most of it.'

Learnt helplessness

Learnt helplessness occurs when a person is persistently confronted with a negative situation that appears to be out of their control. Despite having the power to do so, the person makes no attempt to change their circumstances. The term 'learnt helplessness' was coined in 1967 by the American psychologists Martin Seligman and Steven Maier, who showed that it can cause, or be caused by, post-traumatic stress disorder, anxiety and depression. As a young Black professional, you can easily become discouraged when you consider the small number of Black people employed in the corporate sector. In the United States, there are currently four African-American CEOs running Fortune 500 companies, and all of them are male. Historically, there have only been two Black women CEOs of Fortune 500 companies. African-Americans make up approximately 13 per cent of the US population: based on that proportion, there should be about 50 African-American CEOs.

In South Africa, the data is even worse. While Black Africans make up approximately 80 per cent of the population, very few people from this demographic lead the largest companies in South Africa. In your corporate environment, you may not see many Black leaders. Maybe you don't see many working mothers or women in leadership positions in your community. Maybe you don't see younger people in leadership positions, or maybe they aren't even acknowledged or heard in your organisation. Perhaps you've never seen anyone from your neighbourhood, village or town graduate from university, let alone attend a graduate school.

One of the symptoms of Black tax and the you-need-to-work-twice-as-hard mentality can be that you give up altogether. You might feel as though the whole system is working against you, so why would you even bother trying?

Remember that every person who has ever been the first at anything – the first university graduate in the family, the first to get a postgraduate degree, the first to buy a house – had to face that daunting uphill climb. Nevertheless, they were able to achieve it despite their circumstances and the evidence that proved the contrary. All you can do is focus on your situation, your gifts, the value you bring, the effort you put in and any other factors that you can control and influence. Don't let whatever it is you see or don't see in your working environment discourage you. You *can* be the first or one of the first. You *can* combat learnt helplessness by mastering your craft, building your resilience, learning to be optimistic, being compassionate to yourself and building your internal self-worth.

> Use these limitations that others try to put on you as a reminder that your work quality needs to be excellent, that your communication skills need to be tight, that your analytical skills need to be on point. Use these as a motivator for excellence." – *Artis Brown*

Investing in you

Our mindset is our most powerful asset, so build yours up daily. If any of these mindsets resonated with you, ask yourself: are these mindsets, beliefs or ways of thinking serving me or not? Are they helping or hurting my desire to have an impact in my workplace? How are they holding me back from making progress and building relationships? Once you realise which mindsets are not in your best interest, you might ask, what do I do now? Below I highlight a few ways which we can build up ourselves and our mindsets.

Reflect on your story, strengths and accomplishments: Many bright people are so driven that as soon as they accomplish one thing, they are on to the next challenge without taking a moment to reflect. I've been guilty of this myself many times. Take time to reflect on your strengths, what you've accomplished and the obstacles you have overcome. This will help you build confidence and resilience: if you overcame hurdles in the past, you can do it again. Knowing your story reminds you that nothing is permanent; hard times do not last forever. Reflect on the situations and people from your past and determine what meaning you attach to them. You can't change the past, but you can change how you interpret and feel about it. Think about the role you played in situations and how you could be different in the future.

Remember that your areas of development do not represent the sum total of who you are, no matter how much you or other people fixate on them. Many people are so obsessed with their 'faults' that they forget that those are only a portion of who they are. Ask your closest friends, family and colleagues to tell you what they think your strengths are. On a more practical level, consider taking the CliftonStrengths Assessment – a test that has been taken by millions of people around the world – to get a research-backed analysis of your strengths. Once you know what they are, try to put yourself in positions where you can leverage them. Also, think about ways you can use your strengths to address your 'weaknesses'.

See your differences from the majority as an asset: Think about how your gender, race, religion, age, etc, is an asset to your team. Think about the unique perspectives that you can bring because of your difference from the majority of people in the company. Spend time thinking about how you can leverage your attributes to add value to your working environment.

Pause and reprogramme your self-talk: It's hard to have a positive mindset and life if your self-talk is negative. Take note of and consciously interrupt your negative thought patterns. Show yourself some compassion. It's not enough simply to not be negative; you need to fill that space in your mind with positivity. Consider incorporating positive affirmations into your daily routine. Here are a few examples: 'I am destined for greatness. I am strong and capable. I can improve and bounce back from disappointments. Everything is working out for my good. I am open and receptive to all the goodness that the universe has to offer.' In the business world, we often talk about having a strong fact base for moving forward in a certain direction or with a certain course of action. A fact base supports a decision; without it, moving forward is not advised. I treat my thoughts in the same way. If I have an unhelpful thought, I ask myself: 'What facts support my thinking?' I make a point of challenging my thoughts, no longer accepting them as gospel. I no longer allow them to take hold of me and run me off course into an emotional vortex.

Conduct an emotional inventory: Conducting an emotional inventory will help you to understand your self-talk, your emotions and the energy you're emitting in your professional and personal life. Over the course of a week, write down every emotion you feel. Are you happy, frustrated, sad, lonely, excited, content, etc? Jot down the details of each situation and assess them at the end of the week. Did you notice any themes or patterns? Are your emotions more positive than negative, or vice versa? Are there certain situations, people or times of the day that trigger certain emotions for you? How does the energy you bring to situations fluctuate with your emotions? What can you change about the situations or your perspective on the situations? What can you change about yourself? What can you do more of? Get feedback from people in your life (personal and professional) to understand how they experience you.

Examine your inner circle: I read somewhere that you can tell a lot about a person if you look at the five people they spend most of their time with. Does your inner circle affirm your greatness, challenge you and/or tell you when you're wrong? Are they celebrating your successes and encouraging you to reach for that stretch goal? Or do they tear you down, telling you to play it safe so you can avoid failure? Are they trying to better themselves? What do you talk about when you're together? The future, your goals, plans to achieve them? How to be better leaders? Will they be a sounding board for you and provide support when you experience setbacks and feel down? Can you be authentic, vulnerable and share your feelings with the group without their taking advantage of you or belittling you? It's difficult to have a positive outlook on life when your inner circle is negative and disrespects you. Always examine your inner circle to see if they are a help or a hindrance to managing your mindset.

> It's powerful to have somebody that supports you and lifts you up when you feel lost – somebody who primes you for the positive and the good. Having that level of support helps you be fearless and be the person that you can be, the person who you have the potential to be." – *Dr Jennifer Madden*

Read books on professional development: Evaluate the type of materials and information that you consume. The books you read should build you up, helping you to focus on your strengths and address areas of development. They can help you to unpack your story, the meaning you've attached to your story and what elements are propelling you forward or holding you back. Good books also provide tips to help you reframe your story and your mindset.

Invest in yourself and master your craft: When you know that you know your subject matter, you have the confidence to speak up in a meeting, to engage with a client or a customer, to push back on a colleague or raise your hand for a challenging assignment. Be a lifelong learner who is constantly upskilling. Take advantage of online and internal learning opportunities. The world is ever-changing, so focus on staying relevant.

> Just because you're already on a path where you're learning a lot – maybe if it's in a new environment or a new job – it doesn't mean that it's enough. You might feel like you're growing and learning a lot, but there's always so much more. How do you keep pushing yourself from a learning point of view in the same way you would if you were back in university or college? Don't just do work that's given to you; soak up as much knowledge as you can get." – *Damany Gibbs, co-founder and Chief Financial Officer, Nova Pioneer Education Group*

Meditation and spirituality: Meditation is a powerful tool to centre yourself and shut out the noise of the world so that you can hear your own voice and your life's greatest longings. It also helps you to fully experience and enjoy the moment you are in without obsessing over the past or worrying about the future. Guided meditations help me to practise deep breathing, relax and stay in the present – something that improves your listening skills too. Having a spiritual base can help you feel connected to a power and a purpose that is greater than yourself. For me personally, knowing that God, the Creator of the universe, loves me, never gives up on me and that He created a great plan for my life, gives me a tremendous amount of hope and expectation for the future regardless of what is happening in my life right now.

Live a healthy lifestyle: Being a healthy person helps you bring your best self to work. Regular physical exercise releases endorphins that reduce pain, increase pleasure and elevate your sense of well-being. Exercise also reduces stress, helps you sleep better and, importantly, helps keep your mind sharp. Building your physical strength and pushing yourself physically helps to build up your mental strength and confidence. Find some form of physical exercise that you can commit to doing consistently. Getting enough rest helps to improve your memory, makes you more alert and boosts a positive perspective that assists in decision-making. Drinking plenty of water lifts your mood, reduces fatigue and helps with managing your weight. A balanced diet helps to energise you and builds up your immune system.

Practise learnt optimism: Earlier in this chapter, I mentioned Seligman and Maier's concept of learnt helplessness. But Seligman also conceived a concept that counters learnt helplessness: learnt optimism. This is when we develop our ability to speak positively to ourselves and to explain our situations in a more balanced and productive way. People who are more optimistic achieve more, are healthier and live longer lives. Conversely, those who are less optimistic tend to give in and give up more easily, and thus achieve less. They are more easily depressed and have worse general health. Pessimists see the world as it is, while optimists see the world as better than it is; where pessimists see reality, optimists see possibility. The biggest difference between pessimists and optimists is how they explain what happens to them in their lives. These explanations are based on three dimensions: personalisation, permanence and pervasiveness.

Personalisation – the extent to which you believe that whatever happens to you is all your fault and that there are no environmental factors or extenuating circumstances that may have contributed to the specific outcome. *Ask yourself:* was I the sole reason this situation turned out the way that it did? Or were there other circumstances that played a part? This helps you to take responsibility for your role but then also acknowledges that there were other factors at play that perhaps you couldn't control or influence.

Permanence – the extent to which you believe that this situation or the consequences of it will last forever. *Ask yourself:* will this last forever or am I just in a temporarily stressful, disappointing situation or setback? If the situation is temporary, then it can change and you can have a role in turning it around.

Pervasiveness – the extent to which you believe that the characteristics in you that contributed to the situation are traits that can't be changed. *Ask yourself:* do I believe that I can grow my intelligence, that the more effort I put in, the better my skills will be (more of a growth mindset)? Or do I believe that there is nothing I can do to change my situation because of who I am?

We might be born with a certain amount of optimism, but we can always grow it; the same applies to our resilience. Learning how to be more optimistic also ties in with your ability to be resilient. The more we intentionally think differently, the more we can build our resilience and optimism muscles.

> Whether you believe you can or you can't, you're right."
> – Henry Ford

Therapy or a coach: If you have suffered trauma that is holding you back in your personal and professional life, consider seeing a licensed therapist or a certified coach. Historically, therapy has been a bit of a taboo subject in our communities, but more and more people are talking about and taking advantage of it. If you had a broken arm, you would go to a doctor. Why wouldn't you take the same approach for your emotional or mental wounds? Take advantage of this resource to make sure you're able to show up at work as the most whole version of yourself.

Practise gratitude: In her book *Option B: Facing Adversity, Building Resilience, and Finding Joy*, Facebook COO Sheryl Sandberg talks about writing down three joyful things that happen to you every day. It could be as small as appreciating your cup of coffee in the morning, or that the radio played your favourite song. Practising gratitude is about acknowledging small joys, which reminds you of, and orients you towards, the good things in your life.

Setting intentions: A few years ago, I became very deliberate about setting my intentions. What type of energy do I want to put out into the world? What is my aim, my goal for my work? For my interactions with others? What feedback have I received and what were my intentions with it? When I have thoughts or behaviours that don't line up with my intentions, or when I make mistakes, I remind myself: here is a sample of my list of intentions for myself and how I interact with others that I repeat out loud every morning before I go to work. My intention for myself is to have impact, to take ownership for who I am and how I behave, to interact from a space of love (as opposed to ego or fear) and to be distinctive in all areas of my life. In terms of how I relate to others, my intention is to connect, to listen and learn from others, and to be aware and sensitive to the emotional, mental, spiritual and physical needs of others

What is *not* on my list is to be right, to make others feel small, to overshadow others, to be perfect, to deflect or to make excuses. Do you have subconscious intentions? Consider exploring them further. Are they going to help you to create impact in your professional and personal life and build relationships?

Don't expect that negative thoughts or thought patterns will stop immediately. Remember that cultivating a balanced, positive mindset is a long game. If you've held certain opinions, perspectives and thought patterns for a long time, it will take a while to overwrite them. Expect that, with time, you will get better and better at talking yourself out of them. Fifteen years ago, I would beat myself up for two days whereas now I only beat myself up for 30 minutes. You might make progress more quickly on some mindsets than others. You never know: perhaps, in five or ten years from now, and with the proper effort, the mindsets that you struggle with now could be a distant memory. #growth #progress

Chapter 3
People matter

Imagine that you're visiting your friend's house for the first time. After a while, you need to use the bathroom. Since this is your first time there, you clearly don't know where the bathroom is, so you wouldn't dare wander around to find it. Instead, you would ask your friend and you would need him or her to show you around. It's the same at work. You need the people already working there to show you around.

Regardless of the type of organisation you work for, having great relationships with the people you work with and for is extremely important. This is probably one of the biggest differences between work and school. When I use the word 'relationship', I don't mean just being able to 'get along'. Instead, I'm referring to the type of relationship where a colleague is willing to look out for you, open up to you, tell you how the environment works and tell you when you do something well and when you don't. This is someone who will introduce you to important people in the organisation, create opportunities for you and pound the table for you when you're not in the room where bonuses, salary increases, promotions and step-up opportunities are being decided. This person is someone who will coach and mentor you and school you on the unwritten, unspoken rules of the company. Ideally, this is someone who will want to see you win and who will do his part to make sure that happens, because he understands you and wants to invest in your success. In your workplace, who is excited about you? Do any of your seniors know of your skills? Know your story? Consider this: how can someone be excited about you if no one knows you? Remember that you will not be in the room when the most critical decisions that affect you and your career are made, so you cannot lean solely on your intelligence to help you stand out from the crowd.

Relationships are the cornerstone and foundation of business. Whether it's the relationship between you and your teammates, your manager, your company and its customers, clients or suppliers, or between you and the CEO and the board of directors, relationships matter most. Every business sells something or provides a service to people, and every job within it is enabled or performed by a person or persons. If you look at your job through this lens, you will take a totally different approach to your work.

We often talk about hard work as an ingredient for success and I firmly believe that it is. But when we speak of it, we usually speak solely about putting in the long hours and making sacrifices in order to master our craft and be excellent. However, I'd like to challenge you to think more broadly. Hard work also includes the energy and effort you put into building and sustaining your working relationships.

> In 2014, after a spell of unemployment, I got the job of my dreams at a well-known professional services firm. This was the third time I had applied for that job, so I was convinced this was it! But five months later, the relationship between my manager and I had broken down and I was under performance management, even as my internal customers praised my work."

The above quotation is taken from a post on the blog Working While Black. When I first read the post, it made me wonder: what could this person have done differently to make the relationship with his/her manager an asset rather than a liability?

CHAPTER 3

> "The secret to success, whether it's an individual or an organisation, is down to people. That was always the bits that made the difference." – *Thokozile Lewanika Mpupuni*

From my experience working with young professionals, I've noticed that, instead of focusing on relationship-building, Black people across the globe are often obsessed with degrees. When I started working at McKinsey, my mother's first question to me was: 'How many degrees does your manager have?' My hypothesis is that we have been socialised to believe that degrees, certifications and qualifications are the only things that matter. We have been socialised to think that they will take us wherever we want to go in our careers. While your intelligence, qualifications and degrees are the price of admission to an organisation, the key driver for advancement and success in your company is relationships. The better you are at building and maintaining relationships, and at working with others, the more successful you'll be.

I also believe that many of us spend a lot of energy getting those degrees, and then, when the time comes for us to start the job, we have very little energy left to work on our next challenges – many of which we didn't know even existed. It is as if someone moved the goalposts midway through the game! Understandably, we can become frustrated, but, to be honest, the rules governing corporate environments have always been the same. You just didn't know them. This is the consequence of being marginalised, of standing on the outside looking in. Because nobody told us the rules we made them up, and the ones we made up were all about degrees. We need to acknowledge the insufficiency of this belief.

One of those major challenges (those ones you perhaps didn't know existed) is building relationships. In Chapter 1, I discussed the concept of working *in* versus *on* your career. This concept also applies to our relationships. Working *in* your relationships includes the activities that you and your team members or manager engage in to get the work done. They include the following:

- ☐ Establishing expectations and project goals (ie, what does success look like?)
- ☐ Discussing the status of projects (What are the key milestones? What progress has been made to date?)
- ☐ Understanding resources needed (What do I need to complete this project?)
- ☐ Establishing and negotiating timelines (When is the project or task due? Can I push the deadline back? Can I have more time?)
- ☐ Unpacking obstacles (What is hindering you from completing the project?)
- ☐ Determining key stakeholders (Who do I need to consult and keep informed during the course of this project? Who has a keen interest in how this work is done? Who will be impacted by my work? Who can influence the success or failure of this project?)

Working *on* your relationship, however, involves taking a step back to understand, manage and enhance the dynamics of your working relationship(s) with your colleague(s). It includes considering the following questions:

- ☐ How is each of us feeling about the work?
- ☐ What stresses and pressures are each of us under?
- ☐ Do I feel that my colleague cares about me as a person? Does my colleague feel that I care about him/her?
- ☐ Do I feel that they want me to be successful? Do I want them to be successful?
- ☐ Do we feel supported to meet and exceed the expectations?
- ☐ How do we feel about our interpersonal dynamic (how we communicate in person or via email)?
- ☐ Do we have unaddressed tension in our relationship(s)? If so, how should we handle it?
- ☐ Do I understand what my partner's areas of development, strengths, values, trigger points, etc are? And does he or she understand mine?

❐ How do I feel after having an interaction with my colleague? And vice versa? Do either of us feel demotivated, anxious, uninspired, de-energised? Or do we feel motivated, peaceful, inspired and energised?

Working *on* your relationships highlights an important point: often, we don't want to address interpersonal dynamics. We just want to focus on the work. But it's important to remember that the quality of our output and the general outcome of a task correlates with the quality of our relationships. I have been super guilty of this in my career, exactly because I didn't understand the connection between my work and my relationships. In the past, I used to set aside any negative interpersonal dynamics and focus all of my energy on the outcome. A part of me didn't think that relationships were important: if the product was great, all that other stuff didn't matter. What I quickly learnt, though, was that 'the other stuff' never went away. In fact, negative relationships just got worse.

If you and a colleague get along, he or she will be more willing to help you, which means that you don't have to spend any of your energy thinking about, trying to avoid or unpacking the tension between the two of you. With a good relationship in place, you can focus all your brain power on solving the problem. (Anyway, who wants to come to work every day and deal with passive-aggressive comments, tension and side-eye?) In order to get to this point, you might have to put your agenda and that project aside to discuss the working dynamic between you and your teammate and/or manager.

People matter

Working *In* vs Working *On* Your relationships

Working *in* your relationship discussion topics	Working *on* your relationship discussion topics
• What are the project due dates?	• How do I feel about the work?
• What are the roles and responsibilities?	• Do I trust you?
• What are the specific tasks that need to be completed?	• Is there unresolved conflict in our relationship?
• What are the critical project milestones?	• Do I feel as though I am being properly supported to get the work done?
• What roadblocks am I encountering?	• Do I feel that the expectations from the other side are fair?
• What resources and support do I need?	• What are your emotional trigger points?
• How often will we meet to discuss the project's progress?	• What are you trying to achieve?
• What elements of the project do you want to be kept abreast of? And with what frequency would you like these updates?	• What are your strengths?
	• What are your areas of development?
• Should I bring an agenda to those meetings?	• What influences you the most when you are making decisions (data, vision, process to achieve, who else supports the idea, etc)?

From theory to practice

One of my former coaching clients is a senior executive at a branding and marketing firm. She told me that she does not trust or connect well with a certain member of the board of directors of her company. The lack of trust between them, she said, affected their ability to communicate effectively and exchange ideas in a mutually beneficial way.

'What does this board member *value*?' I asked her.

'Money, numbers and financials,' she responded.

'And what do *you* value?'

'I value leadership. When I communicate with him, I speak about numbers and financials because I know that is what matters to him. I don't feel like he makes the same attempt.'

'Let's switch gears for a second,' I replied. 'Tell me about your business partner. I know you're close to her.'

'She's very different from me. I'm much more "big picture" and she is more into the details. She wants to know the metrics and important numbers that are associated with whatever I want us to do. Once I talk to her in the language that is most important to her, then we can talk about the areas that are important to me.'

So I asked: 'How did you get to this point with her, especially since you are so different?'

'We've known each other for seven years,' she said. 'She's like a sister to me. We have a great relationship.'

'So, since you've been working in this business, how much time have you spent building a relationship with that board member? Have you ever had a non-work-related conversation with him? Have you ever gone for coffee or lunch to understand who he is, his journey and why he values what he values?'

She looked at me sheepishly. 'No.'

'If you don't trust him, he isn't going to trust you either,' I said. 'He can sense that you don't trust him regardless of whether he has said anything or not. Regardless of how professionally and respectfully you have communicated with him, people can sense vibe, energy, body language and tone. People have to trust you before they trust your ideas. So if you want to maximise your impact in this company, then you'll have to take the first step to build and repair this relationship. You're going to have to start to understand who he is, what his story is and why he values what he values.'

I continued: 'Relationships matter most in business and that trust is the most important factor in those (or any) relationships. If trust is lost, then the working relationship is doomed and you'll never be able to have the impact that you want to have until you fix it. Building or repairing this relationship should be your number-one priority. Take time away from your to-do list and spend time on this. Make the sacrifice of time in the short term and it will benefit you, your team and the organisation as a whole in the long term.'

As with anything in life, your approach to relationships starts with your mindset. Here is a perfect example. I was speaking with a young Black professional who was about to start a new job at a global management consulting firm. I asked her how she was feeling about the job, and she said: 'I'm nervous because this is the first job I've ever had where I have to get people to like me. I'm also someone who has a lot of pride, so . . .' I finished the sentence for her: 'So you don't want to have to grovel to get people to like you.'

I told her that if she wanted to be successful in her new role, she had to think about it in a different way. It's not about getting someone to like you. It's about building a mutually beneficial relationship where each party adds value to the other person. The senior person adds value by mentoring and coaching you and giving you feedback, and you, in turn, add value by giving that person an audience for their experiences and maybe an extra set of hands when they need help on a project. Because of the relationship that you've now cultivated with that person and the quality of work you deliver, that person will be more than happy to pound the table to support you during performance reviews and recommend you when step-up opportunities arise.

> It's important to remember that a person is a network, not an individual. So always treat people as a network and not as an individual. So you have to leave that relationship in a way that's good enough that if they ever have influence over you in a different scenario or through other people, you would still leave a positive impression with them no matter how hard it is." – *Thokozile Lewanika Mpupuni*

I've seen a lack of relationships keep people from promotions they rightfully deserved. On the flip side, I've also seen how relationships help people keep jobs that they should have been fired from long ago.

> I tried to understand and collaborate with a lot of the departments. I tried to understand how my work affected others, and vice versa. This led me to having a great network internally and externally. Nurture those relationships always, even after you've left. You want to leave a good name wherever you go." – *Nomfanelo Magwentshu*

Relationship currency evolves over time. When you first start a job, building your relationship currency means that you have to get to know people and allow them to know you, so that they will show you the ropes and invest in your development. The first person you want to build that currency with is your direct manager. However, don't stop there: build relationships with your teammates. They might have skills that you don't, or maybe they've been there longer and can help you understand the culture, the expectations and how the organisation works. Plus, having friends at work makes work more enjoyable. Some of us spend more time with our colleagues than we do with our families and friends, so it stands to reason that you would want to have real, genuine, authentic relationships at work.

If you become a manager, your relationship currency will extend to the people who report to you. As a manager, your job is to achieve results through others, but if you are a horrible manager with a high attrition rate – if you're constantly recruiting, rebuilding and training a new team – you will never be as effective or impactful as you would like to be. And, even with peers on a managerial level, you want to be able to show up to work every day and have positive interactions with them. If you become part of what is known as 'the C-suite' (positions such as Chief Executive Officer, Chief Human Resources Officer, Chief Financial Officer, etc), you'll need to develop great relationships with your direct reports as well as your company's board of directors. Show me a company that is not performing well and I'll show you how poor relationships have contributed to the breakdown of that business.

> Engage with others and understand each one's journey and not just in the formal environment. Engage in the formal and informal environments. In the lift. At the coffee station. In the parking area. In the informal one-on-one feedback. Just be open to interacting and engaging with people. You will learn more about them and you will learn a lot more about yourself in the process." – *Nomfanelo Magwentshu*

If building relationships comes naturally to you, congratulations. For those of us who don't naturally think about doing this, building relationships has to be an intentional decision and a goal. I am naturally more of an organic relationship builder. I just let it happen, as opposed to being intentional about it. I am also someone who has a natural preference for action and execution. Getting things done energises me, so I am always focused on the task at hand and love checking items off my to-do list. However, over the years I've realised that I needed to intentionally set aside some time to get to know people and for them to get to know me.

In preparation, I asked myself two crucial questions: first, what are my boundaries, and, second, what small steps outside my comfort zone am I willing to take to build relationships? In other words, what am I unwilling to sacrifice in order to build relationships? And which of my preferences and aspects of my usual way of being am I willing to sacrifice? I realised that I have one main boundary: I wasn't going to be dishonest in an effort to build relationships, nor was I willing to spend time building relationships with people who clearly weren't interested in building a relationship with me. Other than that, I was willing to make adjustments and be flexible.

For example, during my time at McKinsey, I shared an office with two other people. Colleagues would often come into the office to speak to one of my office mates about work-related matters, but, because of my natural bias for action and my almighty to-do list, I would greet them and then turn around to keep working. However, I decided that if a colleague came in just to chat socially, I would turn around and join the conversation as well. It didn't cost me anything except a few minutes away from my to-do list. In addition, it gave people an opportunity to get to know me and for me to know them. I gave them a chance to access me in a non-business, non-task-affiliated way. It helped people see a different side of me, and vice versa. In the long run, these short interactions made future business interactions easier, exactly because we had established rapport beforehand.

What are your non-negotiables? Is everything on your list non-negotiable? When and how can you be a little more flexible? Are you willing to make compromises? Keep in mind that if everything is important, then nothing is. An easy step that you could take is to eat lunch in the break area with your teammates instead of at your desk. Are you willing to sit with people that you don't know? Could you spend a bit more time at the coffee machine if a colleague is engaging you? Are you willing to sacrifice a bit of your Netflix time to join office drinks on a Friday or at the monthly networking event? Start small, but start somewhere.

> Networking is about genuinely being interested in people." – *Jocelyne Muhutu-Remy*

Building relationships is a skill. Trust is the primary foundation for any personal or professional relationship.

One of my favourite Harvard Business School professors, Frances Frei, says that trust is made up of three components: logic ('Are you competent?'), authenticity ('Are you real?') and empathy ('Do you care about me?'). There are two key takeaways from this formula. First, a deficit in any one element affects your overall trust level. And, second, the more your actions seem focused on and about you, the less trusted you will be. If you ever have a relationship that you are struggling to make work, look at one of these elements to see what the root cause of your issue might be.

When you're deciding what you will share to build trust, I'm not suggesting that you reveal your deepest, darkest secrets. But be willing and be prepared to share some side of yourself that is not connected to work to help you connect on a human level with the people you work for and with. Be vulnerable to a level that you're comfortable with. It draws people to you. It humanises you. It helps people be honest with you. Plus, knowing your human side makes people want to invest more in you. Consider this: when was the last time you trusted someone you knew nothing about?

> Who are the people you need to collaborate and work with to deliver value for your company? Know who is in that value-creation chain of your world and connect with them authentically, because there's nothing more off-putting than that transactional newbie. Every time you go to someone, it can't just be because you want something from them. Take an interest in and facilitate the success of others." – *Thokozile Lewanika Mpupuni*

Determine what you want to achieve and what type of support you need to achieve those goals. The next step is to determine the key stakeholders and what type of support you need from each person. Use the relationship-building plan template below to organise your thoughts on those key relationships.

Working *In* vs Working *On* Your relationships

Goal	Name	How can this person help you achieve your goal?	How can you be helpful to this person?	Current Relationship Status	Desired Relationship Status	Action Plan to Shift Relationship	Progress

Keys to building great relationships

Now that you know who you want to build great relationships with and what support you need, let's focus on four key elements that will help you do just that.

1. **Do your due diligence:** We often assume that others are just like us, want the same things or will automatically know what we want. We tend to play this game of assumptions and wait until conflict or tension arises between ourselves and others. Wouldn't it be better if we had conversations upfront to communicate what each person needs and wants so that we could be more intentional about how we interact? On page 125 there are 17 topics that we can discuss upfront to better understand the individuals that we work for and with.

In an ideal world, you want to know what your preferences are so that you can communicate them to your manager. If you're early in your career and still learning what your preferences are, spend this time learning how your manager operates. Once you and your manager have shared your preferences, see how big the gap is between you and this person. The bigger the gap, the harder you will have to work to make the relationship work. Keep in mind that these questions do not have to be answered in one sitting. Take a few sessions to discuss them. They can also be posed to a team member that you are trying to build a relationship with. Another great source of information is to speak with people who currently or previously worked with your manager or teammate.

2. **Be accessible:** This may sound like an obvious point, but in order to build a relationship, you have to be available – quite literally – for those conversations. You have to work *on* your relationships with your colleagues, which means you have to create space and time for you to get to know each other. I know it can be difficult if you are the only Black person, the only young person or the only woman at work: I've been in those circumstances as well. It's just easier to go and sit with the people in the break area who look like you, speak the same language and come from the same culture. But does that help build the necessary relationships that you need to be successful and have maximum impact? No, it doesn't. This doesn't mean that you can never sit with those who look like you; what I'm saying is that you can't do that all the time. Life is about stepping outside your comfort zone, and you're never going to grow if you stay firmly within its boundaries. Growth is inevitably about discomfort, so if you want to grow, be prepared to be uncomfortable sometimes. Is it hard? Yes. Does it suck? Sometimes. Is it unfair that you have to and others don't? Absolutely. Does it still need to be done? Yep.

> "People have a yearning to see themselves in others, to mirror each other. Sameness gives us a sense of belonging, a sense of safety, reduced anxiety, cognitive rest and optimal survival. Diversity poses a risk, because anybody that looks different may be a threat to our well-being. The brain is extraordinarily drawn to sameness for survival. In a corporate world, our evolutionary biology of being attracted to sameness doesn't always serve our social goals. So if you want to serve your social goal of being more inclusive and diversifying, you've got to override the brain's desire to stay in the same group." – *Timothy Maurice Webster*

3. **Be curious, and listen:** We often use our time to share something about ourselves, but sometimes we need to ask questions and learn about others. A good tip to building great relationships at work is to show genuine interest in who your colleagues are: where they come from, how they got to where they are now and what they care most about. We celebrate those who can string words together eloquently in TED talks or on social media, but we rarely celebrate the skill of listening. Let's differentiate between hearing and listening. Hearing is passive and involuntary. If you do not have a hearing impairment, you will be able to perceive sounds. Listening is active, voluntary and requires concentration. Listening requires you to engage your brain and process meaning and generate questions based on what the other person is saying. You can't be a great communicator without being a good listener. Everyone wants to be heard and supported in terms of how they experience situations and people. This skill will also help you tap into what is most important to that person. This knowledge can help you shape your messaging so that it appeals to who you're talking to and what they're trying to accomplish. People enjoy sharing their stories and they'll open

up even more if you demonstrate genuine interest in learning more about them and appreciation for what they bring to the table.

Before you start a conversation with someone, ask yourself whether you're truly open to listening to what the other person has to say. Are you willing to expand your thinking or are you merely looking for an opportunity to validate your opinions? During a conversation, you need to listen to what the person is saying and how they are saying it, and to pay attention to his or her body language. You shouldn't be simply thinking of what you're going to say next or waiting for the person to take a breath so that you can insert your point into that gap.

In a July 2016 *Harvard Business Review* article titled 'What Great Listeners Actually Do', Jack Zenger and Joseph Folkman show that great listeners don't just silently sit there or repeat word for word what someone else has said. Instead, good listeners ask thoughtful questions that clarify assumptions, and they ask questions that let the speaker know that they have understood what was said. They even ask additional questions to gather further information about what the speaker has said. Great listeners are empathetic and acknowledge the feelings and emotions of others. Make sure you're in the right frame of mind to listen; if you're not, move the conversation to another time when you're in a better headspace. Stay open and don't make assumptions. Practise listening even when it is painful to hear what the other person is saying. What emotional baggage do you have that keeps you from staying in the moment and listening to what the other person is saying? I believe poor listening skills, combined with our own baggage, keeps us from listening, especially when we're in a conflict situation or when we're receiving feedback. We listen through the filter of our baggage. You and someone else can hear the same statement but interpret it differently because of your experiences and perceptions. When someone challenges you or gives you feedback, does it dredge up emotions from people and situations in your past? If so, that is your baggage. Spend some time unpacking it.

4. **Grow your empathy:** Being able to understand the context, situation and associated feelings that a person has is critical to building rapport and relationships with others. A prime example is when a leader in a company acquires a new client and then approaches a consultant to see if he or she might want to work on that particular business project. I used to tell consultants that before they said 'no' with a disgusted look on their face simply because they're not interested in the project, they should think about all the effort and months of work it had taken for that leader to close the deal. I encouraged consultants to think about all the back-and-forth those senior leaders probably experienced; how could they, as consultants, have the nerve to tell the leader in such a dismissive way that they weren't interested? It's similar to someone telling a new mother that her baby is ugly. Whenever I used that analogy, people seemed to get it.

   I am not telling you to feign interest in a project. Rather, I encourage you to think about how you convey a message. You can honour your truth *and* the efforts of the other person in a way that fosters the relationship and does not tear it down. Empathy, like any skill, is something that you can develop. Start by practising empathy in small ways. When starting a new project, take a few minutes and put yourself in the shoes of your teammate or manager. Think about the context of that person's reality, all that the person is balancing and feeling, and how your work fits into that person's overarching goal.

> With empathy you can reach anyone." – *Jocelyne Muhutu-Remy*

People matter

	Key questions	Knowing self	Knowing Others (Teammates, Peers, Managers, Direct Reports)
Story	What was your journey up to this point? What were your biggest lessons learned?		
Goals	What are your goals for the project? What are your goals for yourself? How does this project feed into your personal and professional goals? How does your work fit into your professional and personal goals? Are there certain elements of your work that are more important to you than others?		
Strengths and values	What are your strengths? What do you value (eg people, relationships, outcomes, timeliness, excellent execution, etc)?		
Development areas	What are you currently working on professionally and personally? What would you like to get better at through this project?		
Handling conflict	How do you feel about conflict? How do you handle conflict when it arises?		
Energy source	Where does your energy come from – being alone or being around others? How and when do you like to process information – alone or with others? Do you need time to process information on your own or can you do it on the spot?		
Big picture or detail?	Are you a detail-oriented person who wants the facts and figures or do you prefer the big-picture overview? Or are you somewhere in the middle?		

	Key questions	Knowing self	Knowing Others (Teammates, Peers, Managers, Direct Reports)
Structure	Do you prefer order and structure or are you more comfortable with chaos?		
Triggers	What types of behaviours or attitudes upset you?		
Preferred communication method and frequency	What method of communication do you prefer (email, phone call, in-person, etc)? How frequently would you like us to communicate?		
Feedback method	How do you like to give and receive feedback (eg on the spot, formal meeting)? Do you share strengths and areas of development?		
Management style	What management style do you prefer? What is your management style? Visionary, transformational, coaching, democratic, autocratic, servant, laissez-faire, transactional? Something else? Some combination of these?		
Energy highs and lows/cycle	How does your energy ebb and flow during the day? When are you most and least energetic?		
Decision-making	What is your decision-making style? What is the process you go through when making a decision?		
Influence	What type of information influences you the most? (eg analytical data, the big-picture vision, how an idea affects people and relationships, the step-by-step breakdown of a process, something else?)		

Personal boundaries or constraints?	Do you have certain personal boundaries that are important to you? Gym, leaving the office at a certain time, morning start time, space to work alone, etc?
Apology and appreciation language	What do you like to see or hear to believe that someone is truly apologetic? What makes you feel appreciated? When you do something great, how do you want to be recognised?

The reality about managers

Years ago, I worked for a manager with whom I never really gelled. After a few years working for her, our entire team took the Clifton-Strengths Assessment (which I describe in Chapter 2). When I compared my results with hers, I realised that the heart of the reason why we didn't get along was that we did not have the same strengths, which meant that we did not value the same things. We were basically on opposite sides of the strengths spectrum.

When you and another person don't value the same things, there is a good chance that there will be tension. Now, what if I had known that at the beginning? We probably would have had a completely different working relationship. I would have known that I needed to work harder to bridge the gap between us. Maybe I would have been able to influence her more had I appealed to her in areas that she valued. Maybe I would have volunteered to help her in areas where I knew that I was stronger, instead of being frustrated when she didn't do the things I expected her to do well. Had I valued her strengths, maybe I would have tried harder to learn from her in those areas. Maybe we would have had a better relationship if she felt that I valued what she brought to the table. Ultimately, not trying to understand each other's differences got in the way of our having a fruitful working relationship.

In most conventional corporate settings, your manager has a tremendous amount of influence over your career, your on-the-job training, your development opportunities and how others in the organisation perceive you. Remember that your manager is not just a manager: he or she is a human being with fears, insecurities, triggers, strengths and weaknesses. Regardless of how senior, how talented, how tenured your manager is, or how confident they may seem, they may have deficiencies in areas that will affect, annoy or even anger you. Sometimes you might even find it difficult to identify anything to respect about your manager.

Because many of us (including myself) have grown up with such a focus on competence, and because we're told that we have to be great at our jobs, we assume that everyone in a leadership position deserves their position, based solely on their competence. I had to learn the hard way that adults are in positions for many reasons and sometimes those reasons have absolutely nothing to do with competence. Sometimes people get (and keep) jobs because of their loyalty to the organisation. Other times, a person has a certain job because she has great relationships with senior people who would never fire or demote their friend, no matter how incompetent that person is. And even if your manager is competent, he or she may not bring everything that is needed to do the job well. But remember: your manager is also trying to survive, navigate and thrive in the same complex world as you. Be sensitive to that and spend time trying to understand this person.

I'm sharing this so that you can manage your expectations about the quality of your manager. I know I've had high expectations of my previous managers, and when they didn't meet my expectations, I found it hard to build relationships with them. My advice is to work hard to find something you can respect about the person – be it education, their path to their current position, tenacity, work ethic, knowledge about the organisation, their network, their ability to build and maintain relationships, their sense of humour ... something, anything. Your respect for the person needs to emanate from a genuine place; if not, it will have the opposite effect and your relationship will disintegrate.

> Make good friends at work. Don't make your co-workers your enemies. Make them your allies. Find that one good ally." – *Zimasa Qohole Mabuse*

One of the biggest surprises in my career has been how each company, culture and set of circumstances that I have chosen to be in has taught me something about myself that I didn't know. Sometimes these revelations appeared quite subtly. Sometimes I didn't even see them until I reflected on the situation. And sometimes they popped up in an unprofessional way because I was not sufficiently managing my emotions, which led to my work relationships going south. The coaching I've received, the personal reflection that I've done and the assessments that I've taken have given me a window into a better understanding of myself. Once you are armed with that self-knowledge, you are no longer taken off-guard when a situation triggers you because you've 'seen this movie before'. You don't react without thinking because this situation is familiar to you and you know how to manage it. It's better to continue to learn the lesson of *you*, because if you don't, you'll repeat the same mistakes and wonder why you keep getting the same outcomes.

Once, during a one-on-one meeting with my manager, she turned to me and said: 'I feel like you don't trust me.' I was shocked, because I thought I was being professional and respectful, so I could not for the life of me understand how this person could sense anything was wrong. I had not spent a lot of time examining how I felt about her, but clearly she had detected what I hadn't even realised or admitted to myself. I had two choices in that moment: I could either tell the truth or I could lie. It would have been easier to lie because then I wouldn't have to face the elephant in the room. I wasn't sure of the repercussions if I told her the truth. Would I be on the fast track out of this company? Would she be angry, upset?

Would she start crying? Regardless of the possible outcomes, I decided to exercise courage. I chose to tell the person the truth. I looked at her and admitted: 'I don't trust you.' The person responded: 'Is it a values issue or is it that you don't believe that I have the team's back?' 'I don't believe you have the team's back,' I said.

What I realised at that point was that any person can sense tension and whether or not you like, trust, value or respect them. I learnt that people sense your energy, your body language and your tone, and that I wasn't fooling anyone. It was a big lesson for me. If I knew that I wasn't fooling anyone or hiding how I felt, I might as well have been honest with myself and unpacked my emotions about the person. If I had done that, I would have had to address those issues head-on in a respectful and thoughtful way with my manager. From that point forward, if I had an issue with my manager (or anyone else), I decided to address it as soon as possible. Remember that the person may never articulate that she or he knows you don't like him or her; nevertheless, that person knows it and will proceed to interact with you in a way that is based on that knowledge. Pretending as if your feelings are not what they are doesn't work. Hoping that the problem goes away also doesn't work. In many ways, and in most situations, it just makes it worse.

Managing up

One of the first and most important relationships that you should invest in is the one with your direct manager. One of your goals should be to make your manager's work life easier. The better the relationship you have with her and the more you understand her, the easier it will be for you to achieve that goal. You want to make your manager feel that you are on top of things and that you are communicating proactively with her before she even asks. The more she feels like you are on top of things, the more autonomy she is likely to grant you.

Just imagine what a powerful impression you could make on your manager if you said the following to her at the outset of your relationship: 'Having an effective relationship with you is a big priority for me. I want us to work as best we can as a team and as part of the larger team. So I would like to sit down with you and discuss how you like to work and what you're expecting of me. I would also really love to hear more about you and your professional journey. There is so much I can learn from you, so I would love for us to grab a cup of coffee, schedule lunch or for me to shadow you. Please let me know if you would be open to this and the best way for me to get on your calendar.'

'Managing up' means creating mechanisms and ways of working that honour what you've learnt about your manager during the Relationship Conversation Starters exercise. If you know that your manager is a big-picture thinker, as opposed to someone who is focused on the details, communicate the big picture in your emails and presentations and then bring attention to the details afterwards. If your manager doesn't like to digest information in the moment, plan your work so that you can send her the document the night before to give her time to formulate her thoughts. If a certain project is high-priority for your manager, create recurring weekly calendar invites with her so she can be kept abreast of any updates. Bring agendas to your weekly or semi-weekly meetings and make sure you first cover the items your boss cares about, just in case you run out of time. Use this time to problem-solve with your manager or alert her to obstacles that you're running into. Alert your manager immediately to pressing issues that simply can't wait. Bring proposed solutions to her, not just problems.

Check in with your manager to make sure that your plan and approach are still working and adjust as necessary. Projects and priorities shift. What your manager cares about today may change tomorrow. Maybe your manager was fine with biweekly check-ins for your previous project, but now she may want weekly check-ins because the stakes are higher.

CHAPTER 3

Managing conflict

If you start to feel that there is unaddressed tension in any of your work relationships – with your manager, peers, clients or any stakeholder that is key to your delivering your work – address it. It doesn't have to be a dramatic conversation. You can simply say, 'I'm sensing some tension between the two of us and I really want to talk through it. Is there something that I have said or done that is causing the tension? If so, please tell me what it is so I can address it.' As a junior employee, this type of tension has a disproportionate impact on you and your work, so it behoves you to step up and initiate the courageous conversation. So many young people just hope that conflict, hurt feelings and tension will magically go away. On the surface we say, 'Oh, it's fine. It's not a big deal. I'm over it.' But, secretly, we are noting each offence, each slight and each misstep in our mental notepad. I call it the SLOO – the Secret List of Offences. With every addition to the list, the offender digs a deeper and deeper hole that becomes harder and harder to get out of. With every slight, the gap widens between you and the other person until it reaches a point of no return.

Secret List of Offences (SLOO)

1. Colleague A really kept interrupting me during the weekly meeting.
2. Colleague A sent a really snarky email and copied our manager.
3. Colleague A took all the credit for our work in the weekly meeting.
4. Colleague A wouldn't make time to give me some advice for my project.
5. Colleague A gave me some really bad feedback on my performance.

People matter

We often make assumptions about people's behaviours, motivations and intentions, and nine times of ten our assumptions are negative. Usually, we don't give people the benefit of the doubt. And the longer the list of offences grows, the more sinister the spin is that we put on our assumptions. There is a chance that you are the type of person who sincerely gets over things and moves on, but if you aren't, it's best to address those issues and give others the opportunity to explain their side of the story. Even after hearing from the other person, you still may not like what he or she has to say, but at least you've given them a chance to share their perspective. And maybe, just maybe, you were wrong and the person's behaviours and motivations were not what you thought they were. All of this helps to lessen – or even close – the gap. This will help you establish a genuine working relationship with that person, instead of you just saying the right words to make the person believe that the relationship is good.

When we don't address conflict, one of two things is likely to happen at some point. We either explode because we can no longer suppress our feelings of hurt, anger, disappointment or betrayal, or we completely mentally cut off the other person. There are obvious career-limiting consequences that come with exploding in anger at your manager. Cutting someone off might be much less destructive, but people will usually sense your feelings even if they don't verbalise them. Unfortunately, this will create an invisible wall between you and the other person, and he or she might no longer want to actively contribute to your development, growth and advancement in the organisation.

Sometimes we have to work with people that we don't have natural chemistry with or that we don't like or respect. We have to find a way to make the relationship work, because you're not going anywhere and neither is the other person. Before you know it, you and the other person have characterised each other in such a negative way that it becomes increasingly more difficult (read: impossible) to close the gap or to even return to a point of neutrality.

You have to figure out what type of person you are in conflict: do you have a fight, flight or freeze response? Fight people become more controlling and aggressive. Flight people run from the situation in fear and want to be left alone. Freeze people just stand still and they look okay but they are not comprehending or engaging.

When someone offends you, the first thing you need to do is ask yourself: 'Am I bothered by what happened? Or am I bothered by something else?' The worst thing you can do is to take your frustrations about another situation out on your colleague. If you reflect and realise that the issue is not important enough to raise, then you should move on. If you decide that you are bothered by the offence, you have three options: ignore the offence and have a gap develop between you and the other person; raise the issue and address it with that person; or decide that the issue is not important enough to address and genuinely move forward.

Over the course of my career, I have sometimes done this well and sometimes very poorly. These have been some of my biggest lessons. What has worked for me was to create some space between me and the other person so that I could calm down and think about what was going on between us. I would reflect on what I didn't know about the person or the situation, what my role was in that tension, what I was willing to give up, how I could change my thoughts and behaviour, and what I needed from the other person for the relationship to move in a more positive direction. Then I would approach my colleague. In addition to sharing how I felt, I would make sure to ask questions, as opposed to making statements or assumptions, about how he or she felt or why he or she behaved in a certain way. Another crucial technique is to pause the conversation. Maybe it's for ten seconds, ten minutes, a day or a week. If the conversation is getting too heated, it's okay to step away so that one or both of you can calm down. Even pausing for a few seconds allows the more rational, conscious part of your brain to kick in so you can respond in a more thoughtful, intentional way.

A few years ago, I was selected to join a very prestigious leadership development programme. This was my dream job at the time

People matter

and I had wanted to be part of the programme for four years prior to applying and finally being selected. The person I was reporting to was a career educator and I felt that at times he was quite resistant, aggressive and borderline angry when I shared new ideas with him. Instead of dealing with the tension head-on, I chose to 'ignore' it and focus on the work. I wasn't going to let anything or anyone get in the way of enjoying my work or having the impact I wanted to have. I chose the flight response and avoided him at all costs. When he asked me to come to his office, I would walk in and then slowly back away towards the door until we were finished speaking.

His responses to me in further incidents became more and more aggressive until it all exploded. One day, he came to my cubicle quite upset and said: 'I know what you're doing and I want to talk to you in my office.' It was on like Donkey Kong. It was on and poppin'. I had pushed every affront down and now every single one of them was going to come out without my having any control over them. I can still remember the sound of my heels on the plastic runner between my cubicle and his office as I stomped over. American comedian Amanda Seales talks in one of her stand-up routines about the scale of Blackness: from Stacey Dash (a conservative American political pundit) to Nat Turner (a slave who led a group of slaves and free Black people in a four-day rebellion in 1831). In that moment, I was definitely tap-dancing all over the Nat Turner side. The gloves were off and I was prepared to be the Blackest version of myself that I had ever been. I listened quietly as he proceeded to tell me what he thought of me (for the record, none of it was positive). Once he was done, I totally unleashed (in a rather loud voice) all my suppressed anger, which was born from every instance where I felt he had been rude, aggressive, insecure and territorial towards me.

When I was finished – and I'm ashamed to admit this (sorta, kinda ... well, not really) – he began to tear up. By the time those tears welled up in his eyes, my heart was ice cold towards him and

I felt no sympathy. He apologised to me and I just walked out of his office, breathing hard and with my chest still heaving from the unmitigated rage I felt. Once I had calmed down (which took me a minute ... okay, hours), I had to ask myself three questions: how did we get here? What part had I played? And what would I do differently to make sure I never ended up in a situation like this ever again with him or anyone else?

I didn't have to look too far or too deep for the answers. We were here because I didn't know one could have a calm, rational disagreement, and thus I was ill-equipped to handle conflict. I thought my two options were silence or rage. I subconsciously believed that I could be successful and have impact in spite of the dysfunctional relationship with my manager. I had chosen to suppress my emotions and feelings every time I was upset at something he said or did. I told myself that it didn't matter how either of us felt. In other words, I had lied to myself. I tried to tell myself that the latest slight didn't matter and that I had forgotten about it, until one day I exploded because I could no longer suppress my emotions and feelings. Sometimes it takes us a while to learn certain lessons. I knew I hadn't handled it well. Luckily, not long after that incident, my reporting relationship was changed so I became his peer, reporting to his manager. I didn't have to deal with him or put into practice the lessons I learnt from that situation. If I could go back in time, I would have addressed those situations where I felt he was rude or aggressive to me in a calm manner, especially if I was still upset a few days later.

Another lesson I learnt was to gather the context when you start working. I had no idea that my manager had been demoted prior to my joining. I believe he was quite insecure because of the demotion and I think the tremendous hype around my arrival only made it worse. In his mind, I was a Harvard hotshot who was coming to take his job. Had I spent time gathering the context, I would have known about the demotion and I would have couched my new ideas and suggestions slightly differently. I would have made sure that he knew that my intentions were not to usurp his job but rather to make the team (and him) look good and our output even better.

> Sometimes we are challenged in ways that might cause us to feel very emotional. But even if you're right, when you blow up, you're going to be wrong. It doesn't matter what was said to you. If you get into a shouting match in the middle of the trading floor with John, a whole bunch of other people see you and they don't know exactly what happened. All they know is that you and John are screaming at each other. Even though he instigated it, that's not the point. You're now guilty because you are in a professional work environment in a company that is paying you for your qualifications and education. And now you've tarnished your reputation because you're volatile in their eyes." – *Artis Brown*

Mentors and sponsors

> If someone has the right mindset, you give them the benefit of the doubt and you spend the extra hours coaching them. I look at potential and mindset to determine who I mentor. If someone comes to me without me knowing the person's potential, I will help them because they are humble and want to learn." – *Stefano Niavas*

A mentor gives you wise counsel and they share their experiences to guide you in the right direction. They motivate you, provide support and set an example. You should have mentors both inside and outside your company. External mentors can give you a perspective on the industry, how other, similar organisations work, and what you need to do to stay relevant in your industry. Your internal mentors can help you understand how your company works, but they might struggle to help you understand the industry overall if they've been in that same environment for a long time. Remember that you can have mentors for different topics. Maybe you also have a mentor who has a similar personal life structure as you; this person could be especially helpful to you because they help you think about how to juggle professional and personal demands. Either way, you need to be clear about *why* you want a mentor, *what* you want to get out of the relationship and what you want to *give* to the relationship.

Remember that there are differences between mentors and sponsors. A sponsor is someone who works in your company who does not just have a senior title but has influence, decision-making power and a seat at the table when the decisions that affect you most are being made – decisions about promotions, developmental assignments, performance ratings and bonuses. Because you won't be present in discussions where some of the most important decisions about your career are being made, you'll need someone in that room advocating on your behalf.

A sponsor, specifically, needs to meet certain criteria. He or she is someone who can create opportunities and open doors for you within your organisation; otherwise, the person cannot do much to actively help you on your path. A good sponsor helps you to build your visibility and credibility. However, before you get to that point, you should have impressed him or her with your performance, because this is how you earn their support. Sponsors are earned; mentors can be requested. As soon as a sponsor has first-hand knowledge of your abilities, he or she will be willing to put their social capital and reputation on the line to back you. It's ideal if you have multiple sponsors backing you, for two reasons: first, in case one of them leaves, you don't have to start from scratch; and, second, it's advantageous to have multiple people helping to build your reputation and open different doors for you.

Your relationship with your mentor or sponsor should not be a one-sided, transactional one. Find ways to add value to that person. It may not seem like you have anything to offer since this person is so much more senior to you, but you do. For example, if this person works in financial services and you see an article that might be interesting to her, send it her way. If you know that they are working on a big proposal and there is some number-crunching that needs to be done or a PowerPoint presentation that needs to be created, offer to help. And, as I've mentioned before, if you need help unpacking feedback you've received at work, ask your mentors and/or sponsors to help you interpret it. Mentors and sponsors also get a kick out of sharing their wisdom with a young, talented person, being a part of your development journey and developing the next generation of leaders. If a senior person invites you to lunch or to grab coffee, take it seriously and accept the offer. It's unlikely that that person is offering to spend time with everyone, so he or she obviously sees something special in you. Even if he or she cancels on you five times, keep rescheduling. Capitalise on the opportunity to build that relationship.

Based on my own experience and insights from Professor Rosalind Chow of Carnegie Mellon University, I've created a chart that highlights the key differences between a sponsor and a mentor.

> "I got an email from a young man and it said: 'I read your profile. Would you be my mentor?' But I wondered: what kind of relationship did he want? What was it specifically that he needed? A more effective approach is to ask specific questions. He could have said: 'I saw that you are interested in so and so. Could you please give me some insight on that?' Mentors can speak words of correction and give you perspectives that you wouldn't have had otherwise. I'd say to a new mentee that your mentor can learn as much from you as you do from them." – *Obenewa Amponsah*

Mentor vs Sponsor

	Mentorship	Sponsorship
Who is the mentor vs sponsor?	Mentor – very experienced, could be internal or external to your organisation	Sponsor – Senior and influential in your organisation
Who chooses whom?	The mentee chooses the mentor and asks the mentor for mentorship.	The sponsor chooses the mentee. The mentee can ask for sponsorship after establishing credibility and a value proposition.
Who bears the risk? If the mentee fails, who is impacted?	The mentee, since the failure is a reflection on him or her.	The sponsor, since she is putting her name on the line to vouch for the mentee.
What is the purpose of the relationship?	To mould, shape and change the mentee to better fit into the organisation.	To provide opportunities for the mentee to show up authentically in a way that changes how the organisation and other people see the mentee.
What is the nature of the relationship?	Help comes in the form of one-on-one interactions.	Help comes usually when the mentee is not present during critical decisions around salary increases, bonuses, step-up opportunities and promotions.
What is the resource provided?	Time, willing to sit down with the mentee.	Social capital, willing to take risks and advocate for the mentee.
Suggested questions to kick off the relationship	I'm interested in X and I know that you have expertise in this space. What was your journey in this area? What were your lessons learned?	How do I navigate the organisation? How can I prepare myself for the next level or a promotion? How can I get access to opportunities that will raise my visibility with decision-makers and influencers in the organisation?

> Everyone deserves a mentor. Mentorship is equal opportunity. Sponsorship is earned." – *HBR podcast* Women at Work.

People of colour are very familiar with the concept of a mentor, but many of us have only recently learnt about the importance of a sponsor. I would say that many of us are over-mentored and under-sponsored. If I were to choose between having a mentor and having a sponsor, I would choose a sponsor. They can bang the table for you to get that increase, promotion and/or stretch assignment that is critical to your advancement. Even though you might be at the same company with people at the same level as you, you probably are not all having the same quality of professional experience. And not all work opportunities are created equal. A friend of mine used to work in investment banking at Goldman Sachs and a lesson he taught me was that not all deals are the same. You want to make sure you're on teams that manage deals with the best opportunities for learning, and with the most influential leaders in the office.

Your sponsor will help you gain access to premium opportunities such as these. Whereas some junior employees have to figure things out on their own, others have sponsors on their side who can give them the inside track, thus helping them to better understand and more effectively navigate the environment. If you have senior leaders who are excited about you, and who sing your praises, they can help strengthen your reputation in the eyes of other seniors. Which leaders at your company are excited about you and your potential? If no one is excited, ask yourself why. What can you do to build your credibility and a value proposition (the unique contribution that you bring to those you work with) so that leaders become excited about you?

> I was the first of my family to go into corporate America, so there wasn't a pathway, but I knew I needed to talk to people who were senior in the organisation. Get

with people who know what's going on. I knew that I couldn't survive this on my own; I needed to be in lockstep with someone. Always look for people who you can partner with that can coach you, mentor you and help you see around those corners. Stick to that and you'll gain a lot more confidence." – *Tina Taylor*

If your goal is to build your network, how will you know if you've built your network with the right people in the right way if you're not specific? A better way of tackling your goal is to be specific about how you want to attain it. For instance, you could frame your goal of building your network in the following way: 'By the end of 2021, I will be able to include person X as part of my network. Person X will be able to connect me to opportunities and introduce me to other people to help me build my network further.'

Once you've mapped out your plan to meet and/or build a relationship with person X, you have to execute it. The first step of the plan should be to begin to cultivate that relationship. To be honest, the kinds of people that you would want to have as a mentor are usually very busy, so a vague question such as 'Will you be my mentor?' can be daunting for them. When you ask a busy person this question, they might think, 'What does this mean? What kind of time commitment is involved? I'm not sure I have that kind of time. I don't know this person that well. What are we going to talk about?' As you can see, mentoring you can become work for them and, trust me, they already have enough on their plates.

Be specific about what you want to discuss and about the frequency of your conversations. When you approach a potential mentor for the first time, you could say the following in your message:

> [Person X], I'd love to chat about three topics when you have some time. Firstly, I'm very interested in the work that you're doing and I'd like to learn more about your journey and lessons you've learnt. Secondly, I would like to share with you some of the

feedback I've been getting to better understand what I need to work on. Finally, I'd like to run by you some of the opportunities that I've been offered. I'd like to get your thoughts on which ones are the best fit for me if I want to do work similar to what you're doing. Could I reach out to your assistant to set up a time to get on your calendar so that we could discuss this further?

With these few sentences, you've expressed an interest in this person's background *and* you've told him or her exactly what you want to speak about. And the cherry on top: you're asking exactly how to get on his or her calendar. You're showing that you're serious, so once the person agrees to meet with you, you have to make sure you follow through on your request.

> I didn't mind taking the tough assignment, living in the most rural areas or moving multiple times. That's when I grew the most – when I had the most difficult personal and professional growth experiences. I gained mentors and sponsors when they saw that I raised my hand to take those tough jobs. Only much later in life I realised that they were working some things behind the scenes."
> – *Tina Taylor*

One of the biggest lessons I've learnt from my corporate experience in the US and South Africa is that, as a young professional person of colour, you're going to have to let go of the idea that you only want mentors and sponsors who look like you. In some companies, there are just not enough Black senior leaders to mentor and/or sponsor every young Black person in the organisation. At this point, the numbers just don't add up. One Black senior leader cannot mentor 60 junior Black employees. Your options are therefore to go without, clamour for the attention of a few Black leaders or learn how to build and maintain relationships with older, senior people who will likely be male. (Sadly, women still have a way to go to level the playing field.)

At this stage, most of the people who are in power are old(er) men and many of them are not comfortable with, nor accustomed to, trying to find commonality or build relationships with people of a different (younger) generation, ethnicity or gender. As much as we would like our leaders to reach out to us and make us feel at home, some of them just don't have the capacity to do so. And, trust me, you need them more than they need you, so you're going to have to be the one to extend and keep on extending yourself.

> "The minute I walked in there as a market analyst, the African-American VP grabbed me. He said, 'Kapungu, we're having lunch every week.' He basically forced this on me. He saw something in me that I didn't see in myself. You need someone to believe in you even more than you believe in yourself. They push you to do more than you thought you could. They create opportunities for you. I would not have been able to get sponsored to attend Harvard Business School, get the support to move to Africa or have many of the opportunities that I've had had it not been for those people in my life." – *Fungayi Kapungu, Chief Financial Officer, Infinite Foods*

Even if you work in an environment where everyone looks like you, or comes from the same cultural or ethnic background as you, you will still have to work hard to connect, build and maintain relationships with people who differ from you. They will likely be older than you, might have different ideas about work and think differently from you. While all these differences add richness and colour to the work environment, they can also be a source of tension and judgment, so we have to work extra hard to connect and find commonality in the midst of these differences. The ultimate goal is for you to learn to appreciate and fully leverage these differences in order to have greater impact and better serve your customer or client.

Remember, your relationship with your mentor and/or sponsor is not an equal one: you need them more than they need you. So if your intention is to learn, grow and cultivate supporters among the seniors in your company, you need to understand that knowledge, mentorship and sponsorship can come from people who don't look like you. Might it be uncomfortable? Yes. Might it take a bit more work to find common ground? Probably. Will it be hard at first? Yes. Does it have to be done? Absolutely. When I reflect on my career, the majority of people who have created opportunities for me have been people who are different from me – either of a different ethnicity or gender or both.

An example of when I had to put this principle into practice was during my second stint at Deloitte. At the time, I was not performing as well as I had hoped. I had gotten quite rusty while I was away at business school, especially in terms of managing stress and dealing with demanding clients. The head of my department decided to assign me a mentor: Eileen, a senior executive in the same consulting group as me. I wondered what I could possibly have in common with her. She was white and at least 20 years older than me, if not more. Plus, I assumed that, because she was in a senior position, she had had a pretty straight trajectory to the top. How was she going to understand the challenges I was facing?

Prior to our first session, I had to answer a list of questions about my life and was told to bring them along. Little did I know that Eileen also had to answer the same list of questions. When I arrived at the session, I was quite nervous, but as she started to share some of her own – very personal – failures and mistakes, I realised that we are all human beings underneath the titles, big salaries and physical characteristics. We are all just trying to successfully navigate a very complicated world. Her transparency encouraged me to open up and I instantly sensed that I could trust her. This experience taught me that everyone has a story that I can learn from and that no one has had a straight, obstacle-free path to the top. I also learnt that in being vulnerable as a leader – when you remove the leader mask – you become much more relatable to those you lead. I filed this away as a key leadership trait that I wanted to emulate and an exercise that I would do with my mentees and direct reports at some point.

> I looked for mentors who looked like me and had similar experiences to mine. Because I couldn't find them, I stopped looking. I found different mentors for different reasons – Black women entrepreneurs, white males in tech. Find mentors who are looking out for your personal best interests." – *Aisha Pandor, CEO, SweepSouth*

If you reflect on your personal relationships, they began with your getting to know other people. *Where are you from? Where did you grow up? What do you care most about? What do you value? What was your professional journey? What are some of the most valuable lessons that you have learnt during the course of your career?* Just as we spend time getting to know people, their stories and their family make-up, we need to spend time doing the same thing at work. When you've established a good relationship with a mentor or sponsor, make sure you pay it forward as soon as you can. If you've been at a company for six months, you know more than the person who just started yesterday. Make sure you offer what you know and any tips and tricks that can make that person's transition into your organisation smoother.

The connection between EQ and your relationships

> You might have a colleague that you're not getting along with and you could go in and be the mad Black woman or the mad Black guy and take them on. But you have to choose how to navigate these situations and how to

navigate people; you have to be comfortable with the potential outcome or knock-on effects. To me, it's like mind chess: you have to know how to navigate that over time. Know the different pieces on the chessboard, who's who in a room and who has allegiances and connections. Really reading and understanding but also being honest about yourself." – *Ronald Tamale*

One of the greatest tools in building strong relationships is emotional intelligence, or EQ. EQ, a term coined by Peter Salovey and John D Mayer, is defined as the ability, first, to acknowledge, interpret and regulate our own emotions, and, second, to acknowledge, interpret and persuade the emotions of others. To understand EQ, we need to understand what emotions are. We can say that they are conscious mental reactions (such as anger or fear) that we experience subjectively as strong feelings. These feelings are usually directed toward a specific person or situation and typically accompanied by physiological and behavioural changes in the body.

In my experience of coaching individuals, I saw that people sometimes have difficulty in identifying emotions. This stems from the fact that they intellectualise and/or judge what they are feeling, as opposed to merely *identifying* the feeling. People might also struggle with their emotions because they're focused on not showing perceived weakness or vulnerability, which might result from their expressing their emotions. In other cases, people might lack the vocabulary to express themselves or might never have been given the permission to have and/or express their feelings.

Emotions should never be judged as either bad or good. They just are. However, we do not have to allow our emotions to rule over us. We can choose how we want to express what we feel. Emotions are merely signals that show us that something is out of balance or needs to be delved into more deeply. When you feel overwhelmed by a particular emotion, always ask yourself: what is this feeling trying to tell me? Maybe the anger that you are experiencing is telling you that you have some unresolved hurt that you need to work through. Maybe the relaxation that you are feeling about a recent decision indicates that you made the right choice.

> "Many people don't appreciate what emotional energy they're exuding. They don't know the vibe that they're bringing unless they're conscious of it. You bring that energy in the way you talk to people. You bring that energy in the way you look at people, your body language, a lot of things. And it can impact your decision-making." – *Artis Brown*

In many Black families, the focus is on merely surviving and moving on with life. We do not create the space to spend time on, or to investigate, emotions and trauma. Historically (and even still today) in Black culture, we have not been comfortable talking about mental health. Many of us have not had widespread access to, or even trust in, mental health professionals to help us understand, process or give voice and language to our emotions. If we are ever to fully master ourselves, I believe, we have to be able to know what is going on within us. We have to be able to own and interrogate what we're feeling so that we can intentionally choose how we want to respond to those emotions. When we don't, we run the risk of unleashing those negative emotions onto other people. If we want to understand others, we need to understand ourselves first.

A great way to get to the root of your feelings is to close your eyes, speak from your heart and say the following: 'I feel [fill in the blank]' or 'I felt [fill in the blank].' You could feel angry, sad, anxious, hurt, embarrassed or happy; try to use one of the words (or even a variation of them) to express how you feel at heart. If you are unable to recognise and understand your feelings, it will be very difficult for you to manage them. You'll also find it very hard to recognise, understand and influence others' feelings. One of the most important skills I have cultivated – and which has helped me develop my EQ – is sitting with my emotions and understanding their roots.

The famous American academic and author Brené Brown talks about how we are better at offloading our emotions onto other people than at sitting with them ourselves. If we feel isolated or sad, she says, we yell at or are brusque with others, instead of dealing with those emotions ourselves. In the workplace, this is not the type of team member you want to be, and neither is this the type of person you want on your team. You definitely do not want to be on the receiving end of a team member's emotional offloading, and you wouldn't want anyone to be on the receiving end of yours either.

Offloading creates tension, insecurity and a general sense of unpredictability in a team, all of which undermine trust, which is the first building block of any relationship. Consider the following: how can you trust someone if you never know when he's going to snap? How can you trust someone if you never know which version of that person you're going to get? The same is true of ourselves. If we're aware of how we feel, however, we can deal with it or ask the people in our lives for help by letting them know that we're feeling a certain way. Or, if they notice a certain change in our mood or behaviour, they might be assured that it has nothing to do with them.

> It's about cultivating maturity. It's about being honest about your emotions, but also about being able to deal with them for what they are and not to let them define you, your actions or situations." – *Obenewa Amponsah*

When you're able to identify a certain emotion in yourself, your next step would be to ask yourself if the situation that triggered those emotions really unfolded in the way that you perceived it.

You could learn how to understand, work through and manage your emotions by thinking through the following: could you have attached meaning to someone's behaviour or words that the person didn't intend? Did you make assumptions, which then triggered you to feel a certain way because you treated those assumptions as facts? Are there certain situations, comments or types of people that trigger certain emotions within you? Once you identify those patterns within yourself, you can begin to examine the root of those emotions. You might be stuck in a particular mindset, or you might be framing a situation in a particular way, which causes you to feel triggered.

The process of unpacking your emotions and understanding yourself is a lifelong, layered one. This is because different personal and professional situations with specific circumstances and types of personalities trigger us in new ways. As you begin to work through your own emotional identification, assessment and management, you will become more skilled at seeing what is going on with yourself and with other people, thus building and strengthening your EQ. You will not necessarily be able to label others' emotions or the root causes behind them, but you will be more emotionally attuned. You will then be able to help other people take a step back to identify and understand their emotions too.

> For smart people, logic and sound arguments tend to be the default for making a point. Leaders need the ability to make sound arguments, but it takes more than that to influence others. As your leadership develops, you'll realise that you aren't just managing people; you are managing people's emotions. You aren't just managing their work; you're managing how they feel about their work. Sometimes you can use logic, sometimes you can't. If your default stays at logic, you will stumble at least half the time." – *Chaka Booker, Managing Director, The Broad Center and Forbes.com columnist*

We have to understand who we are – the good, the bad and the ugly. Remember that the importance of understanding yourself is not just for your own benefit: it also benefits the people who will work on teams with you and follow you in the future. Your preparation to be a great leader of others starts with being a great leader of self. You lead from who you actually are, not who you want to be. The more you know yourself, the better, more authentic and more mature a leader you will be in the future. You will know what your strengths are and thus your true sources of distinctiveness. This self-knowledge will give you the confidence to voice your opinions and firmly position yourself at the table where decisions are made.

You have a sense of self and self-confidence that the world can't touch. You know who you are and you stand firmly in your power. Conversely, you also know what your areas of development are, which helps you understand who you need around you, both to complement you and to provide those skills or perspectives that you lack. Knowing your own limitations helps you to remain humble because you know that you don't bring everything to the table. It helps you to be open and sometimes to defer to the opinions, perspectives and ideas of others. Understanding your emotional triggers helps you to know what types of situation might upset you so that you can try to either reduce or eliminate the chances of being in those situations. Additionally, you can develop techniques to help manage negative emotions or you can work on changing your perspective so that those situations and people no longer elicit the same emotions in you. Harvard Business School professor and former Medtronic CEO Bill George says that 'the hardest person you will ever have to lead is yourself', and you are the only person you can control. How can you expect people who report to you to be mature if you are immature? How can you expect them to respond in a professional, calm way if you don't? Being able to lead by example starts with examining who you are, what your personal and professional goals are and what might get in the way of your being and doing all that you want to be and do. The type of leader of others that you will be begins with the type of follower that you are now.

> Many people have never really done an emotional inventory. For instance, let's say you're in a meeting and you think someone is challenging you on something. What is your response? Are you going to respond professionally with a well-thought-out, calm answer, or are you going to respond emotionally? Frown up? Get loud? A lot of folks don't acknowledge which camp they fall into." – *Artis Brown*

The most important story

> Understand how to say, here's my interest, here's why, here's my story. Understand your story and own your path. Make sure people around you know your story, make sure it's believable, and then you go out and perform."
> – *Fungayi Kapungu*

Reflecting on and understanding your story is a big part of unpacking the source of your emotions. It helps you understand why you might struggle to change in a certain area. We might logically know that we need to change but we might have a hard time doing so because of some underlying needs, fears and ways of thinking and feeling.

Here is a clear example of how your story can affect your performance at work. A consultant once came to me and said she was struggling to ask for help. I decided to take her through the behavioural iceberg model, a psychological tool based on the work of Sigmund Freud (1856–1939), the father of psychoanalysis.

Behavioural Iceberg Model

Behavioural Iceberg Model
What are you saying and/or doing that is not serving you, your team and/or your organisation?

Thoughts & Feelings
What are you thinking and feeling during this behaviour?

Assumptions & Beliefs
What are you assuming and believing during this behaviour?

Needs & Fears
What are you afraid of?
What need of yours is being met or not?

Freud believed that what drives us most is not visible to the human eye. Our behaviour can be likened to the ten per cent of an iceberg that is visible above the surface of the sea. However, what drives us most, he argued, corresponds to 90 per cent of the iceberg that is below the surface. There are questions that we can ask ourselves to uncover our innermost thoughts, feelings, assumptions, beliefs, needs and fears that are 'below the surface' – those emotions hidden within our psyche or subconscious. When we get a grip on these, we can start to understand what drives our behaviour.

As the consultant and I worked our way through the model's questions, she realised that her story played a huge role in her inability to ask for help. The consultant had grown up with her two siblings in a single-parent home. Her father died when she was very young and her mother was left to raise three children on her own. Her mother worked a lot to keep food on the table, a roof over their heads and the school fees paid. As a result, she and her siblings had to do many things on their own. As such, she learnt to be very independent and self-sufficient, not giving herself permission to ask for help.

Fast-forward a few years, and she lands at McKinsey. McKinsey is a fast-paced organisation, and asking for help is expected so that consultants can get up to speed more rapidly, thus delivering results more quickly. This consultant's upbringing and the McKinsey environment were in conflict, so she had to adjust. She never realised that her upbringing had resulted in her inability to ask for help. I mapped out her struggle to ask for help on the behavioural iceberg:

Current State of Behavioural Iceberg Model

Behaviour
Q: What are you saying and/or doing that is not serving you, your team and/or your organisation?
A: Not asking for help when I need to.

Thoughts & Feelings
Q: What are you thinking and feeling during this behaviour?
A: I should know. I am expected to know. This is stupid. That person knows how to do it.

Assumptions & Beliefs
Q: What are you assuming and believing during this behaviour?
A: If I ask, it's going to look like I wasn't paying attention or I haven't thought about it enough. There is something flawed in me if I can't do it.

Needs & Fears
Q: What are you afraid of? What need of yours is being met or not?
A: I fear a loss of trust and the perception of being incapable or lazy. I need to not be a burden and I need to be independent.

When she became aware of this, she understood that she could not allow her old fears to take over. She knew to take deep breaths to centre herself, to interrupt her negative thoughts and fears, and to write down her thoughts on where she needed help.

Another great use of this model is to work your way up the other side of the iceberg to reimagine or rewrite your needs, fears, assumptions, beliefs, thoughts and feelings to produce a new set of desired behaviours.

Future State of Behavioural Iceberg Model

Behaviour
Q: What are you saying and/or doing that is serving you, your team and/or your organisation?
A: Ask for help when I need it.

Thoughts & Feelings
Q: What are you thinking and feeling during this behaviour?
A: I don't always have to be right or know everything.
I have the time and space to figure things out with others.

Assumptions & Beliefs
Q: What are you assuming and believing during this behaviour?
A: Others want to help me and see me do well.
Others are asking for help as well.

Needs & Fears
Q: What are you afraid of? What need of yours is being met or not?
A: I need to know that it is okay to reach out to others for help when I need it.

It's important to note that just because we become aware of our unhealthy behavioural patterns, it doesn't mean that we won't slip back into them. However, with focus, we can recognise them more quickly, understand where they are coming from and take steps to stop the pattern so that we get different results. Changing our mindset is not easy and we have to be compassionate with ourselves on the journey, even in spite of our missteps. Another crucial step is to rewrite your story, because the most important story is the one you tell yourself. For example, in this consultant's situation, she saw asking for help as a negative option, based on her childhood experiences. Now, however, she could rewrite, overwrite or reframe her story in the following way:

> My mother was our sole provider and was very busy working to provide for my sisters and me. I honour her for her hard work and sacrifice. An unintended consequence of our family situation was that my mother did not have enough time to help my siblings and me. I know that she would have spent more time helping us if she had the choice and the time and if she knew that we needed her help. It's not bad to ask for help. It just wasn't available to me at that time, but that doesn't mean that it is not available to me now. I am in a different set of circumstances. People want and expect me to ask for help. Asking for help benefits me because it increases my speed and accuracy at work, which ultimately benefits the team and me.

After she had taken some time to reflect on the new framing of her life story, it became her dominant, most useful, interpretation. In time, this allowed her to have a neutral or even positive perspective on the idea of asking for help.

> From a neurological perspective, there's no real unlearning. There is rewriting and overriding information. You can diffuse and mute old thinking patterns, but they're still there. Rewrite or rewire in such a way that it dominates the patterns and discourse that you've learnt." – *Timothy Maurice Webster*

I was recently asked to review an essay by a South African friend who was applying to Harvard Business School. Although his essay was great, it didn't have a uniquely South African perspective, and neither would it give the admissions committee an idea of his unique voice, perspective or life story. I told him that his unique voice is shaped by his story and he should bring it into every room he enters. Taking my advice, he made some changes to his essay and was subsequently admitted to Harvard. I don't think that his essay was the only reason he was admitted, but it was definitely part of it. Remember that your story – even the unhappy parts – helps you to connect with others and build your empathy and resilience.

Embrace your story because that is what sets you apart from everyone else. Your story is your competitive advantage. It is also the source of your greatest pain, purpose and, ultimately, power. Reflect on and write down your thoughts so that you can begin to uncover who you are, and identify patterns, key situations and people in your life that have shaped you in a positive or negative way. How can you leverage your story to stand out more and make more of an impact in the workplace?

> It's important to understand the chemical dynamics of emotional intelligence because somebody could tell someone repeatedly, 'Be emotionally intelligent, be mindful, be aware', but all those impulses could still continue. Understanding what's been passed down from generation to generation is key because all of these dynamics impact emotional intelligence. There are certain things you can do to rewire the brain but there are some things that go a little bit deeper. I don't think people of colour have enough conversations about historical scarring, trauma, early childhood exposure and those experiences that have caused us so much damage. We just write it off as generational curses or trauma, [we tell people to] get over it and force people to carry on without having sufficient inquiry into what could be happening in the brain. I'm very interested in looking at the full spectrum of inputs and experiences into the brain while having that emotional intelligence conversation to ensure that we don't write people off because they're struggling with certain things." – *Timothy Maurice Webster*

Below is an exercise that will help you to reflect on your life. On the timeline below (you could even draw one yourself), mark all the significant events, people, places and turning points in your life thus far. This exercise will help you to reflect on your past and give you insights into, and understanding of, who you are as an individual.

Born ●———————————————————▶ **Now**

Be a student of you

There are various types of assessments that you can take to help you understand yourself better. The MBTI (Myers-Briggs Type Indicator) highlights your preferences in terms of the source of your energy and if you prefer chaos or order, among other areas. I took the MBTI for the first time in high school (shout-out to my ENTJ brothers and sisters!); however, I just thought, 'Oh, that's interesting' and then put it aside. I took the test again in business school and again at McKinsey. Next, I took the CliftonStrengths Assessment in 2014 as part of the McKinsey leadership development programme I was running. Everything started to click for me there. These personality assessments were giving me a bird's-eye view of my strengths, what energises me, what my values are, how I like to be managed, my trigger points and the type of personalities that I would clash with. The CliftonStrengths Assessment really helped me understand what types of activities energise me. Because those activities energise me, I will naturally do them over and over again, which means that I will become more and more distinctive in them. The better I get in these activities, the more I will be able to set myself further and further apart, specifically in terms of the value I bring. If you are struggling to understand yourself or what your strengths are, I strongly advise that you take one of these personality tests and have an experienced facilitator or coach walk you through your results. Just remember: the tests are not the sum total of who you are. Nevertheless, they're a great place to start.

The level of reflection and introspection I have described in this chapter is what many people call 'doing your work'. It allows you to show up in the best way for yourself and others. This sentiment is best expressed by a series of questions from Thomas DeLong, a professor of management practice at the Harvard Business School. During my second year there, I took one of his courses, called 'Managing Human Capital.' He would often say to us: 'When people have an interaction with you, do they walk away feeling motivated, energised and inspired? Or do they walk away feeling demotivated, de-energised and uninspired? And how are people experiencing you? And which experience do you want people to have with you?' These questions have stuck with me for 14 years. They keep me motivated to continue to do my work so that I can be the most authentic version of myself, thus inspiring and connecting with those around me.

Chapter 4
Developing your cultural intelligence

Would you ever go to someone else's house and say, 'We put our feet on the table at my house, so I'm going to do the same at your house'? You would never. You would sit back, observe how your hosts conduct themselves and adjust your behaviour. Out of courtesy to your hosts, and out of respect for their rules and guidelines, you'll try to adapt to your new environment (within reason, of course). The same principle applies when you're a new employee at an organisation. Your company is someone else's house and you have just arrived. So why don't we bring this attitude to our places of work?

Cultural intelligence (or cultural quotient, CQ) is a person's ability to interpret, understand, become comfortable with and operate within a culture that is different from their own. Just as building your EQ starts with understanding and managing your own emotions, building your CQ starts with examining your beliefs about your own cultural upbringing, and then adjusting them to your environment. Our cultural values are a product of our education and socialisation. Understanding your own culture will also help you understand why there might be tension between your own and another person's or organisation's culture. A number of years ago, I discussed the idea of CQ with one of my mentors. We talked about the difficulty of performing well in a culture that differs from one's own, and he gave me the following advice: 'Adaptability is key. Be flexible in style, learn the culture and calibrate.' He encouraged me to 'remove the judgement of "my culture" versus "their culture"' and to 'allow different parts of [my] personality to play out in different situations'. 'Our personalities are broad enough,' he advised, telling me to 'differentiate between [my own] values or core identity and style.'

> As a woman, especially in my particular industry where most of our customers are Indian Muslim [men], it is not acceptable for me to be talking to them. So you learn to understand where they come from. Many times I have extended my hand and then I take it back because they don't shake hands with women. So you learn to understand your industry and adapt to it." – *Connie Mashaba, Manager, Amka Products and Former CEO of Black Like Me*

Considering the global nature of the economy and how connected we are, you will likely work within different organisational cultures with people of different cultures and possibly even from different countries. Building your CQ is therefore an important skill. Understanding and assessing your own culture against another is like a muscle that you have to exercise consistently to build and maintain relationships with different people.

As I've shown in the previous chapter, effective relationships are key to making an impact at work and serving your clients or customers well. Consider the following: if the cross-cultural team of a company cannot get along, or does not communicate effectively with each other, how can they deliver the best solution, service or product? They can't. If different racial, religious and gender groups are not represented within an organisation's marketing team, or if team members who come from different cultures don't have enough power or agency to speak up, it can have disastrous effects. Just think of Gucci's (now discontinued) Blackface sweater, H&M's 'coolest monkey in the jungle' T-shirt or Pepsi's ill-fated commercial with Kendall Jenner.

When I moved to South Africa nine years ago, I had to adapt. As an American, for example, I was accustomed to walking up to customer service employees in stores and launching straight into my question. In South Africa, however, people expect you to recognise them as a person *before* you get to whatever role they have or service that they provide. Today, when I walk up to a person in a store, I greet them first. I wait for the person to respond, and only *then* do I proceed to ask my question. Old habits die hard and sometimes I forget, but I try my best to remember. This way of interacting has become such a part of who I am that I get upset when people don't greet me before asking me a question. It just serves to demonstrate that culture is fluid and it can and does evolve. I'm glad I inquired about the significance of greeting and I'm grateful someone took the time to explain it to me. When I think about it, recognising another's humanity before their role at work is a beautiful concept, and it helps me to remember the humanity in every person I interact with.

> What should you listen to or look for to figure out how an organisation works? You need to observe and understand how people both interact and present themselves." – *Nomfanelo Magwentshu*

All of us look at the world through the lens of culture, but if we don't work hard to understand this, we will be unable to see past or around it. We have all grown up in a particular culture, and some of us have even grown up in multiple cultures: we might have had a certain culture at home, a different one in our greater community, another one at school and still another in our religious community. We judge people based on what *we* think is appropriate behaviour, hygiene, dress, speech, etc, and we choose, befriend, dismiss and/or categorise people based on those filters. But it's important to understand that no culture is better than another; they're just different. Remember that if we judge others' cultures to be less than our own, we're no better than those who deem their culture to be superior to ours.

Criticising other cultures also creates distance between us and those who consider themselves part of that culture. Think back to a moment in your life when you have felt judged by someone. How did it feel? Probably not so great. It definitely did not build a positive connection between you and that person. The negative energy you felt from the person who judged you is the same type of energy we exude when we judge others. In other words: if we can learn to approach different cultures with curiosity, openness and the desire and effort to understand, we will be able to grow our CQ. Do you use culture as another way to separate yourself from or to judge others? Learning about other cultures provides you with the opportunity to expand your world view *and* the world view of others.

My aim in this chapter is not to give you all the answers – I certainly don't have them! – but rather to highlight several different parameters of culture and how those cultural elements show up in various organisations. Hopefully, these examples will help you to identify the points of alignment and difference between you and your surroundings. Differences can be a source of tension, so it's helpful to assess them upfront so that you can proactively address them.

> In corporate Nigeria, if your meeting is scheduled for 10 am, you're probably going to see the CEO arrive at the meeting at 1 pm if you're lucky. That's because Nigerians' culture has permeated into their corporate space. But in South African corporate spaces, you have to work in line with the culture of the corporate space you're in. You have to fit in and manage your own cultural biases so that they don't make you ineffective at work." – *Thokozile Lewanika Mpupuni*

Assess your culture

Before you assess your organisation's culture, it's imperative that you assess your own. If you understand how beholden you are to your culture, you'll be able to see how wide the gap is between your own cultural beliefs and those of the organisation and/or the people that work there. Assess whether your cultural beliefs are helping you to be successful in the company. The three key areas that are useful to examine are your culture, the culture of others and the culture of your organisation.

Geert Hofstede, the late Dutch social psychologist, identified six dimensions (or characteristics) with which you can assess your culture and how strongly you subscribe to its norms. Each dimension is expressed on a scale running from 0 to 100. Think about where your culture falls on the scale of each of the following dimensions:

1. **Individualism:** The extent to which people within a culture are seen as individuals or as part of a bigger community. People within a culture that prioritises the bigger community prefer to do what is in the best interest of the group as a whole, as opposed to what benefits individuals.
2. **Power distance:** The extent to which power is distributed in a culture and the hierarchical distance between those who make the decisions and those who are affected by those decisions. Countries that have a high power distance are comfortable with the hierarchy and do not aspire to equalise the distribution of power.
3. **Masculinity:** In 'masculine' cultures, there is a focus on winning, assertiveness, material success and the ideas 'bigger is better' and 'the more the better'. In 'feminine' cultures, there is less of a difference between the genders.
4. **Uncertainty avoidance:** This points to the level of comfort a culture has with uncertainty, ambiguity and the unknown. The less comfortable a culture is with uncertainty, the more likely it is to have fixed habits, rules and rituals.

5. **Long-term orientation:** The extent to which a culture is focused on the future. Cultures with a long-term orientation are willing to delay short-term gratification (eg material, social, emotional) in order to prepare for the future. People with this cultural perspective value persistence, adaptability, perseverance and saving.
6. **Indulgence:** The extent to which a society allows for the relatively free gratification of basic and instinctual human drives related to enjoying life and having fun. Cultures with more restraint repress the gratification of needs and manage them by implementing severe social norms.

Where on the scale does your culture fall on each of these six dimensions? In what ways does this impact how you see the world and interact with people who are different from you?

> Sometimes we are unprofessional in the way we understand jobs and etiquette. I think it's to be expected, because we don't come from multiple generations of working people. We haven't learnt those mannerisms and, frankly, some aspects of our culture don't serve us well in the classic corporate space." – *Thokozile Lewanika Mpupuni*

Based on my experience, I think there are certain elements of Black culture and how we were raised that can get in the way of our being successful at work. I've provided a few examples below, so see which ones apply to you.

Perspective on time: Many of us grew up in cultures where nothing ever starts on time (think of, for example, weddings, funerals and family events). I feel this has lessened our respect for time. In America, we call it 'Coloured People Time', and in Africa, 'Africa Time'. Maybe there are no consequences in your family and/or social circles if you run late. However, in the working world, time equals money and credibility, so timing has consequences. At work, if you can't do something as simple as deliver a task on time, show up on time for work or be punctual for appointments, how can your employer trust you with bigger challenges and responsibilities? Not sticking to deadlines, for instance, means that your manager might have to stay up late to review your work before it can be finalised. There are repercussions for being late in whatever you do, and you are being judged if you don't honour those time commitments. For instance, I used to tell consultants that showing up on time for a meeting doesn't start the morning *of* the meeting: it starts the night *before*. You have to go to bed on time so that you can wake up on time so that you can leave the house on time (even factoring in traffic) so that you are ready when the meeting starts. Don't make habitual lateness a part of your brand. If you are in an organisational culture that is highly time-conscious, make sure you put the right measures in place to honour that.

> "There is a script in corporate America which wasn't designed for us. They didn't have us nor our culture in mind. The culture of the corporate environment is a different language with a different cadence. All too often, young professionals of colour don't understand that. 'Show up and be on time.' We had to let go of one of our African-American female employees, one of the top ones, a PhD student, because she kept showing up to work 30 minutes late. She was showing up to meetings late. Everything was late. Could she not set her alarm clock?" – *Tina Taylor*

Questioning authority and speaking up: Despite being separated by oceans, languages and cultures, there are some qualities that appear to be common across the diaspora. One of these is that many of us grew up in households where we were seen and not heard. We were not encouraged to challenge or correct our parents or anyone older than us. Our opinions were not valued or solicited. This way of operating may have worked well for our parents in fostering order and discipline at home, but it does not necessarily serve us well in the workplace. Companies hire young people because they want to hear their perspectives, opinions and ideas, and because they might be more aware of trends and what younger consumers want. They hire young professionals to be not just doers but also thinkers. Because of that, you have an obligation to offer your thoughts.

Sometimes we have to disagree, challenge or even interrupt our seniors. Remember that if you don't speak up, you deny your colleagues the privilege of hearing your unique point of view. Over the years, I've seen many people struggling in corporate cultures because disagreeing with, interrupting or challenging seniors goes against their upbringing. Time and time again, I received feedback from managers that a person of colour was struggling to speak up. This was especially apparent during problem-solving sessions at McKinsey. To sketch the scene: during these sessions, a team with members from all levels sits around a table and discusses client issues. These discussions can get quite lively because that is what happens when you put a bunch of highly intelligent, opinionated people in a room to discuss a topic about which they are passionate. In order to get into the conversation, you might have to interrupt someone who is more senior to you. It's a high-pressure, high-stakes scenario because no one wants to look stupid or clueless in that setting. In my experience, very rarely did I hear feedback that a white person had trouble speaking up in these sessions. This made me think that our socialisation as Black people does not adequately prepare us for these types of high-performance, high-pressure environments.

Let me give you an example. A few years ago, a white colleague of mine told me that his family had hosted a foreign exchange student when he was a kid. Before his parents made the decision to host the student, they called all the kids together for a family meeting. The meeting was to vote whether or not the foreign exchange student should come and live with them. Each person, including the kids, had a vote and if the outcome was not unanimous, the student could not come. When I heard this story I was fascinated that the parents even called a vote at all and that each family member's vote had equal weight. I can't think of too many Black parents who would call a family vote! And, even if they did, they would not give an equal vote to each person – especially not to the children.

The idea that children are not to get into grown folks' business is not a bad thing in and of itself. However, it made me wonder: how different would I and other Black people have been had we grown up in homes with a bit more of a democratic culture? Would I have been more outspoken? Would I have found my voice earlier? Would I have been more comfortable challenging authority earlier in my career? While order and discipline are great parenting goals for the first 18 years of children's lives, I'm not sure that that philosophy serves them for the years between 19 and 70. You will spend more time outside your parents' house than inside it. I'm not suggesting that you have to choose between order and discipline on the one hand, and chaos and anarchy on the other. I believe there is a happy medium and I challenge you to find it when you're raising your own kids. They will be the next generation of employees and entrepreneurs.

> "Some of the feedback that I received over the years I took with a pinch of salt. It took maturity. Some of the things, I could tell, came down to cultural differences and others came down to me. I had to be brave and smart. I often understood the feedback, but I was not going to change me, because that's what makes me unique." – *Dr Puleng Makhoalibe*

Asking for help: In some environments, asking for help is seen as a sign of weakness, and being seen as weak is the last thing you want, which is understandable. It feels as though asking for help makes you appear dependent on others, that you are not self-sufficient, that you don't know everything, and it makes you vulnerable. For those of us who have grown up in countries with a long history of racial discrimination, I think we oftentimes feel that we have something to prove. You might feel the same way if you are a woman in a male-dominated industry or if you're the youngest person in your department. We don't want to be perceived as people who don't have what it takes or that we're not as smart as everyone else. Sometimes we have to ask ourselves what is more important: a) my desire to prove that I can do this on my own, or b) my desire to make sure that this piece of work is done to the highest quality and in the most efficient way? Asking for help is critical to being successful at work, especially early in your career, because you are still learning the ropes.

Mistrust of, or lack of exposure to, those that are different from us: Many of us grew up in very homogeneous environments where we were not exposed to people who look and sound different from us. Some of us grew up in environments where we were a minority, and the exposure we might have had with the majority group was not very positive; sometimes, people in our families and communities even spoke ill of people who were different from us, based on their negative experiences. These messages and experiences have shaped our perceptions and they have created in us an inability or unwillingness to establish relationships with people who do not look like us. Regardless of your environment, you are going to have to learn to build relationships with, and garner the support of, people of different cultures, genders, age groups, races or socio-economic status. Examine what stereotypes you might be holding against certain groups. Trying to find what you have in common (for example, professional interests, hobbies) can help bridge the gap between you and the other person.

A former colleague of mine once told me that he wanted to work on his communication skills. I suggested someone in our office who is a great communicator, but he said he was not sure how to build a relationship with a woman. I probed to understand what his issue was. Was he worried about how it would look to others? Was it the fact that she was senior to him? He said no; he had no issue with forming relationships with senior *men* in the office. Then something made me ask, 'How was your relationship with your mother?' 'I didn't have one,' he told me. 'My mother died when I was very young and I was raised solely by my father and was mostly surrounded by men while growing up.' 'Well, maybe that's the issue,' I said. He suddenly had an 'aha' moment: he realised that his past experiences affected his ability to form relationships in the present.

Gender roles: Many of us grew up in cultures where men and women, even girls and boys, played very specific roles in our homes, houses of worship and communities. Unfortunately, we take some of those beliefs to our jobs. We believe that certain genders should behave in certain ways or take on certain roles. We also believe that it is inappropriate for us to take on the responsibilities of other genders. We might also find it difficult to report to, or build relationships with, people who do not fit into our preconceived notions of gender roles. For these reasons, it is important for us to examine the ways in which our upbringing can get in the way of achieving our goals at work. I was raised in Alabama, which is in the southern part of the USA. During my childhood, girls were raised to be demure, subservient and docile. Good southern ladies didn't make a fuss. Unfortunately for me, I took that attitude into my career: I didn't push back on opportunities that didn't help to grow me or that weren't putting my gifts and talents to use.

> We train our boys to be brave, but we don't do the same for the girls. At work, men would put their hands up all the time when new opportunities would come along.

So we would have to go and tell the women that they should apply, too. And they would say, 'No, I don't think so. I don't have [the qualifications and/or experience].' It still is very difficult for women to put their hands up."
– Penny Moumakwa

Individualistic vs collectivistic: Individualistic cultures are all about the individual, while collectivistic communities are about the group as a whole. In an organisation, you have to strike the right balance between these two poles. Your focus can't just be on yourself, but neither should it just be on the organisation. Sometimes you have to make decisions that are right for your career. This means that you might have to turn down an opportunity that doesn't make sense for your career, even though your decision might upset someone in your organisation. At other times you might have to take on certain assignments that you are not excited about but that your organisation needs you to handle.

A big part of working in the corporate world is being able to talk about yourself, what you're working on, what you're good at and what you have achieved. A corporate is much like heaven: there are no group or family 'n friend entry programmes, as everyone is judged on his or her individual merit and contribution, so it's best to be clear on what yours are. I grew up in the US. I've lived in South Africa for almost ten years. I've worked and socialised with Kenyans, Ghanaians, Nigerians, Cameroonians and South Africans. This is a shared experience: in general (although there are always notable exceptions), we as Black people struggle to speak about ourselves and our individual accomplishments.

Admitting mistakes and taking risks: In my experience, we as Black people have a lot of pressure on us to succeed. In environments with a history of racial segregation, many of us are told that we can't fail because it will reflect poorly on the next Black person, and that another Black person will never get another chance because we failed. This was exactly the collective sentiment when President Barack Obama was inaugurated in 2009. Many Black people felt like he couldn't mess this up, because if he did, we would never see another Black president in our lifetime. I believe we take this attitude into our work environments. We feel there is no room for error, so we try to cover up mistakes, we fail to take risks or we are indecisive because we don't want to make wrong choices. The problem with this attitude is that we miss out on the lessons to be learnt from taking risks and making mistakes.

Other aspects specific to your family, country or culture: I once coached a woman from an African country; she had a lot of potential and expressed her aspirations to advance in her organisation. I asked her what was holding her back from going after what she wanted, and she said that, in her culture, they 'wait for things to come to [them]. We don't go after things,' she told me. Let me tell you this for free: if you want something in an organisation, others are not going to figure out how you should go about getting it. You have to figure out what you want and how to get it, and then put a plan in action to achieve it. Assess the difference between your culture and that of the organisation. The bigger the gap, the harder you will have to work to adjust your attitude and behaviour in an authentic way.

> Young Black professionals get tripped up when they don't know how to navigate the spaces they're in. It then starts manifesting itself in other ways and starts looking like laziness or unprofessionalism." – *Kagiso Molotsi*

The issues that have played a big role – and sometimes tripped me up – in my career have been my thoughts on gender roles, my focus on the collective versus the individual, and my discomfort with pushing back on authority. My cultural background led me to take on roles that were not in the best interest of either my career or my own personal development. It is important that we learn how to strike the right balance; it took me a long time to get it right.

Regardless of where you work, you cannot make assumptions about what type of culture the organisation adheres to. We assume that a company will or should have a culture similar to the dominant culture of the country in which it is located. This is definitely not the case. For example, if you work for a multinational that is operating in South Africa, the culture of your organisation could be Western, male-dominated and individualistic because that is the dominant culture of the country the company was founded in. Any South African who wants to be successful in that particular environment will need to adapt to that style of performing, delivering and communicating, which, interestingly, is the antithesis of how most South Africans grew up. It will be up to you to assess your company's culture and decide whether it's for you or not. You will have to do the hard work of deciding what aspects of your upbringing you're willing to relax in order to be successful in that culture.

Understanding your organisation's culture

Up to this point, I've been discussing personal culture, but now I'd like us to shift our attention to organisational culture. Organisational culture is the set of shared attitudes, values, goals, norms, language, behaviours and practices that characterises an institution or organisation. Cameron Sepah, assistant professor of psychiatry at the University of California, San Francisco, argues that, regardless of the values listed on the company website, an organisation's culture is defined by who it recruits, rewards, promotes and fires. Some people believe that *that* tells you everything you need to know about what a company values. I'd like to highlight three frameworks for evaluating culture, each of which presents different elements that you should explore at your organisation.

Organisational Culture Profile: Within this framework, researchers Jennifer Chatman, David F Caldwell and Charles A O'Reilly III identified seven dimensions of culture: innovation (how much risk-taking and innovation are encouraged), stability (how much growth and change are encouraged), people orientation (the extent to which employees and the impact on them are considered in decision-making), outcome orientation (the amount of focus on results versus process), easy-going (the level of competition versus collaboration), detail orientation (the amount of focus on exactness) and team orientation (how much work is structured around individuals or team achievement).

Organisational Culture Assessment Instrument: University of Michigan professors Robert E Quinn and Kim S Cameron developed a framework which looks at six aspects of culture: dominant characteristics, organisational leadership, management of employees, organisation glue, strategic emphases and the criteria of success. The output from this model is called the Competing Values Framework, which, in turn, identifies four areas around which cultures are developed: how internally focused or externally focused the organisation is and how much flexibility/discretion or stability/control exists in the organisation. Based on these four areas, Quinn and Cameron's research shows that there are four types of cultures: Clan Culture, which is entrenched in teamwork; Adhocracy Culture, which is grounded in enthusiasm and innovation; Market Culture, which is rooted in a competitive environment where the focus is on driving for results; and Hierarchy Culture, which is grounded in order and command.

Integrated Culture Framework: This model was designed by Jeremiah Lee, Jesse Price, J Yo-Jud Cheng and my Harvard Business School professor Boris Groysberg. The authors argue that organisational cultures operate according to two sets of dimensions: how an organisation manages change, and how closely people in an organisation work together. The model posits eight types of culture: learning, purpose, caring, order, safety, authority, results and enjoyment. The names of each of these cultures speak to their specific focus.

Each of the abovementioned cultures has a unique style of leadership, value drivers and strategic focus. There is no perfect culture. Some people are better suited to certain kinds of cultures based on their personalities, values and motivations. Each type of culture has its advantages and disadvantages. Certain cultures work better for specific organisations because of the organisation's strategic priorities, the customers they serve and the industries in which they operate. Your organisation's culture may not fit neatly into one of these categories, however: there may be a dominant culture but there can also be different subcultures that exist in various parts of the organisation. While these models focus on different areas, I believe each one highlights an element of culture that you should investigate within your company.

Before you accepted the offer for your position, hopefully you did some due diligence to determine whether or not the organisation's culture was a good fit for you. Nevertheless, there will still be many details about your new employer that you can only learn by being on the inside. In many ways, the recruiting process is like a first date, because everyone is putting their best foot forward. However, you might only see the good, the bad and ugly once you're inside the organisation. Remember that no company is perfect, because every company has imperfect people working for them. Every organisation has its fair share of problems, even though they may vary in severity from company to company.

A big part of your role as a new hire is to understand the culture more deeply and understand how you can fit into it in an authentic way. You were drawn to your chosen company's brand for a number of reasons. In addition, the company has been operating successfully enough to be in a position to hire people for many years – if not decades – and there is a reason why. Now is the time to peel back the layers and learn what makes this organisation tick.

There are the values that every company lists on its website... and then there are the ways in which they play out in reality. To use an analogy: when you've just met someone, you would not like that person to tell you everything that they think is *wrong* with you. In general, it is better to approach people with their strengths in mind. Companies are the same. Focus on the positive, what is working, why this company or brand has been able to stand the test of time and weather various economic and global storms. There is something that you liked about the company and it made you want to join. Focus on those elements and dive deeply into them so that you can appreciate how the company operates.

> I had to almost unlearn what I knew initially and then later on bring what I knew to the table once I had learnt the basics. That humbled me a bit. When you walk into a new situation, it doesn't matter how much you know or how much experience you have, you need to understand that environment." – *Nomfanelo Magwentshu*

Over the course of my career I've worked full-time for six different organisations, and each one had its own distinctive culture. Aon Hewitt, my first employer after university, had a very relaxed, youthful culture. Arthur Andersen, the company I joined next, was very hierarchical, and there was a distinct line drawn between support staff and consultants (those who generated revenue for the organisation). They had strict (and sometimes unspoken) guidelines, ranging from dress code (no sleeveless tops for ladies and no facial hair for men if they wanted to be made partner) to the specific colours to use in client PowerPoint presentations. Deloitte, the next company, was very diverse, collegial and friendly.

Then I joined the Fulton County Schools Board (Atlanta, Georgia), which was hierarchical, with a cultural distinction even in its three-floor central office building. The employees on the top floor wore suits every day, because that was where the Superintendent (akin to the CEO) had his office. The employees on the ground floor dressed much more casually. At McKinsey, too, I quickly learnt that the company had a very specific way of solving problems, of writing, speaking and designing business communications (for instance, in email or PowerPoint presentations). I quickly learnt that if I wanted to be heard, seen as effective or thought well of, I had best learn, practise and perfect what they called 'the McKinsey Way'. After my years there, I worked briefly for a startup where the atmosphere was much more relaxed, and where everybody pitched in to accomplish whatever needed to be done. Know that different environments have different pressures, expectations and personalities, which may trigger emotions or reveal qualities within you that you did not know were there. This is why the process of knowing and understanding yourself is an ongoing one.

Be a student of your organisation

Below, I share a few examples of how the different elements of culture have played out in the organisations that I've worked with and for as an employee and a consultant. Using this information, see if you can evaluate your company's organisational culture and design.

Listen out for commonly used words: The words that I heard spoken at Fulton County Schools were very different from the ones I heard at Deloitte. The words that are used in an organisation speak specifically to what it does and what it holds to be true. What are the most commonly used words in your organisation? Why do you think those words are used so frequently? How do those words align with what the business does and values?

Uncover the unwritten rules for success: The expectation on the part of some consulting firms that their consultants will take part in extracurricular activities to build office morale is not written down anywhere. If you look at a consultant's job description, this additional expectation does not feature in it. Nevertheless, consultants are judged on their participation. At a former client of mine, a new hire has to be properly introduced by a more tenured person with credibility in order to be taken seriously. Without this proper introduction and contextualisation of the new hire's roles, people would not accept meeting invites nor respond to emails from this person. What is expected of you outside your standard job description? What might people be evaluating you on that you're not aware of? When you first join the organisation, how do you need to communicate, show up and deliver in order to build trust in you and your abilities? Historically, what has derailed people who weren't successful in the organisation?

Understand how and why people communicate: McKinsey was the first company I worked for that communicated in a very specific way. They call it 'top-down' communication. It basically means that when you're communicating, you should start with the 'so what' – the most important recommendation or takeaway – of your message and *then* call attention to the supporting details behind it. This is in stark contrast to 'bottom-up' communication in which you start with the details and work your way up to the 'so what'. I once asked a partner why top-down communication was the preferred style at McKinsey: 'We're usually working with C-suite leaders who don't have much time or headspace,' he said. 'So when you get the opportunity to communicate with them, you need to grab their attention with the main idea so that they'll listen to the rest of what you have to say.'

Once I heard that, I understood the reason behind their staunch devotion to top-down communication. What I also understood was that McKinsey partners are the same as C-suite leaders: they, too, don't have much time, so if I wanted to grab their attention, I had to communicate with them in a top-down fashion as well. All senior employees at McKinsey, I realised, were trained to be top-down communicators, so if that is how they were trained, it was highly unlikely that they would want to receive communication in a different way. What is the most commonly used communication style in your organisation? Why is it preferred? How different is the organisation's communication style from your natural communication style?

Notice the physical layout of your office: When I worked at Deloitte, one of my clients was a global confectionery and pet food company. When I arrived at their headquarters, I was surprised to see that the CFO was sitting in a cubicle in an open-plan office. He didn't have a fancy office or an assistant who acted as a gatekeeper to restrict access to him. He was as accessible as the most junior person on the team. That office set-up told me a lot about their culture. It let me know that this was not an organisation for prima donnas or divas. This was a down-to-earth, no-frills type of culture where everyone was valued and the focus was solely on getting the work done.

From my time at McKinsey, I remember how the company prided itself on being a trusted client advisor. A big part of building and maintaining that trust is making sure that client information stays confidential. For instance, non-McKinsey guests were not allowed into the client-confidential areas of the office. On the rare occasions that they were allowed in (always due to space constraints), a McKinsey employee was supposed to walk the path that the guest would walk to ensure that there was no confidential information visible on whiteboards or flip charts. The McKinsey employee was supposed to stay with the guest the entire time to make sure they didn't wander off and accidentally see something they weren't supposed to. If confidentiality is a big freakin' deal for the company, it needs to be important to its employees too. How is your organisation's space configured? Why do you think it's configured in that way? What message does the physical layout convey?

> "A new joiner should ask questions to understand how their position fits into the organisation and business strategy. They should be curious about the values and behaviours that drive the organisational culture of reward and recognition. They should ask if collaboration is encouraged? How are decisions made? How empowered are they? What exactly does the organisation value and what does it look like in terms of the behaviours expected? A new joiner should do their homework to hone their craft and become fully equipped to operate in the culture. I encourage new joiners to seek out a mentor, informal or formal. They should ask about the unwritten norms. What are the things that can derail a career?" – *Shenece Garner Johns, Director, Talent and Organisational Capability, Lockheed Martin Missiles and Fire Control*

Even if they say they are, many people in many organisations are not sincerely open to doing things differently and changing certain elements of their company culture. Looking back at all the people I've worked with, I understand how beholden employees can be to their company culture. Why wouldn't they be? If their company is extremely successful, why should they fix it if it ain't broke? You, too, might encounter a great deal of bias and resistance to change in certain corporate environments. For example, if you have to sacrifice your energy, time with family and friends, maybe even your health and your relationships, in order to succeed in a certain company, you would probably believe your company is the greatest place to work. If not, what would all the sacrifices be for? You'd never make these kinds of sacrifices for a mediocre environment! So it stands to reason that when employees feel they're working for the greatest company ever, why would they ever be motivated to change?

If I had it to do all over again, I would spend a lot more time understanding the cultures of the organisations I've worked for and with. This would have enabled me to tailor my messages and ideas in ways that were more palatable for employees and leaders. Delivering messages in a way that was customised to those environments would have made me even more effective. In hindsight, I realise that walking into a new space and telling people what they need to do differently is like walking into a restaurant for the first time and telling the kitchen staff how to prepare the food faster. Regardless of how great your ideas are, you have to deliver them at the right time and package them in a way that makes it easy for people to digest.

If you want to be an *effective* communicator, understanding the context is crucial. I liken it to feeding children at different stages. You have to mash up a baby's food because they have no teeth. For a toddler, you have to cut their food for them. For an older child, you can serve it as is. While you're serving the same food, you're presenting it differently, based on what they can manage. The same holds for communication: you have to meet people where they are socially and psychologically, and in order to do that successfully, you have to listen and learn. Spend time inquiring, listening and observing so that your ideas are well received and ultimately considered as part of the solution.

The business you're in

> Try to learn as much as possible. Many people that work in a company never pick up the annual report of that company. I interned at Enterprise Rent-a-Car ... it's actually quite amazing, even though I never understood this: Enterprise doesn't make money from renting cars. That's what you would think. Enterprise actually makes money from selling insurance. Read and learn about your company and what they do. At 18 years old I did my job,

but I wasn't very good at it because I didn't put in the time and I didn't really understand how the organisation was structured, so I didn't last very long." – *Ronald Tamale*

For the last few years, I've been facilitating a course for new hires at Bain & Company South Africa, called 'Building Credibility'. As part of the course I ask the newly minted consultants the following question: 'What business is Bain in?' Their answers are always consulting, management consulting and problem-solving. While these are all true, ultimately Bain is in the business of making an impact. A client wants to know that their business is better off for having engaged the services of Bain. One way of describing impact is to say that it is the difference between *before* your organisation's product, service, input, advice and/or actions arrived on the scene and *after* your organisation's product, service, input, advice and/or actions have been consumed or implemented. You need to see your work through this lens. It's not enough to merely complete that Excel spreadsheet or PowerPoint presentation. You need to think about how these insights could have an impact on your clients or customers. You also need to understand how your organisation generates revenue so that you can make sure that your work aligns with and/or supports those efforts as much as possible. What business is *your* organisation in? What is your organisation's value proposition? How can you use this understanding in your daily work? How does the business your organisation is in affect the culture?

Another area for observation is how your organisation is designed. The organisation design speaks to the company's strategy. Look at your organisation chart, or organogram, and see which departments report to whom. Assess why the company was structured this way. Was it organised in this way to better serve its customers and/or clients? Was it to foster collaboration, creativity and teamwork?

> "The different organisational designs are reflections of the organisation's overall business strategy. As business strategies evolve, so do the organisational model and culture. A matrix organisation [where individuals have a dual reporting relationship, usually to a product manager and a functional manager] may lend itself to a culture of agility, customer focus and transformative mindset." – *Shenece Garner Johns*

From understanding to action

One of the biggest challenges in developing your CQ is to become aware of the extent to which you see the outside world through your own cultural lens. No culture is better than another, so we have to remember that we see life through our own biases. This means that we should constantly take a step back to understand that there are other ways of seeing and being in the world. The goal is not merely to tolerate difference but rather to appreciate, embrace and ultimately leverage it for the impact that you want to have for yourself, your team, your organisation and those that you serve.

Decide whether your cultural beliefs are dealbreakers when you enter a new place of employment. If they are, you might have to remove yourself from that environment and find one that is more aligned with your beliefs. Having said that, also recognise that it is highly unlikely that you will find an organisation that is completely in line with your cultural values. And even if by some small chance you find a perfect fit, there is a likelihood that someone in that organisation will not be a perfect fit culturally. As you're learning more about your company, you have probably already found – or are about to find – gaps between your own culture and that of your organisation.

What do you want to accomplish in your current role? What

specific areas will you focus on over the next three, six or nine months that will help you be more effective? What are your CQ goals? How critical to your success is alignment with these cultural norms? Remember that these things don't just happen: you have to create and execute a plan to make it happen. You need to build your awareness and carve out time to increase your exposure to people in the organisation who understand and buy in to the various elements of your organisational culture – especially those elements that you're struggling with. I've created a template that you can use to map out the most critical cultural elements to which you need to adjust in order to be successful in your organisation:

Personal and Organisational Culture Alignment Plan

Element of culture	How it shows up in the organisation	Level of importance to being successful (Critical, Important, Less Important)	Level of difference from own culture and preferences (High, Medium, Low)	Mindset shift needed/ How can I see this element differently?	Authentic ways to close the gap and timing	Feedback on progress

Try to identify the three to five most critical elements that could make the biggest difference in your performance. Determine how you can see these cultural elements through a different lens or figure out how you can shift your mindset on them. Speak with your mentors, sponsors and manager to find authentic ways that resonate with you to close the gap between your culture and the organisation's culture. Also ask them for feedback on how you're progressing and adjust your action plan as necessary. Raising your level of CQ takes time, energy and thoughtfulness, but your personal investment in increasing alignment between your culture and that of your company will be time well spent.

Chapter 5
Building your personal brand

When I first heard the term 'personal branding' during my time at Deloitte, I thought it was complete rubbish, *gar-bahj*. To me, it sounded like: 'You have to fit into a certain box to be accepted into a specific environment, so contort and mould yourself until you fit nice and tight into that box.' I am a very authentic person – what you see is what you get – so I physically and emotionally could not bring myself to be something that I am not. I decided to bow out of the whole conversation. I thought I needed to find an environment where I could just be me and let my work do the talking. To me, the idea of branding myself sounded arrogant, phony and contrived: not only would I have to do great work but I would also have to talk about it all the time, pound my chest and constantly ask people to notice me. It was all Team Too Much and I wasn't willing to do any of it.

It was not until I met Donna Rachelson, a South African expert in personal, team and entrepreneur branding, that the importance of personal branding started making sense to me. I was fortunate enough to attend one of her workshops early on in my tenure at McKinsey, and I had three important epiphanies during the session. First, a brand is the words or emotions that come to people's minds when someone mentions your name. It's the space that you occupy in the mind of your client, customer or anyone else. Second, you have a brand whether you want one or not, so you might as well manage it. And third, you can intentionally and authentically craft your brand in a way that resonates with who you are and what you want to be known for.

The branding struggle

In general, we, as Black people, struggle to brand ourselves. I think much of the reason has to do with the messages we've received about focusing solely on obtaining degrees, being more concerned with the team than ourselves and believing that our work will speak for us. Conversations around our dinner tables did not touch on the topic of personal branding. We lack awareness of and/or comfort with this topic, so how can other people know what value we bring if we are never comfortable talking about that value? How can people know what we can do to help them if we never talk about it? Part of our challenge is that it seems arrogant to talk about ourselves, but there is a big difference between being confident and arrogant: confidence draws people in, arrogance repels people.

People who are confident are certain about what they bring to the table, and they are not shy or selfish to talk about that value. Conversely, confident people know that they are not good at everything. So while they are sure about what they bring to the table, they also create space for others to bring what they know they don't have. Arrogant people don't create that space, and that is what drives other people away. Arrogance comes across as if it's all about that one person. It's as if that person brings all the solutions to the table, or the most important and only skill. Confidence is about 'you and me'. Arrogance is about 'me'. If you ever wonder whether you're being confident or arrogant, look at how people react to you. You can also reference the Self-Confidence vs Arrogance Comparison chart to see the different behaviours associated with each.

Personal and Organisational Culture Alignment Plan

	Self-Confidence …		**Arrogance …**
✓	Attracts	✗	Repels
✓	Understands strengths and areas for development	✗	Believes she is superior to others
✓	Is not afraid to admit her mistakes and learn from those mistakes	✗	Never admits her mistakes. Always justifies her mistakes.
✓	Engaging	✗	Dominating
✓	Shares how she adds value to others	✗	Brags about herself to get attention
✓	Helps others correct their mistakes	✗	Revels in the blunders of others
✓	Is about what she brings and what others bring	✗	Is only about what she brings

A brand that fits you

Branding is not a one-size-fits-all exercise. You don't have to be someone you are not. For example, if you are an introvert, there are ways to cultivate your brand that resonate with your preferences. The same is true for extroverts. You don't have to build your brand in the same way as others do, and they don't have to follow your lead either. Branding differs from person to person. It's not about copying someone else, but rather about finding a way that is authentic and sustainable for you. The first steps that you can take to market yourself are to determine what you want your brand to be, assess your current brand and then create an action plan to close the gap between the two. And, as with anything, you will have to assess the effectiveness of your branding and make adjustments as you go along.

Donna helped me to understand that my overarching mission

in life is to empower other people, which is precisely why I wrote this book. I might empower others through a variety of platforms and topics, but empowerment is the umbrella term under which all my ideas fit. The word 'empowerment' summarises my brand and needs to be woven through everything I do, say, deliver, wear and post online. Ultimately, a brand is a verbal commitment that is not just about you. You are sharing with the world what you stand for, what you will deliver and, most importantly, the value that you can add to their lives through your unique set of skills, gifts, talents and perspectives. Then it is up to you to live up to that promise in every way, every day.

As I began to think about the brands that I love most, I realised that the most authentic brands are the ones with the most impact and longevity. I realised that the same could be said for my own personal brand. The brand identity and approach that would be perfect for me would be one that is authentic, effective and sustainable. Remember that having a great brand encourages people to invest in and support you, which in turn increases your skill set, your profile and your access to high-impact opportunities. All of this increases your ability to work with people on projects that have more impact in your organisation.

I really had to wrap my head around the idea that I had a brand, whether I wanted one or not, and that I had to manage it. People who met you five minutes ago have an impression of you, so the people who have worked with you for days, weeks or months certainly have an impression of you, too. As part of my role as the manager of the leadership programme at McKinsey, I had to secure high-profile speakers to talk through their leadership stories with the programme participants. I always invited the broader office to these events as well. My predecessor had always managed to find well-known speakers, so when I took over the programme I knew I had to maintain – if not raise – those standards. I was constantly hustling for speakers: I attended talks by experts at local universities, I reached out to McKinsey alumni who had extensive connections, and I even asked speakers who turned me down to reconsider my invitation. I was able to book inspirational speakers, including a South African cabinet minister (equivalent to a US cabinet secretary), the CEO of a media/magazine empire and the CEO of a healthcare company. One day, someone asked me if I knew a particular high-profile person because I was known to have this amazing network. I was taken aback. I never saw myself as *that* person. I just saw myself as someone hustling to do her job well. Nevertheless, this had become part of my brand at the office, whether I wanted it or not.

Let's talk about three myths and truths about personal branding:

Myth 1: Personal branding is all about bragging, self-promotion and being the colleague that works our last nerve.
Truth 1: Personal branding is about sharing the authentic value that you bring through your work. It is about delivering on and communicating a promise and occupying a certain space in your client or customer's mind.

Myth 2: Personal branding is only done well by extroverts and men (so if you happen to be an introverted female, you're screwed).
Truth 2: Branding doesn't have to be done in a loud and boisterous way. It has to be done authentically, and everyone has the capacity to be authentic.

Myth 3: The visibility that you get from personal branding is a finite resource.
Truth 3: The sun is large enough to warm the entire world. No one ever says, 'If you get sunshine then I can't.' There is enough sun for all of us to get some shine. We all bring different things to the table, so we can all be recognised for our individual contributions.

> "Patterns matter. There's a term that I've been reading about recently called patternicity. In a society where there's so much stimuli that people are facing, there is so much chaos and uncertainty, people rely on familiar patterns. So there are principles in behaviour science around heuristics and why people take shortcuts. People take shortcuts when they are under pressure. The workplace is under pressure, so people are taking shortcuts. Create patterns that help you become familiar and visible quicker – patterns such as creating relationships with someone senior in a mentoring relationship. Be part of conversations that are important to the company. Anything that's pressing, etc. Try to create a link between yourself and a pattern to really show that your personal brand ecosystem is interested in the pressing things versus just going about things randomly." – *Timothy Maurice Webster*

Branding yourself is much like marketing a product. Imagine that you devote your entire career to researching, developing and manufacturing the world's greatest product, something that could save lives. If you don't talk about the product – what it's made of, its benefits and how to access it – no one will ever know about it. In other words, awareness and communication are key. Let's take the Coca-Cola Company as an example. It has been around since 1886 and Coca-Cola is the most successful and well-known soft drink in the world. Coca-Cola spends billions of dollars each year to create awareness and differentiation of its brand. Every year, the company works hard to occupy a certain space in your mind, making sure you continue to think positively, and feel certain emotions, about the brand.

If Coca-Cola still brands itself after almost 150 years and billions of dollars in revenue, don't you think you should do so too? The brand that you develop and market is called You Inc. Regardless of what your role is, you have customers or clients that you serve. Who are your customers and clients? Do you have internal and/or external clients/customers? For example, if you are in a support function (human resources, IT, finance), your customers/clients are other employees in the business. Your work serves them and meets their needs. If you are in an external-facing role (sales, marketing), your customers/clients are outside your organisation. What space do you want to occupy in your customers'/clients' minds? And what is your plan to ensure this?

> Whatever you do, it's important to understand your [customers]. Don't think, 'Because I know the business, I should do things this way.' Try to understand the customers' needs and give them what you promised them; in that way, they will embrace you *and* your product. Never underestimate what you want to give or what the consumers are looking for." – *Connie Mashaba*

During my time as the leadership programme manager, I continued having Donna facilitate a personal-branding course for each new cohort in the programme. I discovered that there is often a disconnect between who we think we are and how others experience us. Donna's workshop included her gathering and aggregating anonymous feedback on strengths and areas of development from the participants' friends, family and colleagues. I remember how one participant in the programme was very upset that some of the people who gave her feedback said she had an anger issue. As a result, she had trouble being fully present in the class because she was stewing and brewing over the feedback. Fast-forward a year after the course, when I had to deliver some negative feedback to her. During our session, she became angry and ended the discussion abruptly. Clearly, this was someone who was disconnected from the reality of who she is and how others experience her. This example highlights a trait common to us all: we have blind spots when it comes to ourselves. This is why feedback is so critical when we are cultivating our personal brand and trying to grow in our careers. How else will we be able to maximise our personal brand if we don't know where we're starting from and what adjustments we need to make?

When I started my career, I knew that I wanted to stand out. I wanted people to know what I was capable of. I wanted to be recognised for my contributions and given opportunities to do more of the work that I loved and that energised me. I realised that if I needed to brand myself to get an opportunity to do those things, I was more than willing to do so. I decided that I needed to change how I looked at the process of branding. If branding could help me stand out without forcing me to compromise my values, then why not? In a busy, time-constrained environment, the average person is too busy worrying about themselves to be thinking about all *your* accomplishments and talents, so it's your job to remind them of those, as well as what you're passionate about.

When I was getting ready to leave McKinsey, Donna asked me what my plan was as I left the company. 'I've submitted my resignation letter,' I said. 'I'm leaving in a few weeks.' 'No,' she replied. 'Are you going to summarise all the great things you did while you were here?' I had to admit that I hadn't even thought about it. Her advice to me was that I should create a document outlining all my accomplishments during my time as the leadership programme manager and send it to the key leaders in the office. It had never crossed my mind, so I had to think about it. Would it violate my personal values or boundaries in any way? No. Would it leave a lasting impression on the company leaders and help them understand my contribution to the office? Yes. After reflecting on my answers to these important questions, I decided to give it a try. So I created the document and I sent it to the Africa office leader, the Johannesburg location manager and another influential senior partner whom I respected. Surprisingly, they all responded very positively and thanked me for all that I had done. I'm sure no one ever created a document like that upon exiting the firm!

My tenure at McKinsey was the first time in my life that I heard behind-the-scenes feedback on consultants. I sat in performance reviews and listened to real-time feedback on employees. This was when I realised that personal branding, apart from being a reflection of your work, talents and accomplishments, also includes everything you say, do, wear, deliver and put on social media, because it shapes people's perceptions of you and thus your brand. Perception is reality, so you need to be intentional about creating and maintaining an authentic personal brand that aligns with who you are.

Keeping it real

You can't do what everyone else is doing and expect to stand out from the crowd. So how do you differentiate yourself? I often hear young people say, 'I can't be fake; I am who I am.' Remember that building your personal brand is not about being someone that you're not. It's about being the best version of your authentic self and making sure everything you do – how you dress, speak, write, deliver a message or a presentation, engage with others, your online presence – aligns with what you want to be known for. Rather than viewing yourself from an either/or perspective – 'I am either this or that', 'I am either fake or authentic' – consider viewing your personal brand on a continuum.

Let's say that there is a continuum of authenticity and it is structured from levels one to ten, with ten being your most authentic, unfiltered version of yourself. This might be the version you display when you are with your family and closest friends. However, if you're in an interview, you might tone it down to a five or six because the interviewers might not be able to handle you on ten. Always consider your audience and determine how your message will be received if you present it on level ten. In addition, if your family and friends could see you during an interview or when you're at work, my hope is that they would still recognise you and how you're acting. But the reverse is also true. If your co-workers were to come to your house and see you hanging out with your family and friends, I hope they would recognise *some* version of you, even if it is a more unfiltered version.

Remember that not everyone might be able to handle you at authenticity level ten. Keep this in mind in the workplace, especially if your goal is for your message to be well received. It is not merely for you to just be and say what you feel. Yes, authenticity is important, because, psychologically speaking, it can be tiring to be two complete opposite versions of yourself. However, there is a way to find a good middle ground. Finding that space on the continuum allows you to be yourself while using your energy to solve the problem at hand and reach your intended audience.

Again, the importance of authenticity cannot be overstated when it comes to branding. Bring your full self, which is the totality of who you are: your personality, experiences, sense of humour, strengths, areas for development, quirks, interests and perspective on the world, people and situations. Everything that has happened to you has shaped you into the unique individual that you are today. The way you see the world is your source of distinctiveness. My advice is to determine what authenticity means for *you*; only *you* will know how it looks and feels. I cannot tell you what authenticity looks like because it manifests itself differently for everyone. What is common to all of us, though, is how authenticity *feels*. Authenticity is when you feel at ease. It feels effortless. It is when you don't feel a need to behave in a certain way to protect yourself or convince others to like you. Authenticity doesn't come from a place of pain, trauma or brokenness. If you strip away all that is external and physical, it is the core and essence of who you are. During the 'Building Credibility' course that I lead for Bain, one particular question always gets to the heart of what I mean by 'being authentic': who are you when you're with the person(s) that you trust the most? And who are you with complete strangers or those who have hurt you in the past? The answers to these questions represent the opposite ends of the continuum of authenticity.

> "We're so obsessed with career peaks. I will say the career peak is reaching 'the list'. I'll say a career peak is reaching *Forbes* and because we're so obsessed with career peaks, we only show the good. No one is showing the long hours. No one is showing the crying in the bathroom. No one is showing this is what my boss said to me today. We're only showing that today I made top 40 under 40, we're only showing that today I'm on *Forbes* 30 under 30. I wish we were more open and honest with each other about what we're all going through. If we're more open with each other, I think we will achieve a lot more." – *Zimasa Qolohle Mabuse*

If authenticity implies standing up for your values, it also means that you might be called to do so in the face of authority, or when it might be unpopular. Authenticity means that you feel so strongly about your values and beliefs that you are willing to go out on a limb and risk failure, embarrassment, being wrong or upsetting your seniors. Authenticity also means having the courage to take risks and ask for help or additional clarity when you don't understand something. If you're ever in a public or professional setting with me, you'll find out that I ask a lot of questions. If something doesn't make sense to me, I will keep asking questions until it does – even if it makes me look dumb or as if I wasn't paying attention. My aim is not to look smart. My aim is to get clarity so that I can do my job well. (I can't tell you how many times people have walked up to me after a meeting or discussion is over to say, 'That question you asked . . . I was wondering the same thing but I didn't want to ask.') Finally, authenticity is also about admitting when things are not going well. Being true to yourself means being real about your performance at work and taking the necessary steps to help you turn the situation around.

> "When I was 24, 25 years old, a senior officer at my company once called from another country and asked us to go back on contracts we signed in good faith. I leaned in and said: 'I am uncomfortable with this because it shows a lack of integrity on our part.' There was a gasp in the room. I didn't think anything of it and sat back down. The senior leader said that he appreciated my comment and that I was absolutely right. He explained that he didn't want every contract to be reopened, just the uncompleted ones. That's when other people jumped in and they started asking questions. Speak your truth. It may not be the most welcoming environment and you'll have to live with the consequences, but you have to live your truth and do what's right."
> – *Tina Taylor*

When I say that everything you do contributes to your personal brand, I mean *everything*: how you speak, dress and deliver. Sometimes people think it is only in certain situations that excellence counts. For example, at McKinsey, consultants would often be asked to help senior leaders with client development proposals. Sometimes consultants would blow this work off or not take it as seriously because they didn't consider these projects to be 'real' client work. This lack of effort on the part of consultants definitely tainted senior leaders' perceptions of those individuals. After working on a proposal with a senior leader, you may never work with that senior leader again, but she may give feedback on you to someone else in her network who trusts her opinion. When you are early in your career, your attitude and output at work plays a huge role in building your brand. When you turn in an Excel spreadsheet with incorrect numbers or poor logic, it reflects on your brand. When your PowerPoint presentation contains misspelled words or the wrong numbers, that is how you've chosen to brand yourself. Is that what you want to be known for? The person whose work can't

What Authenticity Feels and Looks Like

What Authenticity Feels Like Internally	What Authenticity Looks like Externally
You feel at ease with who you are, your strengths and areas of development. Who you are and who you want to be are pretty consistent.	People experience you as someone who is congruent. Your behaviour and your words align. People are drawn to your authenticity, confidence and balanced sense of self.
You know what is important to you and you operate from that space.	People know what you stand for and where they stand with you.
You are aware when you don't know something and need to ask for help. You know when you are wrong about an idea.	You ask for help, admit that you're wrong or don't know something. You raise questions. You acknowledge that you are wrong and that someone else is right.
You know when you have treated someone poorly.	You apologise.
You believe that your perspective matters even if it might be wrong. You will not let fear hold you back from taking a risk.	You share your perspective even when it might seem unpopular or challenge the status quo.
Your goal is to gain clarity, not protect your ego or appear smart.	You request a second or third explanation in order to gain the necessary clarity.
You are honest with yourself about how personal struggles affect you.	You share personal struggles with those you trust and you ask for their advice on how to solve them.
You realise that you have a performance problem and your role in that problem.	You are honest with the relevant people about where you performance is, and you ask for their help to determine what you need to do to turn it around.

be trusted? Now, mistakes will always be made, but you want to try to avoid silly mistakes and repeat offences. Even if your spell-checked and number-checked work leads to nothing in the short term, it still shapes your reputation at work, which affects the feedback you will eventually receive and the opportunities you will subsequently be offered. At this stage in your career, you don't understand the organisation well enough to decide when you should or should not be excellent, so always try to do outstanding work. Performing well is not only a great way to build your brand, but it is also the best way to draw mentors and sponsors. This is why it's important to understand what is important to your company and then develop a way of working that maximises those particular areas. Your personal brand will be that you are someone who works efficiently, effectively and always with your mind and hands directed firmly towards the customer, client and/or end goal.

Another interesting aspect of your personal brand is how you speak about yourself. Carla Harris, a Harvard Business School alumnus and the Vice Chairperson and Managing Director of Morgan Stanley, once came to speak to one of my classes. During her talk, she told us that she wanted people to see her as someone who could take on the challenges of being in the competitive world of investment banking. In an effort to shape her colleagues' perception of her, she started referring to herself as 'tough' in every conversation. She would say things like, 'Well, you know I'm tough so I can handle it' or 'I'm tough enough to take that on.' Eventually, people started referring to her as 'tough' too.

Carla shaped how people spoke about her through the way she spoke about herself. She was deliberate and intentional in shaping her narrative. How do you speak about yourself? Do you take every opportunity to let people know what you're involved in, what you stand for and what's important to you? When a senior person asks you how you're doing, do you take that opportunity to tell her about your passions and projects? Perhaps suggest meeting up with her to discuss a common interest. If you do this, you not only share your interests and your projects, but you also open the door to strengthening the bond between you and that senior leader. In addition, it creates the impression that you've researched that person or, at the very least, remembered what someone told you about her. In that moment you've differentiated yourself, and *that* is the goal.

> "You can't change people's perceptions about you if you're not excited about yourself and passionate about what you do. Go out of your way and do your work to the best of your ability, even if it is for a small request."
> – *Nomfanelo Magwentshu*

Dressing for impact

> "Grooming. Image. It matters. You can have earrings in your ears and your nose, you can wear what you want, but if that keeps you from becoming a CEO who can make an impact in society, what's the point? Think about the bigger picture. In my experience, speaking as a person of colour, I think we've held ourselves back because we've focused too much on politics than on the impact we can make, too early on. Sometimes, people of colour need to learn that to enter a space and establish their credibility through their work is more important than to engage in politics. Only once you do your work can you change the things that need to change. *Then* you can introduce politics because then you have an audience. Your image and managing your politics is very important." – *Thokozile Lewanika Mpupuni*

You may think that the only thing that matters is what's in your head. How you dress, how you wear your hair, how you accessorise are all representations of who you are and what you believe is important. But let's be honest: first impressions matter. We judge people every day based on what they are wearing, how their hair looks and the accessories they are wearing. You are being judged in this way *especially* at work. When you walk into a room, no one knows how bright you are, where you went to school or that you graduated top of your class. Even though it's not ideal or fair, people categorise others based on their outward appearance.

My philosophy has always been that I want people to pay attention to what is coming out of my mouth – my ideas. As such, I have chosen to dress and wear my hair in a way that does not distract from that or undermine my credibility. Remember that your goal is to be impactful in the workplace. How you choose to present yourself should be dependent on the type of environment in which you work, so this is what you have to gauge. It's all about assessing and understanding your environment and understanding what the professional dress code is. In a professional-services environment, you will have clients who are likely to be older than you. They might question what you, at the tender age of 22 or 23, could tell them that they don't already know. Even when we are older, our melanin and the old adage 'Black don't crack' can work against us and make us look much younger than we actually are. In those types of situations it is always about establishing credibility, which will give you licence to offer advice and challenge them on established ways of doing things. Credibility helps them take you and your advice more seriously. The way you dress can either add to or detract from your credibility.

Women have many options when it comes to fashion, but an abundance of choice is a double-edged sword. It can be a blessing and a curse. Because there are so many options available to us as women, we also have more opportunities to get it wrong. I remember sitting in an annual performance review where decision-makers were talking about how inappropriately a specific employee was dressed on multiple occasions. It was then my job as the programme manager to convey the message to her. 'Carice, you need to talk to her about how she dresses,' they would tell me. 'Her clothes are too revealing, she's showing too much cleavage.' Often, these individuals were not poor performers – in fact, they were doing well at their jobs – but their dress overshadowed their performance. Once I had spoken to those employees, they would always be mortified to know that their appearance (and not the quality of their work) had been given significant airtime during their performance review. Regardless of the environment, you don't want decision-makers to spend one second of your performance review talking about how inappropriate your dress or grooming is.

> "You don't know the game. You think you have a nice tie on, but again, there is no one grabbing you by the shoulder and saying, 'Don't wear that tie with the little Santa Clauses on it' or 'Don't wear the lime-green shirt with a tie.' No one is telling you the things that somebody is telling the Jewish kids at Goldman Sachs."
> – Ronald Tamale

I often ask people: do you want people to pay attention to how you dress, wear your hair and accessorise or to the quality of your work and the depth of your relationships? Figure out what the dress code is at work. If it's a written policy, abide by it. The old saying 'Dress for the job you want' is relevant here.

Even if there is a written dress code at your company, there can also be unspoken, unofficial rules. When I worked at Arthur Andersen, the dress code strictly prohibited women from wearing sleeveless shirts or dresses. Even though this rule was clear to everyone, there were other rules that were not. Once, an executive assistant for a senior leader told me that one of my co-workers needed to get rid of his facial hair. When I inquired as to why, she replied: 'Look at the partners in this organisation. None of them have facial hair.' I had been at the company for almost two years when she told me and I had never noticed. When I was early in my career, I never paid attention to how leadership dressed or how they were groomed.

My advice to you is to look at how seniors in your company dress and groom themselves. But also understand that in some environments, senior leaders are given the latitude to express their eccentricity through their dress because they've proven themselves in that environment. This might not be the case for more junior folks. If you work in a more creative environment, the style of acceptable dress might be more expressive and personal because of the industry, and because people might encourage you to dress in a more unconventional, fashion-forward way. Look across the board at a wide variety of people, getting an average feel for how people present themselves. This will ensure that you're not basing your choices on one example or one outlier. And if it's still not clear, have a conversation with your manager or mentor.

> Nelson Mandela wore a power suit until he became an icon and only then he put on that funny shirt. That funny shirt came as a result of 'I got a Nobel [Peace] Prize and I'm a world icon.' But when he was fighting, he wore a power suit. If you're trying to get to a position of power, there may be some sacrifices you'll have to make, but once you get it, you can set the terms. As soon as you're able to dictate the terms, try to put new conversations out there. Try to reinvent spaces. Wear that cultural attire; people will start taking it seriously." – *Timothy Maurice Webster*

Ultimately, it is down to you to decide what is more important to you: expressing yourself through your appearance or expressing yourself through your ideas. The choice is yours. Here are a few gender-specific tips for dressing professionally in the workplace.

Women: Ladies, you need to make sure that your clothes are appropriate from every angle. I call it the '360-degree check'. Get a full-length mirror and see how high that skirt sits in the back.

Sometimes a skirt can be an appropriate length in the front but not in the back. Bend down at the waist (not at the knee) and pretend you're picking something up off the floor. Notice how high your skirt or dress comes up in the back when you do. Also, sit down and examine how far your skirt comes up when you sit down. Skirts or dresses might be the appropriate length when you stand up but reveal too much when you sit down or bend over. When it comes to your neckline, lean on your desk and notice how much of your cleavage is exposed. Can you sit comfortably in that dress or do you have to keep adjusting it every few minutes in order to be comfortable and not expose too much? Be sure to invest in the proper undergarments that give you the right level of support. Visit a department store or women's speciality shop and invest in properly fitted undergarments. Many women wear the wrong size and/or type of bra or undergarments. Properly fitted undergarments can make a huge difference in how our clothes fit and look.

And another general tip: if you can head right to the club from the office, you're probably dressed inappropriately for work. If you're one to wear make-up, consider getting a make-up consultation to make sure you're wearing foundation and powder that match your skin tone well. Also, however you choose to wear your hair, get it done regularly enough to keep it looking like you take care of it. Although I'm a proud, uncompromising naturalista and have worn my natural hair since 2004 in every professional environment I've worked in, I've always worn it in conservative styles. As I've mentioned, I don't want my appearance to be a distraction. Whatever style you wear – be it a weave, wig, braids, Afro, etc – be prepared to make the investment to keep it looking good.

> There's something around professionalism in terms of dress. There's this senior partner, Vivian [Hunt], and in one of her speeches she says, 'Ladies, you have a job now. Please get your hair done. Look like you have a job.

You're not a student anymore.' And it's really true. It's not saying your hair has to be a certain way. It just needs to be properly done. And if you choose to wear it natural, a wig, whatever you do, just make sure that you do it. Make sure your clothes fit properly. Make sure your dress isn't too short. Make sure your hands aren't ashy. I know these are small things but people notice them. There are some gaps [in what people know about] how to dress for work, how to come and show up in a professional way. We had to have a dress code in our office because some people thought the office was the club. They would just wear the same outfit for the whole day and all night. They could just go straight from the office to the club." – *Tiffany Hinton, Senior Global Talent Manager, McKinsey & Company*

Men: Gentlemen, you're not off the hook. While you might feel that you don't have as many options as women, it doesn't give you the permission to be sloppy. I've seen men with untucked, wrinkled shirts and trousers that are too tight, too big or too short. Be willing to invest in a bit of tailoring so that your clothes fit your body type (yes, men have body types too). Don't try to stuff yourself into a shirt or trousers that are now two sizes too small or large. The 360-degree check also applies to you: take a spin in front of your full-length mirror and make sure your outfit looks good from all angles. Check the hems on those trousers; if they're frayed, get them repaired. At McKinsey, an external image consultant once came to do a presentation on professional dress. What I found most interesting was her tips on how men can elevate their style to look more mature and put together. She recommended having a properly fitted suit and wearing a matching belt and shoes to top off the look. She also mentioned that smaller prints on dress shirts look more sophisticated, professional and expensive than larger prints. Finally, get your hair cut regularly by a professional, and if you're going to have facial hair, keep it well-groomed consistently.

Men and women: Before the advent of a new season or change in weather, try on your work clothes to see what fits and what doesn't. Your weight can fluctuate and it's not safe to assume that your outfits from last season will still fit you this year. Assess what needs to be altered or mended and take those clothes to your nearest seamstress or tailor to be repaired. Determine what needs to be donated or replaced. The same rule applies to your shoes, too. Check how worn out the heels of your shoes are and get your shoes shined to keep them looking good. Keep in mind that dressing professionally is not about breaking the bank or buying expensive designer clothes, shoes or accessories. Instead, it's about making professional choices that are smart, strategic and cost-effective.

> Understand your environment. Just because you see someone of your particular skin colour wearing a tank-top dress does not mean that you can do the same. Both of you would be in violation. The message that that dress sends to all of the leaders and all of the people looking at that individual is: 'They don't care about themselves so why should we care about them?' Just considering your appearance, always respect the environment that you're stepping into. Understand it and make sure people are respecting you." – *Tina Taylor*

Unique brand elements based on organisational culture

In the previous chapter, I discussed understanding your organisation's culture and values. You need to make sure that the elements of your personal brand align with and speak to what is important in that environment. You also need to understand the speed of judgement in that environment. How quickly do people form opinions about other people? Is it possible to rebound from a bad impression? How forgiving is that environment? If the environment is quick to judge and slow to forgive, you will have to quickly adjust your working style to deliver and build your brand in the ways that matter to the organisation.

Once you find out those values, you need to map out a plan to deliver on them. For example, at McKinsey, speed of delivery and accuracy are *very* important and a consultant is judged on both. It's not enough to be accurate; you must be fast as well. Time is of the essence in that environment. Remember that different organisations work at different speeds, so it's important that you assess the speed of work accordingly. Engaging others at the right time (after you've applied your mind to the problem) and in the right way is a non-negotiable, and your ability to do this well is a key component in being able to deliver in a timely and accurate fashion. Understanding how to think about your work, and how to engage others, requires thought, planning, seeking advice and removing a large part of your ego.

Imagine that a junior consultant is asked to produce a slide in PowerPoint. She will spend hours working on the slide to make it *perfect*, making sure that all the numbers are right and that the boxes and lines are all straight. The consultant then presents the slide to the manager on the team . . . and hears that the slide isn't anything close to what the manager was looking for. So let's start over, from when the consultant first was tasked with creating the slide. She should have spent 30 minutes to an hour applying her mind to the problem, *then* she should have sketched out with pencil and paper how she would design the slide. Following that, she should have shown her sketch to the manager to see if she was on the right track. She might have gotten feedback, which could have led her to co-create the slide with her manager. They could even have gone back and forth for a couple of iterations on pen and paper, with the manager giving feedback and the junior consultant making changes until finally they landed on a workable draft. Only *then* should the consultant have spent time creating the slide in PowerPoint.

This example illustrates the point that there are two very different ways of working. One way involves trying to go it alone; the other involves balancing individual effort, speed and accuracy and doing what is best for the team and the problem at hand. At McKinsey, some junior consultants had to learn this the hard way: in trying to be perfect, they would waste valuable time, which is one of the top currencies in that environment. When you reflect on your company's culture, what are the values that are most important? How can you work in such a way that your brand aligns with what matters most in your organisation's culture?

> Personal branding is an evolving term that is about positioning a story and an identity that has value for some sort of commercial exchange. For me it's about stories and narratives that can be exchanged for value. I always say to anyone who's trying to build their personal brand: be clear about your story and your patterns and figure out where you have leverage, whether it's corporate, as an entrepreneur or as an influencer." – *Timothy Maurice Webster*

Now that we've talked about what a personal brand is, let's discuss the eight steps to build yours.

Step 1. Reframe what personal branding means to you and determine your why: How do you feel about personal branding? If you have a negative view of personal branding (eg if you think it's about being fake or fitting into a box), the chances are very high that you won't do it. If you only develop a personal brand because I'm telling you to have one, you also probably won't do it, or, if you do, it won't be sustainable because the desire is not coming from an authentic place. What will having a personal brand create for you? What is your *why*? What is the purpose of your brand? How will you use it to serve others?

Step 2. Embrace your story: Building a brand starts with having a voice, and a big part of your voice is based on articulating and owning your story. What are the elements of your story that influence who you are today and what you are passionate about? Let me give you an example: many years ago, I attended a talk by Howard Schultz, the former CEO of Starbucks, at Wits University. As a child, Howard's family sank deeper and deeper into poverty after his father was injured on the job. At the time, there was no workers' compensation and his father did not have health benefits. In his presentation he mentioned that he wanted to create the type of company his father never had the chance to work for. That is part of the reason why Starbucks was one of the first companies in the US to offer full-time benefits to part-time employees. Today, Starbucks also covers the cost of tuition for any of their employees who want to finish their undergraduate studies while continuing to work at the company. Howard Schultz's approach to supporting his employees and his leadership of Starbucks was therefore directly influenced by his childhood experiences – his life story.

Step 3. Define your overall goals and aspirations: As you define your goals for the future and how these could shape your brand identity, reflect on the following questions:
- What do you really want? What does success look like at this stage in your life?
- What do you want to be known for?
- What value do you want to bring? What impact do you want to have?
- What type of person do you want to be?
- What do you *not* want to do in the future?
- What skills and experiences do you need to make progress?

Step 4. Research and determine brand attributes: If you think about people who excel at the type of work that you would like to do, what skills and experiences do they have? What are they great at? What are they known for?

Step 5. Understand how others perceive your brand by getting feedback about your strengths and weaknesses:
- ❏ What do those around you – your friends, family, colleagues and others – say is your brand? How do they experience you?
- ❏ What kind of impression does your online presence create? Do your posts and comments on social media reflect the brand that you want to convey?

Step 6. Evaluate the gaps between your current and desired brand and create an action plan to close the gaps:
Consider the following questions:
- ❏ Why do you believe there are gaps between your current brand and your desired brand?
- ❏ What can you do differently to move closer to the brand you want?
- ❏ Who do you need to build relationships with? What support do you need from each relationship?

I recently saw an article on Forbes.com that outlined the various degrees of support that individuals can provide. Do you need each type of relationship? If not, which degrees of support are most important, and do you have someone (or multiple people) who falls into each category? If not, how can you build your brand and ultimately a relationship with that person so they feel comfortable providing that level of support? What are you trying to achieve? Who are the people who are critical to your success, growth and access to opportunities? What is the status of that relationship? What do you want or need it to be? And how will you close the gap?

One school of thought on relationships that I found interesting comes from Herminia Ibarra, a professor of organisational behaviour at the London Business School. She theorises that there are about five different levels of support: the Mentor, the Strategiser, the Connector, the Opportunity-Giver and the Advocate. As I showed in Chapter 3, the role of the Mentor can be defined as a 'trusted counsellor or guide' who will coach you and offer his or her wisdom and experience. The Strategiser provides inside-track information to help you determine how to get ahead and will help you figure out who the right people are for you to get in front of, the right opportunities for you to participate in and the timing for each. The Connector will take it a step further by opening up their network to introduce you to the right people. This person elevates your personal brand by speaking well of you with his or her peers or within his or her network, and takes a more public role in supporting you than do the Mentor and Strategiser.

The Opportunity-Giver, in turn, provides high-visibility opportunities for you to increase your status or be seen in a different light in the organisation, demonstrate competencies that other projects haven't allowed you to and/or work with key influencers and decision-makers in the organisation. And, finally, the Advocate pounds the table for you to get the promotion, salary increase, bonus or step-up opportunity that you need. This person is in the room when the most important decisions about your career are being made and puts his or her name on the line to vouch for you. The Mentor and Strategiser roles are far more private than the roles of Connector, Opportunity-Giver and Advocate. Make sure you're cultivating your brand with multiple people in the categories of supporters that you deem most important.

Step 7. Monitor your progress by gathering feedback: After you've implemented the necessary changes to your brand and its image, gather feedback once again. We all have blind spots when it comes to ourselves, so feedback is critical and should be ongoing.

Step 8. Live your brand every day and be prepared to evolve your brand as you evolve: Remember that in ten years' time, you may want to be known for something else or you may have changed occupations. In that case, be sure to assess what you want your brand to be and then make changes to make it a reality. For example, if you were a great individual contributor in your company but were recently promoted to a managerial role, you would want your brand to reflect that. In your previous role, you wanted to be known for your great work, and now, as a manager, you want to be known for achieving great results through others. How can you position your brand differently now that you are in a new role?

8 Steps to Develop and Maintain a Personal Brand

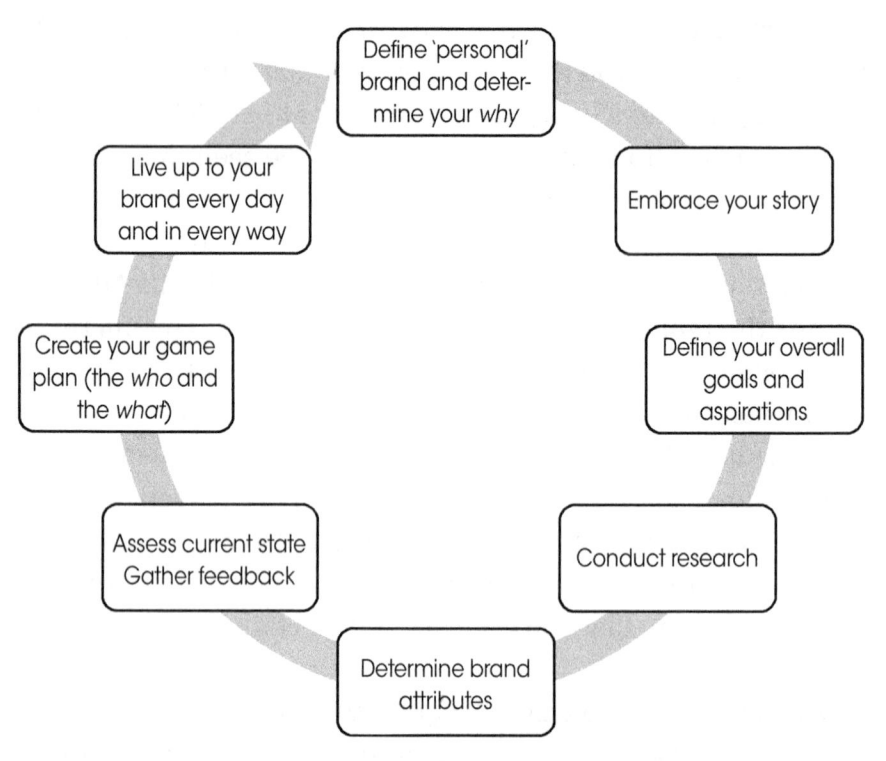

- Define 'personal' brand and determine your *why*
- Embrace your story
- Define your overall goals and aspirations
- Conduct research
- Determine brand attributes
- Assess current state Gather feedback
- Create your game plan (the *who* and the *what*)
- Live up to your brand every day and in every way

> I would tell my younger self that you can always reinvent who you are professionally. You're not locked into one thing; don't let anyone tell you that. I would tell myself that you can do whatever you want. I give myself the permission to do that and all that encompasses it."
> – Tina Taylor

Branding tips for your personality and lifestyle

As I've shown in this chapter, branding can look different for different people. If you're an introvert, you might be thinking, 'I'm shy. I hate networking events and I feel awkward at them.' Or, if you're very busy, you might be saying, 'I am really time-constrained and I don't have time to be at all these events.' Here are a few examples of branding tips for introverts and busy people.

Branding tips for introverts:
- ❏ Think about what makes you comfortable and makes you feel authentic. Start there. Start somewhere! To continue to do nothing is not an option.
- ❏ Use social media. You can use social media to display your knowledge and brand yourself as an expert in your field.
- ❏ Use one-on-one opportunities to connect. If you're uncomfortable at large events and prefer one-on-one meetings or small-group sessions, reach out to individuals and schedule coffee chats to share your knowledge and to learn more from those people.
- ❏ Use your preference for alone time to hone your craft. Then convey what you've learnt when you're at work or in a meeting with decision-makers, influencers and your manager.
- ❏ Use your environment to demonstrate your expertise. If you're in an environment where education is valued, talk about your

university and graduate school experiences. Hang up those degrees and certificates in your working space. It can be a conversation starter, help people learn more about you and see you in a different light.
- Look for opportunities to share what you know. Mentor junior people in your office. Volunteer to show your expertise in a lunch 'n learn or at a professional event. Other people will start sharing how knowledgeable you are and how much value you add.
- Step outside your comfort zone. Once you're more comfortable with branding, consider pushing yourself to attend a networking event. Think about two or three people you want to talk to before the event and start a conversation with those people.

Branding tips for busy people:
- Be strategic. You can't go to every networking event, so try to figure out which ones are the most important and attend those.
- Be fully present from 8 am to 5 pm. Be engaged when you are at work. Resist the urge to be on social media. Take advantage of lunch-time chats or coffee-break conversations to give people a chance to know you and what you're working on.
- Be prepared to offer your thoughts. If you're going to a meeting, understand what is being discussed and come prepared with two to three points you'd like to make during the meeting.
- Get your manager's help. Tell your manager that you are trying to raise your visibility to build relationships in the organisation. Communicate your goals for your career and be as specific as you can in terms of where you need her help. Try to align your aspirations with your manager's goals or challenges so he or she is even more incentivised to help you. Ask for your manager's feedback (what you're doing well and what you could do differently) as you build visibility to make sure you're on the right track.

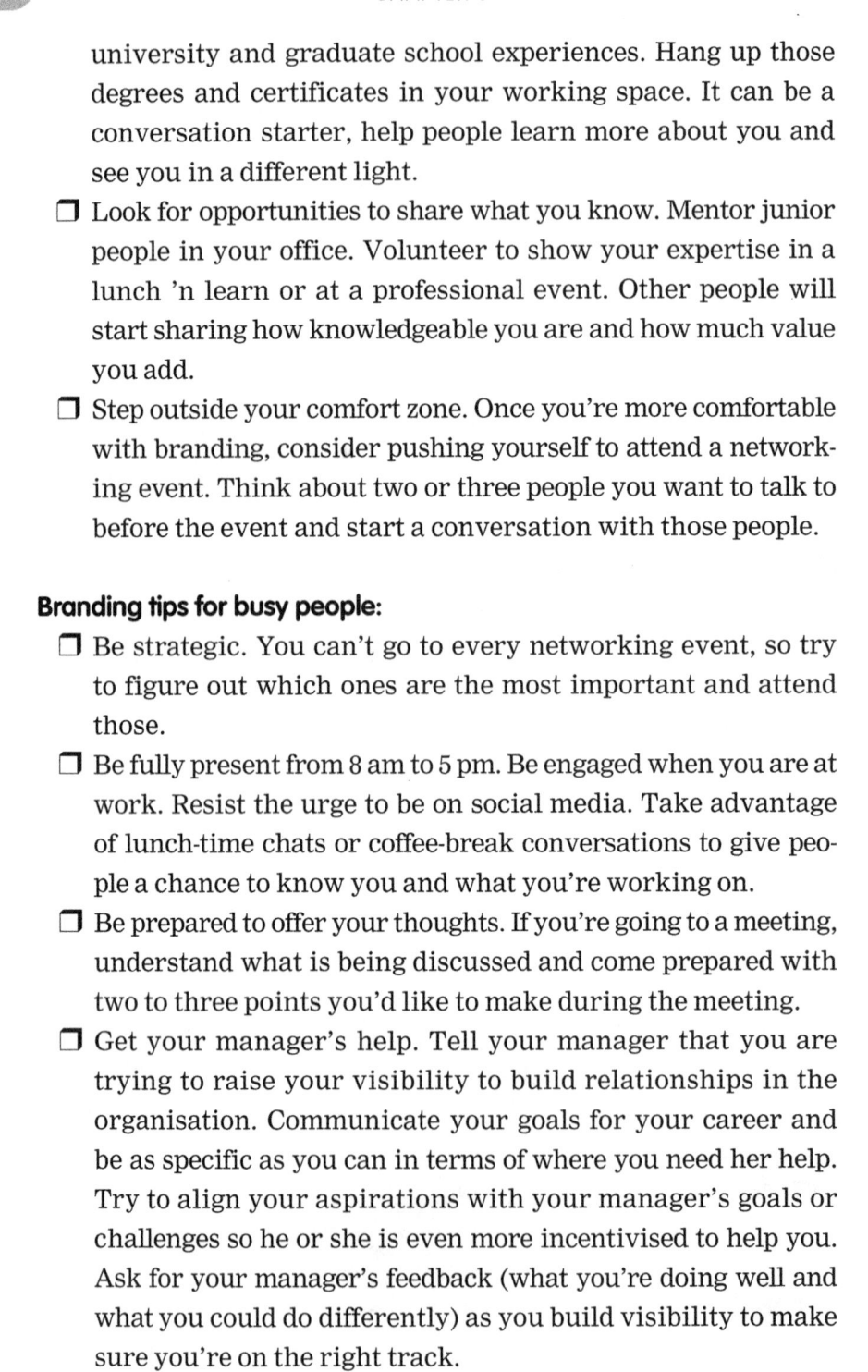

Respect and understand your company's brand

A mistake I've made in the past – and one I've often seen young people make – is questioning the brand right after joining an organisation. The way a company operates is the *why* and the *how* behind that brand. They have that brand because of how they operate and how they deliver. I realised I couldn't be a fan of the end result (the brand) without understanding the method behind the brand. We try to change (read: don't like) the very things that helped create the brand that we love.

Another key point to remember is that, as an employee of a company, you are also actively contributing to how others perceive the corporation that employs you. When clients, customers and/or people in social settings meet you, they form an opinion about your company based on their interactions with you. Be intentional about your behaviour and how you communicate and think about whether it reflects the brand in the most positive, authentic and professional light.

In conclusion, remember that *you* are a brand. You are the CEO of You Inc and everything you do contributes to how others perceive you and your organisation. You always have to ask yourself: is what I'm about to say, do, deliver and/or wear reflective of the things that I want people to say and think of me and my company? Will these help me have more or less impact? One of the biggest keys to building an enduring personal brand is being a great communicator. In the next chapter, I provide a few tips on how to communicate in a way that builds the brand that you want.

Chapter 6
Communication is key

Learning how to communicate effectively is probably the most important skill to master in the workplace. Not only does it help you to develop and sustain your personal brand, but it also helps you to maintain healthy professional (and personal) relationships, which plays a critical role in delivering great work. Communication is how we express respect, admiration, frustration, expectations, boundaries, confusion and anger, and get clarification, among many other things. If self-awareness is the cornerstone of your personal and professional development, communication is the brick laid right next to it.

When it comes to your personal brand, you want to be known as a clear and concise communicator. Most of your professional work will be collaborative, iterative and time-constrained in nature, so communication plays a tremendous role in making that back-and-forth process as efficient and effective as possible. Your ability to deliver your work in an excellent way depends on your listening skills but also, importantly, on your ability to clearly and concisely articulate your understanding of the assignment. You should also be able to articulate your questions if you lack clarity about your task. The way you communicate shapes people's perceptions of you and your level of expertise. Skills such as communicating a sense of urgency, tension between competing priorities, requests for help and appeals to move impossible deadlines account for the difference between a trustworthy, mature team member and someone who isn't.

A key part of communication is understanding your audience. You want to communicate with people at a level that they can understand and to speak to what is important to them. The way you would talk about a subject with your five-year-old cousin will differ from the way you address your colleague or your grandmother. Your purpose in communicating, especially in corporate environments, should be for your message to be received, not just to speak your mind. Understanding your audience means you have to reflect on what is important to them, anticipate the types of questions or objections they might have and develop your thoughts to address those issues. In a presentation, this also helps you appear more prepared: if you've spent time thinking about those questions and preparing fitting responses, the chances of your being caught off-guard are reduced.

Here is an example of how you can think about tailoring your message based on your audience. Let's say you're working at an ice-cream shop. During a team meeting you try to convince the owner and the team that another flavour of ice cream should be added to the menu. To meet the needs and address the concerns of each team member, you might want to emphasise the following points. For the sales rep, you could mention that the ice cream has a delicious, dark-chocolate flavour and that it's dairy-free (something customers have been asking about). For the shop owner, you could say that the ice-cream supplier has agreed to a 60-day payment turnaround (as opposed to a 30-day turnaround). And for the ice-cream-supply manager, you could highlight the fact that the ice-cream supplier is willing to make daily deliveries so the store would not need to keep a lot of the product in stock.

> When you get a big opportunity, you've got to know your audience and you've got to knock it out of the park. You have to know and believe that you know what you're talking about, and that you can get their confidence in running your business. That's fundamental." – *Artis Brown*

One of the first steps in improving your communication skills is to understand what communication is. But let me start by saying what communication is *not*. Communication is *not* just about saying whatever comes to mind. It is not about waiting to respond while another person is talking, formulating in your head what your next point will be. Neither is it about winning an argument. It is not about being right. It is not about manipulating, cajoling or strong-arming the other person into agreeing with you. It is also not about saying what you think people want to hear. Instead, communication *is* about being deliberate about your tone, choice of words and body language so that the other person receives your message and you receive theirs in turn. And this involves the ability to listen. If you are not a great listener, then, unfortunately, you won't be an effective communicator either.

If you are a great lecturer or speaker, you cannot assume that you are a great communicator too. Remember that communication is supposed to be a dialogue: it is about sharing your perspective *and* listening to what the other person has to say. It is about being open to new ideas, new perspectives and how the conversation unfolds, and communicating in an authentic way that honours your and the other person's truth and experience. It is about sharing in a way that strengthens, preserves and grows the relationship and helps you deliver an excellent result. When you are communicating with someone – or even prior to the conversation – make sure to check what your intention is. Is it to be right, to manipulate or to control? Or is it to sincerely hear what the other person is saying and to reach some common ground that will serve as a strong foundation for your relationship and ultimately the impact you want to have? In my experience, many people have never been taught how to communicate effectively, especially when they are in an emotionally charged state or when it comes to sharing thoughts or perspectives that may cause tension or disappointment. To be honest, it's scary when you're unsure whether you're saying the right thing at the right time. You don't want to upset or disappoint others, but you also don't want to dishonour yourself by not sharing your truth.

There are a number of techniques that could help you communicate in a way that honours your and your audience's perspectives. But before we get into those techniques, I want to present another concept: Bruce Tuckman's 'forming-storming-norming-performing' stages of group development. Tuckman believes that the 'forming' phase in group development is when a team is first created and each team member is feeling the other team members out and figuring out what the goal is. The 'storming' phase occurs when tensions arise and team members are in conflict because of their different communication and working styles. The next phase, 'norming', is when teams have learnt to appreciate others' strengths and differences and the goals and roles are clear. In my opinion, communication is one of the key factors in helping a team find their way through uncomfortable times. If they're able to do this well, they ultimately come out at the other end with top-notch results (the 'performing' phase).

Let us explore the storming phase, as this is where many relationships and teams get stuck. I believe that if we expect to encounter tension within our teams, we would not be so surprised by it and thus not get stuck in it. Consider your sibling or a close relative, someone with whom you share DNA. You have probably grown up with similar values in a similar culture and, from time to time, you have had communication breakdowns or conflict with that person. Doesn't it stand to reason that you will have conflicts with a colleague, too? Someone who isn't connected to you genetically and hasn't grown up with the same values or in the same culture as you? Shouldn't you spend time understanding how your colleagues think and communicate? Our experiences influence how we see and experience the world, and they are based on all of the facets that make us who we are: gender, race, religion, culture, sexuality, strengths, areas for development, preferences, education and many more. Companies often hire different types of people because of the differences they bring to the table. Unfortunately, though, very few companies show their employees how to successfully navigate the conflicts that arise from those differences. Being able to navigate these is crucial so that we can build relationships and leverage differences in a way that helps the team deliver at an optimal level.

Communication is also one of the key building blocks for creating psychological safety on a team. This term, coined by Amy Edmondson, is defined as a shared belief held by members of a team that the team is safe for interpersonal risk-taking. Psychological safety, Edmondson argues, creates an environment where people feel accepted, can ask for help, suggest innovative ideas and bring up problems and tough issues without fear of negative repercussions to their credibility or career advancement. As a member of a team, you play a role in creating psychological safety by how you communicate. Researchers are finding that psychological safety may be the most critical driver in building successful, innovative teams.

> One of the things that sets us apart would be communication, and vocabulary plays a big part in communication. For me, communication isn't about sounding good; it's not about accents. It's about having the words to express yourself, whatever your accent is. We underestimate the importance of vocabulary. That's so important in the working environment, not just for building relationships, but also for presenting your work well. Work requires you to communicate well so that people can appreciate the significance of your work. We could do a lot more to ensure people have the right tools to communicate effectively about their work." – *Thokozile Lewanika Mpupuni*

Before we can discuss key topics for communicating and tips on how to do it well, it is critical to examine your current beliefs on communication. You are not a blank slate, and your belief on communication is your starting point for moving forward. Unpacking your approach and mindset on communication will give you insight on what areas of your communication style and mindset you need to leverage as a strength and which ones might get in the way of your being an effective communicator. Do you believe in the value of effective communication? If so, what value do you believe it brings? How would you define effective communication? When you reflect on how your family communicated when you were growing up, think about the communication style of your different family members, as well as the lessons you learnt and habits you picked up from those styles. Think about your usual approach when are you are in a high-stakes conversation. Are you staying present and listening? Or are you mostly focused on formulating your response and merely waiting for an opportunity to respond? If you struggle to stay present, reflect on why that is the case. Examine how important you think it is for you to share your thoughts and feelings on a topic. Do you believe your perspective has value and should be heard? Reflect on whether you believe that courageous conversations are a zero-sum game where you either win or lose. When you go into a high-stakes conversation, are you open to the idea that there might be things you don't know about the other person's experience or perspective?

The top three types of courageous conversations to master in your career

Language is important. What we call something – the way we describe something – attaches meaning to it and shapes whether we see it as good or bad. This is especially important when we have courageous conversations. These conversations are often called 'difficult', but I prefer to use the word 'courageous': when the stakes are high and strong emotions are present, courage is what you need to have the conversation and move forward. Courage is not the absence of fear but the ability to do what needs to be done despite it. When I reflect on my career and the experiences of people I have coached, I can identify three types of conversations that you need to learn to master early on (and even as you advance) in your career: professional delivery conversations, professional development conversations and personal dynamics conversations. Professional delivery conversations relate to the discussions you might have with your manager or colleagues when you deliver work that has been assigned to you. During professional development conversations, you are asking for or receiving coaching and feedback on your performance for your overall development in your career. These types of conversations also occur when you give feedback to others on their performance and development. Finally, during personal dynamics conversations you are discussing your boundaries, desires or the dynamics between you and another person.

All three types of conversation are inextricably linked. When the personal dynamic between you and someone else is unhealthy, it affects others' desire to want to coach and develop you. This dynamic ultimately affects the quality of what you deliver, which, in turn, affects the team's ability to deliver the best product. If you are not delivering in the way that others expect, it will affect the level of investment people make in you, thus affecting any feedback and development opportunities you may receive. Below I've provided several conversation starters and guidelines under each of the three areas. These are explored in more detail in the scenarios that follow. While they are not exhaustive, these tips can help you to be effective in each area, which will put you on your way to becoming a trusted, reliable team member.

Professional delivery conversation starters
- ❏ 'I just received a new assignment.'
- ❏ 'I need help.'

- ☐ 'I don't know what the priority is.'
- ☐ 'I don't have the capacity for additional tasks.'
- ☐ 'I can't meet this deadline.'
- ☐ 'I don't understand the instructions.'
- ☐ 'I don't agree with a certain course of action.'
- ☐ 'I've screwed up.'

Professional development conversation starters
- ☐ 'I have been asked to give upward or peer feedback.'
- ☐ 'I need coaching.'
- ☐ 'I want to ask for a step-up opportunity.'
- ☐ 'I need feedback.'

Personal dynamic conversation starters
- ☐ 'I need to stand my ground on a personal boundary.'
- ☐ 'I need to address tension in a relationship.'

As you prepare for any of these courageous conversations, reflect on the tips below so that the conversation can be as fruitful as possible:

- ☐ What is your intention for this conversation? What outcome is your goal? Is it to be validated? Is it to increase clarity? Is it to get an apology? Is it to stand firm on what you really believe is right? Is it to provide your perspective on the situation?
- ☐ It's always important to put yourself in the position of the person you are communicating with. What is important to you and the other person? Does what you're going to say and/or how you're going to say it consider both sides?
- ☐ What is the other person juggling professionally? How can you make things a bit easier for them (especially if it is your direct manager)?
- ☐ Have you thought about how to concisely and clearly articulate the key insights or facts from previous conversations?
- ☐ How can you show that you have thought through what you

are saying or asking? How can you approach this person with solutions and not just problems?
- ☐ Are you clear about what you're asking for? What do you need from this person?
- ☐ Are you open to the idea that the conversation might unfold in an unexpected way? Are you willing to state your agenda upfront?

Before you have one of these courageous conversations, try practising them with a colleague. Keep in mind the specific communication and conflict style in your organisation. Spend time talking to people who have been at your organisation for some time to understand how to approach these topics. For example, my friend who works at a global management consulting firm says that direct confrontation does not work at her organisation. Instead, she says, you have to use a much more passive, less direct style and vocabulary when addressing an issue with someone else. In her company, saying to someone, 'You did X and it really upset me', comes across as overly aggressive. Language that would be more effective would be something like the following: 'This happened, but what if we had tried a different way of approaching the situation?' Take these tips and test them to see how you need to tailor your message depending on your environment's culture.

Here are my tips for how to approach each of the top three courageous conversations:

Professional delivery conversations

Scenario: 'I just received a new assignment.' Imagine that your manager has just asked you to complete a new task. Understanding what you need to do, how it fits into the larger picture, the level of quality that is expected, any dependencies between your work and others, and the deadline for the task would all be critical factors.

For example, if you are preparing an Excel worksheet, you should ask how it will be used. What sections or pieces of information does your manager expect to see? What format should the report be in, or what template does the manager want you to use? Has the manager (or anyone else) done a similar report before that you could use as a guide? Seven times out of ten, the manager has an idea of what she wants to see and the level of quality she expects. It's better to start off with that. You should still provide other ideas, but at least you'll have an idea of what she is aiming for.

Don't be afraid to ask questions so that you can understand how your work fits into the bigger picture. The earlier in your career you start doing this, the better. It shows that you care about the project as a whole and not just about your part. It shows intellectual curiosity and glimpses of ownership. You should ask your manager when the deadline is and think about the various check-ins or reviews that are needed prior to finalising the work. For example, if today is 1 March and you are preparing a report that is due on 31 March for a presentation, your manager shouldn't see the report for the first time on 30 March. Maybe your manager would like to see a first draft on 8 March and then revised versions on 16 March and 23 March. Be clear with your manager about those deadlines. Schedule the appointments in the calendar now. Those meetings are the time to get your manager's input, clarify questions you have and make sure you're on the right track.

Scenario: 'I need help.' Your manager has given you an assignment with a deadline, and, after working on it for a bit, you realise that you are stuck. You have several ideas but you're not sure which direction to take and don't want to waste time. Don't spin your wheels too long once you get stuck: time is always a precious resource in a business environment. In this scenario, take time to think about and clearly articulate what you understood the assignment to be, what you've done so far, what you're confused about and what you think the next steps could be. You could even formulate an opinion about which option you like best. Once you've done that, approach your manager. It's important that you demonstrate that you have given it some thought and are not just dumping your problem on her. Tell her that, in the interest of time, you wanted to ask for her guidance early enough to make sure that you'll meet the deadline. After she has provided guidance, repeat back what she has said and even consider putting it in an email if you sense that your manager may forget what you discussed or if this is a high-stakes assignment. As you can see, this is a much more thoughtful approach than just simply asking for help. The structure with which you approach her communicates your level of thoughtfulness, ownership and concern for your ability to deliver this project on time. You were mature enough to be upfront and admit to not knowing everything.

Scenario: 'I don't know what the priority is.' Over the course of the last two weeks, your manager has given you four different assignments with various deadlines. She has just come to you with another assignment and you realise that you won't be able to meet all the deadlines. You're also unsure if she realises that she has given you so many tasks. At this point, you're not confident about what the priority is. Managers are often juggling several projects, so they are dishing out assignments as they come. Sometimes they are not connecting the dots that they have, for instance, already given you four different assignments with different deadlines. In this scenario, the onus is on you to help her connect those dots and make sure that you both are on the same page. Initiating this conversation protects you from working on the assignments in the wrong order or missing critical deadlines, which can create tension and disappointment. The onus is on you because this is *your work* and you need to *own it*. If you don't deliver according to whatever expectation she has (which she may not even have communicated), it is your reputation and your relationship with her that will be on the line. Since she gave you that first assignment, she may have changed her mind, or the project circumstances may have changed, which may shift the order of priority for the assignments.

In this scenario, before you approach your manager, assess what each assignment entails, where you are with each of the assignments, how much time each will take and what their deadlines are. You may also want to have a view on what you think the order of priorities is and why you think that way, but be open to the idea that your manager might see it differently. Remember that the purpose of this conversation is not to be right but to gain clarity and alignment on the way forward.

What you juggle vs what your manager juggles on a daily basis

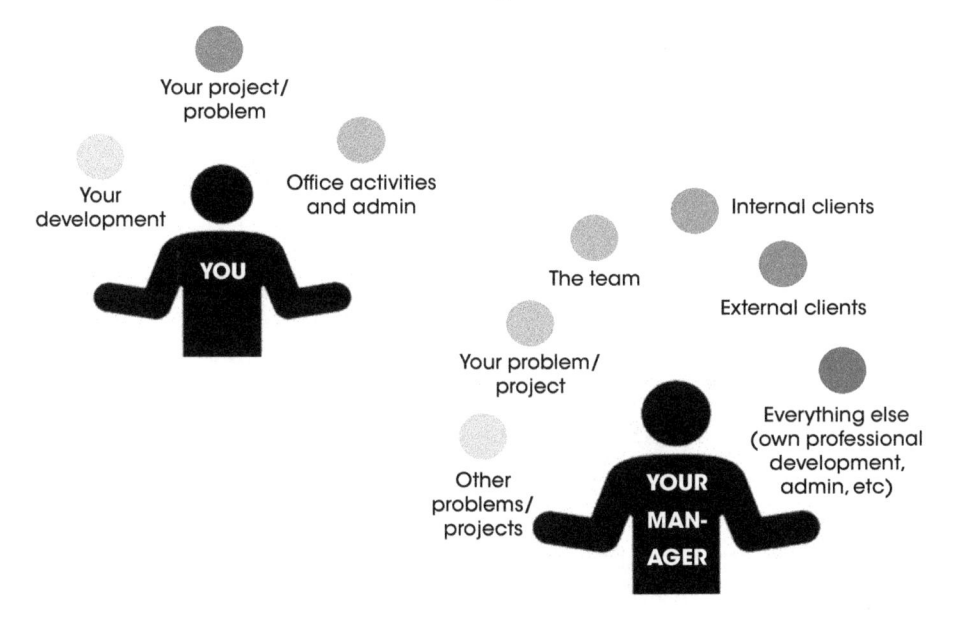

YOU juggles:
- Your project/problem
- Office activities and admin
- Your development

YOUR MANAGER juggles:
- Your problem/project
- The team
- Internal clients
- External clients
- Other problems/projects
- Everything else (own professional development, admin, etc)

I would suggest that you quickly create a one-pager with a table outlining all the information related to your five assignments: it will be much easier for your manager to comprehend your workload if it's in front of her in black and white. Once you approach her, let her know that you want to discuss all the assignments, and that you want to confirm the priorities with her in light of the additional assignment. Walk through the one-pager that you have created with each assignment and your opinion on the order of priorities. With her guidance, draft a timeline of when things can get done, based on high-priority to low-priority tasks. In this way, smaller tasks could be delegated to someone else who may have capacity. Also, ask her how each of these assignments fits into the overall big picture. This part of the conversation might also help her take a step back and think about the order of priorities. And while you have her attention, confirm the instructions for each task. Once you've clarified the order of priorities and any other related aspects, summarise what you've discussed in the meeting and follow it up with an email to confirm the conversation.

Scenario: 'I don't have the capacity for additional tasks.' You are extremely busy and now your manager has added another task to your plate. As much as you might want to be the hero in this moment, you know in your heart that it is not humanly possible for you to meet all of these deadlines. It is important that you are honest with your manager; the worst thing you can do is to make a promise and not deliver. It is much better to be upfront about what you are not able to do. It's important not merely to say, 'I don't have time for anything else.' You always want to be collaborative, open and have a conversation. Express your concern about missing deadlines if you take on another task. Offer other solutions. Could you work on the projects that are furthest along and then enlist the help of another team member to complete the others with guidance from you? Is your manager able to assist? Is there an option to push back the deadline on a few of the assignments? Try to be as solution-focused as possible and let her know that you are willing to put in the extra hours to meet the deadlines, but that you still need assistance. Follow up the conversation with a short email to confirm what was agreed upon.

Scenario: 'I can't meet this deadline.' Your manager has given you an assignment, and at the time the deadline seemed reasonable.

However, as you delve deeper into your task, you realise you will not meet the deadline. The most important element in this scenario is timing. Informing your manager at 4:30 pm that you won't make the 5:00 pm deadline is a very different situation than letting her know at 8:00 am the previous day that you won't make it. The former situation creates a perception of deception and avoidance. You knew long before 4:30 pm that you were not going to meet that deadline, but either you didn't want to admit it or you were in denial.

Remember that this type of behaviour is what breaks down trust between you and your manager. It also does not leave her with much time to intervene or explore alternatives and still meet the deadline. Also, you do not know what the knock-on effect of missing this deadline will have on the rest of the project. It is much better to bite the bullet and be honest. Let's say you recognise at 7:30 am on the day before the deadline that you won't meet the deadline. Sit down for 30 minutes and assess where you are, what you have left to do and how much time it will take. Reach out to your manager with a sense of urgency as soon as possible. Present your assessment of the situation and highlight that you need either more hands or more time to finish the assignment. Determine which option she is most open to and move on from there. Finally, send her a short email to confirm what you've discussed.

> Have excellence and professionalism as standards. If you're going to be late, be late, but let people know – just to be highly professional in your work ethic. Also, try to always do excellent work even if it means you need to renegotiate the deadline. People need to do their work as if it is an extension of themselves. Does your work represent who you are? Do this with the menial *and* the sexy work. People will recognise and appreciate that."
> – *Thokozile Lewanika Mpupuni*

Scenario: 'I don't understand the instructions.' Your manager has given you an assignment and you're genuinely confused about what she is asking you to do. Before approaching your manager, it's important that you're able to clearly articulate what you understood from the instructions and the specific elements that are confusing to you, because you don't want your manager to have to spend time figuring out what you're confused about. Once you're clear, sit down with your manager and confirm your understanding of the instructions. Make sure you have absolutely clarity, even if you have to ask two or three times. This is no time to try to save face or be afraid to look 'stupid'! The quality of your work depends on your understanding these instructions, so when you have your manager's full attention, make the most of it. Once you have clarity, get to work. If you run up against other points of confusion, try to think them through or research them first (maybe 30 minutes to an hour) and then circle back with your manager for further clarity. Your manager may realise, based on your questions or research, that her directions don't make sense. Remember that this is an iterative, collaborative process and everyone gains more clarity as the process goes on.

Scenario: 'I don't agree with a certain course of action.' To challenge a manager or the team on a direction can be scary, but remember that you were not hired to simply be a 'yes' person (at least I hope you weren't!). Think about what you're doing and if it makes sense from your perspective. Now, granted, you are new to this role, this organisation and this industry, so you may not always understand all the nuances. However, sharing your thoughts could make your manager either rethink or reinforce the decision. Since you never know which way it may go, it's always better to bring up your thoughtful ideas and questions. This is your first lesson in influencing. Influencing is about trying to get someone else to see your perspective and, ultimately, to agree with your suggested course of action. Influencing is not a one-size-fits-all exercise and it is not about manipulating people. It is about packaging a message in a way that resonates most strongly with the other person.

Keep in mind that there are many different techniques to influence others. Some people are influenced by data and would want to see the spreadsheet and the calculations. Some people are influenced by the vision, the emotion and the story behind your idea, while others will agree to an idea if someone they really respect supports it as well. Before you approach your manager, think about what is important to her. What is she trying to accomplish? Talk to people she has worked with to see what their experience was with her and if they can guide you on what techniques work best with her. Regardless of how the manager likes to be influenced, make sure that you are always clear about the facts (including people you think support the idea) and assumptions, and double-check whatever calculations you have done that have led you to believe that your chosen course of action is best. How can you approach your manager in a way that resonates with how she thinks and what she wants to accomplish? Also consider how your approach can help her achieve one of her most important goals for the year.

When you've done this, consider both the positive and negative implications of both courses of action. Then approach your manager. Give your perspective and the facts, calculations and assumptions that back it up. If she still doesn't agree with your course of action, maybe make one more push to get her to see things your way. If she still doesn't agree, you have to stand down and defer to her. She is the manager and ultimately she is the one who will be held accountable for the project. Make sure you fully get behind the decision, and that you support it within the team and to those outside your team. Keep in mind that although you are obligated to voice your thoughts, once the decision is made, your obligation is to support your manager and team. If she does agree with your course of action, make sure you align with her on the next steps and deadlines. Agree to touch base a bit more frequently so she feels comfortable with the progress you're making with the different course of action.

> When you have an opinion, voice it, but don't expect it to be followed. And if you make a decision as a team, put yourself behind that decision. That's what it means to be on a team. Being on a team means you have an obligation to speak your mind, but at the end of the day, you need to get over yourself and deliver with the team because the team is always bigger than you are."
> – *Thokozile Lewanika Mpupuni*

Scenario: 'I screwed up.' At the very bottom of the 'Being Human' contract, in the very small print of the Terms and Conditions, is some language around the fact that all of us make mistakes. It is going to happen if it hasn't happened already. The most important part of screwing up is owning that you screwed up. Don't try to dress it up. Don't try to pass blame. I've found that people (including me) have so much more respect for people when they own up to their mistakes without equivocation and apologise for the impact of the mistake. Apply your mind to understand the root cause of the problem and make sure your solutions address those root causes and not just surface symptoms. After admitting your mistake, the next step is to address options for fixing it (if it is indeed fixable, because, sadly, some mistakes aren't). Again, make sure you come with solutions and not just the problems. The next step is to talk about what you're going to put in place so that it never happens again. The last step is probably the most important: forgive yourself and don't let it make you doubt yourself.

There is not a successful person in the world who hasn't made a mistake. I know that because every successful person in the world is a human being (remember, it's in the T's and C's). Apologising can also work for personal-dynamics conversations. Sometimes we say things or step outside our character and we need to apologise.

For some people, apologising is a sign of weakness; for others, there is no value in apologising at all. But to hear the words means a lot to people. For me, apologising is a sign of strength and maturity. It shows that you are willing to put ego aside and admit to your mistakes. You don't hide behind fancy language or excuses and don't throw other people under the bus to make yourself look better. You own up to what you've done, you understand what might have caused your behaviour and you try your darnedest never to let that happen again.

Professional development conversations

Scenario: 'I have been asked to give upward or peer feedback.' Just as you are trying to improve your performance, so too are your managers, senior leaders and peers. Your feedback as a junior person is an important data point in their development journey as leaders. Nobody's perfect, no matter how senior they are or what their title is, and everyone is (or should be) trying to grow. While you may not be able to give technical feedback, you can give feedback on your experience of working with or for that person. You might even have higher EQ, CQ or relationship-building skills than that person, so your feedback could reflect those aspects. Never underestimate the importance of your feedback. I believe that everyone has something to learn from those around them.

You may be asked to provide feedback in a multitude of formats, be it either anonymous 360-degree feedback or in-person feedback (and to the specific manager or peer, or to *their* managers or peers). This might happen in preparation for an annual or midyear review process. It's very important to remember that the person you're evaluating has a career and a reputation that he cares about, just as you care about yours. As such, you should be thoughtful, specific and forward-looking about the feedback you provide. You would not want vague feedback, and neither does this person.

Think about specific examples that highlight the strengths and areas of development for this person. At McKinsey, I used to tell consultants that if they are filling out an anonymous feedback survey, they should use language that they would use in a face-to-face scenario. Your language should strike the right balance between honouring your truth and experience, taking accountability and preserving the relationship. Specific phrases that you might want to use are 'I' statements (for example, 'I felt...' or 'I experienced...') because they help to reduce defensiveness. When you're giving feedback, structure it as follows: first, state the facts of the situation and the person's behaviour as you experienced it. Next, explain how the person's behaviour affected you, others and/or the project overall. Finally, suggest an alternative approach that you believe would be more effective (for example, 'You did a good job on the report but you can take it to the next level by removing some repetitive information and structuring it differently').

Much like the balanced feedback you ask for, make sure that you provide strengths *and* areas for development. Nobody is perfect and nobody is entirely bad. Everyone is great at something, so present that balanced view in your feedback too. If you are in a toxic culture where you feel there might be repercussions for sharing your truth, think very carefully about how much you share and with whom you share it. When you have to give upward feedback, take ownership of your part in whatever situation you find yourself. Here is an example: I once had a manager who asked me to work on a project that was not related to my day job. Nine months later, after many late nights, she told me she had never wanted me to work on the project in the first place. I remember being first confused and then angry. I wanted to karate-chop her in her throat! I am very conscious about how I spend my time, and it infuriated me that I had wasted nine months working on something that wasn't even related to my primary job. What can people do in nine months? Women spend nine months making new human beings! I could have made a person in that time!

I'm sharing this to show you where my anger took me. As I went over and over the situation in my head, the more upset I became. But I finally had to take a step back, put on my big-girl panties, reflect on the role I played in wasting my own time and accept what I could have done differently. I had been working with this manager for several years at that point and I knew she didn't always think assignments through. I knew she probably did not understand what type of time commitment was required for this project or how it would take away valuable time from my day job. Before I accepted this assignment, I should have asked more questions. This would have helped her think through the implications of my agreeing to it. I could even have pushed back and said I wouldn't accept the assignment. So I had to ask myself why I took it on so readily. I realised that a part of me still obeyed authority figures without questioning them. This experience taught me that I needed to do some work on myself in this area. I was not a ten-year-old girl in Catholic school anymore; I was a grown woman and I needed to question certain things. I had the power to ask the questions about how I spend my time.

I could also have chosen to act defensively: I could have blamed her completely. I could have thought, 'She is the manager and she should think these things through.' In that case, my upward feedback would have come from a place of anger. But blaming her would not have helped me, especially not if I were to find myself in similar situations in the future. Remember that you cannot control other people and what they do or don't do. What you *can* manage is yourself, the questions you ask, the expectations you create and the boundaries you set. This situation was not a waste, because I learnt a valuable lesson. It empowered me and made me less of a victim and more of a victor.

Scenario: 'I need to ask for coaching.' Feedback is a reactive exercise. You are finding out how you performed on some task after you have completed the task. Coaching, however, is a more proactive exercise: it is about getting the guidance that you need to do your job well. Everyone needs a coach, no matter how much of a superstar they are. Serena Williams has a coach. Siya Kolisi has a coach. Lewis Hamilton has a coach. I'm going to address two types of coaching: performance and leadership. Performance coaching is about the hard, technical aspects of your role, while leadership coaching is about unlocking your potential so that you can maximise your strengths, identify and address weaknesses and become the most authentic team member, manager and leader.

Early in your career, you focus mostly on honing the hard, technical skills, but as you advance in a company, your leadership skills become more important – how you develop and manage others, how you achieve results through others and how you influence and build relationships with customers and clients. Always have your eye on both aspects, so look for guidance in both areas. In my career, I've found that there are two types of coaches at work – those who are natural coaches and those who are not. I consider a natural coach to be someone who provides guidance and gives direction without being asked. This could be someone who makes changes to a document you worked on and then helps you understand how he went from the old to the new version. This person might also coach you on leadership elements – how your word choice, tone and body language are perceived by others. This is a person who recognises your lack of understanding and is energised by growing and developing others. The other type of coach goes from A (the old version) to Z (the new version) without explaining how she got there. This person might not necessarily appreciate your struggle as a new employee, so they would not sense that you need assistance from a technical and/or leadership perspective. Regardless of which type of coach you get, your responsibility is still to get the coaching you need. Come with a hunger to learn and questions to increase your knowledge.

Communication is key

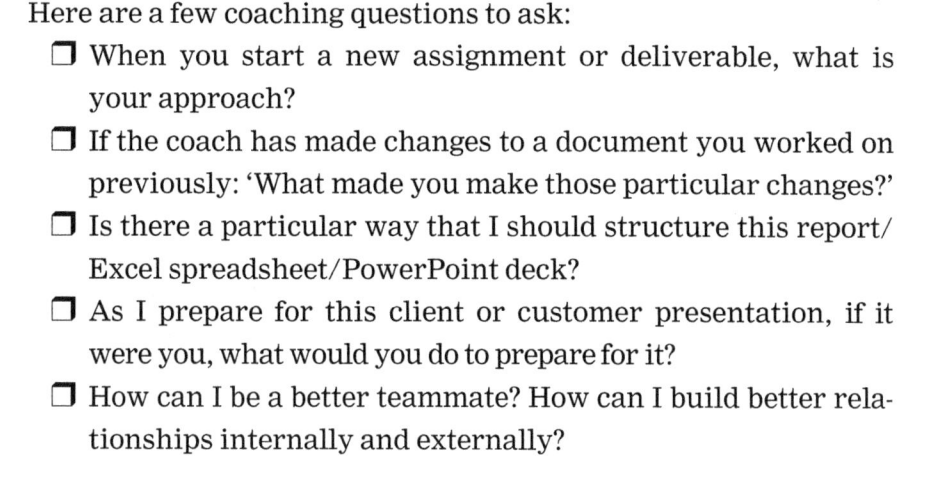

Here are a few coaching questions to ask:
- ❏ When you start a new assignment or deliverable, what is your approach?
- ❏ If the coach has made changes to a document you worked on previously: 'What made you make those particular changes?'
- ❏ Is there a particular way that I should structure this report/Excel spreadsheet/PowerPoint deck?
- ❏ As I prepare for this client or customer presentation, if it were you, what would you do to prepare for it?
- ❏ How can I be a better teammate? How can I build better relationships internally and externally?

Coaching doesn't have to occur within a formal, scheduled time: it can be on the fly. Whenever you are getting guidance on your work, you are being coached.

Scenario: 'I want to ask for a step-up opportunity.' Remember that you own your career, so it behoves you to look for opportunities that will challenge you, teach you new skills or expose you to new environments or people. Let's say that there is an opportunity to work on a project, but it would be a stretch assignment for you, so you would have to ask your manager's permission. Before you do, think about how you are doing in your current job. If you are not doing well, it is unlikely that your manager will approve your doing additional or different work. Look at this from your manager's perspective: if you had to manage a person who was not doing well in the job that you hired him for, would you trust him with additional responsibilities? Probably not.

Some of you might be thinking: 'But, Carice, there are elements of my job that I really hate.' It's important that you learn this lesson now: no matter your seniority in a business, there will always be elements of your role that you do not enjoy! I'm sure Aliko Dangote, Oprah Winfrey, Patrice Motsepe and Mo Ibrahim also have elements of their jobs that they don't like. Learn to see the bigger picture of your work: it will help you get through it. For example, you're working on a spreadsheet and you hate Excel with every fibre of your being. Instead of focusing on your loathing of Excel, think about how your spreadsheet and analysis will be used. Maybe the client or your CEO will make an important decision based on your data analysis. Don't forget the bigger picture when you are busy with those smaller, irritating tasks: the point is that they represent larger ideals such as commitment and reliability. Dig deep and tap into a reservoir of focus and discipline to do the things that don't energise you. If you do them well, you will be given a chance to do the things that energise you. Your manager will probably think: if she is willing to give 120 per cent on something that she doesn't enjoy, what will she deliver on something that she *does* enjoy?

But the reverse is also true. If your commitment and reliability are only for things you're interested in, how can your seniors be sure that you won't lose interest at some point? People want to know that you will consistently show up, no matter what the task or your level of interest. Once, a junior person told me that she had no interest in participating in a client presentation because (and I quote) 'I have no interest in the content at all.' I don't have an issue with someone not being interested in the content; there are times when I am not interested either. However, your lack of interest should not prevent you from carrying your fair share of the team's weight and doing your very best. If *you* were the manager, would you want you on your team? Your goal is to be the kind of team member that you would want to manage.

If you want to ask for a step-up opportunity and you're doing well in your current job, reflect on whether you have the capacity to take on additional work. You don't want your day job to suffer because of this additional project. But if you have the capacity, volunteering for office projects is a great way to give back to mentors and sponsors, and it can put you on the radar of important people in your organisation. Importantly, reflect on your *why*: why do you want to do this project, and why now? Are you going to grow a certain skill set? Will you get an opportunity to work with people you've wanted to work with for a long time? If you are determined to take on this new project, you need to reflect on what sacrifices you're willing to make to put in the additional hours to get your day job and your new project done. Will you commit to working late nights or weekends? Will you sacrifice leisure time? Be honest with yourself, because if you are not willing to make a sacrifice, something is bound to suffer – your day job, the new project and eventually your reputation. If you are confident in your performance, your *why* and your ability to make sacrifices to deliver at a high level on your day job and the new project, then you can approach your manager to have the conversation.

Keep in mind that your manager is going to do her own assessment, so be prepared for a 'yes' *or* a 'no'. If your manager agrees, step up your communication to reassure her that she made the right decision. Provide more frequent updates on your day job and the new project, because these updates are important if she is not managing the new project. She might have no visibility into the new project, so she could assume that you are falling behind on your day job because of the shiny new project. Communicating before she asks, and especially before she starts to get anxious, is the best way to reassure her. If you don't need manager approval, you still need to ask yourself all the above questions, and make sure you step up your communications to anyone you are reporting to and/or working with.

Scenario: 'I need feedback.' From the start of your career, you want to be 100 per cent invested in owning your career and growing as a professional and a leader. Learning how to ask for, interpret and action feedback is one of the most critical success factors in a professional environment. It is also one of the most awkward, nerve-racking parts of working. We all have blind spots when it comes to our strengths and areas of development, which is why it's critical to get a more objective view of ourselves.

> "Seek out feedback and don't be afraid. In the corporate space I was working in, there were not many Black people. People that are not Black or other people of colour shy away from giving you feedback because they may think that they're going to hurt you or that you might not take it well. The same goes for women. Early on in my career I used to make the mistake of not seeking out advice or real-time feedback. You're working on multiple projects during the course of the year. At the end of a project, go to people, ask for feedback and act on that feedback." – Ronald Tamale

Feedback gives us insight into how we are perceived and experienced. Sometimes feedback is objective (for example, 'Your calculation was numerically wrong' or 'Your report is late') and sometimes it can be subjective (for example, 'I felt you communicated harshly in that meeting'). Nevertheless, all feedback needs to be examined to find the grain of truth in it. If you've spent most of your life hearing how great you are, it will be hard to hear that you aren't doing well or that your deliverable was not up to snuff. The only thing worse than hearing the critical feedback is *not* hearing it and, unknowingly, disappointing people. When the former happens, you have an opportunity to hear it, understand it and figure out ways to action the feedback and improve. If you don't, you'll never be able to improve.

> "If your work is an extension of your ego, then you will never handle any form of feedback. But if your work is about adding value and truly making a difference, then feedback becomes your best friend." – *Simon Hurry, Human Dynamics Specialist and Chief Inspiration Officer, PlayNicely*

A common mistake that many people make is to view feedback as a personal attack on them, their abilities and even their likelihood for success. I mentioned the growth mindset in Chapter 2. If you develop a growth mindset, you will be more focused on the process of improving yourself and you will understand that feedback is a key data input to that process. You have limited time, and if you don't get feedback, you won't know where to focus your energy in order to improve. For me, I know that if I trust someone and that person believes I can be successful and is committed to my success, they can say darn near anything to me. Because I know this about myself, I try to build trust-based relationships with people whose feedback I need in order to improve. It helps to lower my defences so I can really listen. You need to determine what makes your defences go down or go up.

Sometimes you will get unsolicited feedback, but you should not count on nor expect it. This is your career, your performance and your future, so it's your responsibility to ask for the feedback. You also have to determine the speed of judgement in the environment you work in. If it's a slow-moving environment that gives people more time to ramp up, then you can space out your feedback inquiries. However, if you work in a fast-paced environment where people are judged more harshly and quickly, you may want to get feedback more frequently to improve your performance before judgements are made and it's too late.

Before meeting your manager (or whoever is providing the feedback), consider whether you are open to feedback or if you are just going through the motions so that you can say that you asked for feedback. What is your intention? Are you interested in growth or do you just want to get your ego stroked? Is it to shift responsibility or is it to share your perspective so that your manager is aware of your experience of the situation? If you are not open to hearing what the other person has to say, then don't even waste your or the other person's time. Because this is a new space for you, accept that it requires skills that you may not have. Accept that you are still learning and that you might not be the best. Your ego might be a bit bruised in the process, but receiving feedback is the only way you'll know what you need to work on.

Giving feedback is difficult for the average person; giving *negative* feedback is even harder. You cannot expect someone to give you honest, constructive feedback when your body language is closed off. You also cannot expect someone to feel comfortable giving you honest, constructive feedback if you are defensive and have a bad attitude. Defensiveness is about shifting responsibility, blaming other people for our mistakes, making excuses or just generally finding ways to preserve our ego and make ourselves look better to other people and ourselves. To help you navigate the feedback process, develop questions that touch on key performance areas. This will also help you drive the conversation to make sure you get clear examples. Those parameters could be quantitative (such as how well you can structure and manage an Excel model) or qualitative (how well you build customer relationships).

Because feedback can be given during a scheduled time or on the fly, be prepared to drive both types of scenarios. Always keep a notebook and pen handy so you can jot down the key insights from the feedback. If you've just given a presentation to a client and you're riding back to the office, ask your manager how he thinks you fared. Always make sure you ask for both strengths and weaknesses. If you are great in one area but completely failing in an area that matters to the organisation, it will affect your or your team's ability to deliver. Develop that area up to a minimum bar at least so that it doesn't overshadow your strengths.

In addition to the questions above, ask your manager the following:

- ❒ Which two or three areas should I concentrate on in the next few months to make sure I am meeting or exceeding expectations?
- ❒ Is there anything else I should have asked you or that you think I should know?

If you work in an environment where people consistently avoid giving negative feedback messages (this is something that you need to investigate), you should formulate questions that are more difficult for people to give soft answers to. Here are a few examples:

- ❐ If you could start this project over again, would you still pick me for your team? If so, why? If not, why not, and what two or three things could I do to turn my performance around in a more positive direction?
- ❐ Would you recommend me to someone else for their team?
- ❐ On a scale of one to ten, how would you rate me on [insert two or three key performance areas here] compared to the best person you've ever worked with at this role and tenure?

I recognise that these are *tough* questions to ask and that the answers might not be what you want or expect to hear. I encourage you to choose long-term growth over short-term comfort so you can get the critical feedback that you need for your growth and development.

> "I won't be offended with anything but be as honest as possible about what you loved about my facilitation, the potential that you see that I didn't tap into, the concerns that you have, and then suggest what I can change. Be as blunt as possible. It will hurt, but it will be worth it." – *Dr Puleng Makhoalibe*

While you receive feedback, be mindful of your body language. A big part of your responsibility in that moment is for your body language to communicate that you are taking in the feedback. Try and make sure your body language is open and relaxed. Are your arms folded? Are the muscles in your face relaxed? Are you asking follow-up questions and summarising the feedback as it is shared, to let the other person know that you are listening and receiving what she is saying to you? Are you jotting down notes to capture the feedback for further reflection later? The more receptive you are, the more comfortable the other person will feel in giving you the feedback. At the end of the day, you are the only one who loses if you make that person uncomfortable.

When you've received feedback, decide what it means and what you will do with it. Below, I've structured these activities into the three A's of feedback: assess, apply, adjust.

Assess: Does the feedback resonate with you? What is the impact of your feedback on the team and you? Which parts of it will you take on and which parts will you ignore? This might surprise you, but you *do* have a choice: you don't have to blindly follow whatever people are telling you. Decide for yourself if the concerns raised are ones that concern you. If you choose to ignore certain parts, have you thought about the consequences? Also, consider what your priority areas are, and whether your goals are specific enough. Are you focused on the 20 per cent that will give you 80 per cent of the impact? Talk through your goals with your manager, mentor and/or sponsor and ask yourself how you can leverage your strengths even more. What behaviours will you need to demonstrate to convey proficiency in a certain area, and what are some specific steps that you can take to improve in certain areas? How will you know if you have reached your goal? What evidence will support that belief? Once you decide which areas to address and strengths to leverage, document those items somewhere you can easily access and review them on a daily or weekly basis. The more specific and time-bound your goals are, the easier it is to track your progress and the easier it is to map a route to get there.

Apply: Put daily reminders in your calendar to remind yourself every day about the plan you have for reaching your goals. Visually seeing your goals helps you to maintain focus. In the hustle and bustle of everyday professional life, it's easy to lose sight of your goals. Put weekly or monthly reminders in your calendar to create space for you to reflect on your progress. Get feedback from people to gauge your progress.

Adjust: Is your plan for improvement focused on the right areas based on your progress, your results and the feedback you've received? What changes do you need to make? Are you leveraging your strengths enough, and are you using them to address areas of development? Share your focus and progress with your mentors, sponsors and the person(s) who gave you feedback. You want to rally people around you, and you want your tribe to know that you own your development. Your mentors and sponsors have a network and you increase the likelihood of their singing your praises of commitment to others if you share your focus and progress with them. Remember that getting feedback is an ongoing process. As your role changes and your tenure increases, the expectations change, so you have to stay abreast of those as well while making sure that you're asking the right questions, getting the right feedback and making the necessary adjustments. This is a lifelong, cyclical process of taking your performance to the next level.

> Always ask for feedback. A lot of the young kids think they're doing a great job. They show up for performance reviews and when we tell them that they're on a performance-improvement plan, they get blindsided. They don't care to ask their leaders and their boss, 'How are you viewing my work? Am I on par? Am I above par?' Put together a 90-day plan and meet with your leader, your direct manager and your manager's manager to make sure that you have goal alignment. Be very deliberate, strategic and proactive in communication and receiving feedback. Document everything: people have amnesia when it's convenient." – *Tina Taylor*

CHAPTER 6

Personal dynamic conversations

Scenario: 'I need to stand my ground on a personal boundary.' A personal boundary is an aspect of your work or personal life that is important to you that you need to show up in the best way. One of the most important things that work is about is figuring out your boundaries. You have to strike the right balance between your boundaries and the team and its objectives. As a working adult, you have some space to create the work environment that will suit you best. I've been working for 20 years and I continue to learn what set of circumstances allows me to show up at my best. A few years ago, I discussed the idea of boundaries with a former Life Healthcare senior executive. I asked him what it took for him to show up in the best way and he said: 'I need four things to be in flow and ready for challenges: time with my wife and children, physical activity, time spent outdoors and being outside of working doing things that stimulate my brain.' He went on to say that he also needs to manage who he works with, but added that it 'only happens as you become more senior and have a greater degree of freedom'. Here are a few examples of personal boundaries:

- ❐ I am an introvert, so during the day I need time alone away from the team to process my thoughts.
- ❐ Working out on a regular basis helps me stay focused, keep my weight down and reduce stress.
- ❐ I am more of a morning person, so I would like to request that I can start early a few days per week.

If managers trust that the work will get done, they are usually not upset if a person sets a personal boundary. Upset usually comes when professional obligations are not met. When I coach individuals who ask my advice on a personal boundary that is important to them, and they want some help in communicating it to their managers, I ask them to think through the following key questions first:

- ❏ Why is this boundary important to me? Is this boundary a nice-to-have or is it absolutely critical for me?
- ❏ What happens if this boundary is not honoured?
- ❏ What am I willing to sacrifice to maintain this boundary? How does maintaining this boundary affect the team?
- ❏ Are there elements of the boundary that I am willing to compromise on?
- ❏ Do I know enough to deliver on my obligations and maintain the personal boundary?
- ❏ What can I do to alleviate any fears that I won't deliver?

Once you've worked through these questions, set up time to speak with your manager. I always advise my coaching clients to use this phrase to communicate the boundary: 'In order for me to show up and deliver in the best way, I need [fill in the blank].' There is not a manager in the world that doesn't want her team members to perform at their best, so this phrasing helps to communicate how important this boundary is for you and how the team benefits as well. If your manager agrees to this boundary, make sure that you deliver and overcommunicate. The more trust you build up, the more latitude you will get. Check in with your manager to make sure you're meeting her expectations: it is human nature for your manager to assume that the personal boundary is playing a factor in your performance if it is not up to snuff.

Scenario: 'I need to address conflict or tension in a relationship.' If there is unaddressed tension in any of your work relationships – be it with a manager, a peer, a client or any other stakeholder – address it. As a junior employee, this type of tension typically has a disproportionate impact on you, your reputation and, ultimately, your work, so it behoves you to step up and initiate a courageous conversation. Because you are so junior, you probably have less of a network and reputation in the organisation than the person you have a beef with. While you are not addressing the mounting tension, that other person is likely to be sharing his side of the story, thus shaping the narrative about you with a larger audience. I don't want to make this sound easy. It isn't. If you come from a conflict-averse culture or community, or if it's just your personality, there is probably an even more intense level of discomfort in addressing these issues. But, as professionals, we have to learn how to do this well. I have never been a person who enjoys conflict, but I realised that it was necessary to develop this skill and make these relationships work. When I first started having these conversations, my palms would get sweaty and my heart would be racing. Over the years, I've gotten less nervous and become better at it.

Before we get into tips about preparing for and managing a courageous conversation, examine your present mindset and history with a topic. When I was growing up, I rarely saw people have calm, high-stakes discussions about topics on which they disagreed. I never saw any real resolution come from the conflict and I didn't have the skills to conduct the conversation in a calm way, so I just avoided conflict altogether. I carried that mindset into my professional career. In addition, I knew that I had a temper, so I could easily go to a place of anger, and I knew I didn't want to behave unprofessionally. I had many misconceptions about courageous conversations and here are a few of them:

- ❐ I don't need to prepare for these conversations; I show up and hope for the best.
- ❐ If the conversation is getting too heated, it's not okay to take a break and revisit the topic later. I have to power through.
- ❐ I don't have the right, authority or permission to confront a senior employee about an issue that I have.
- ❐ The purpose of the conversation is all about being validated and being told that I'm right.
- ❐ I always know all the circumstances of the situation and what the person was thinking or intending when they behaved in a way that upset me.

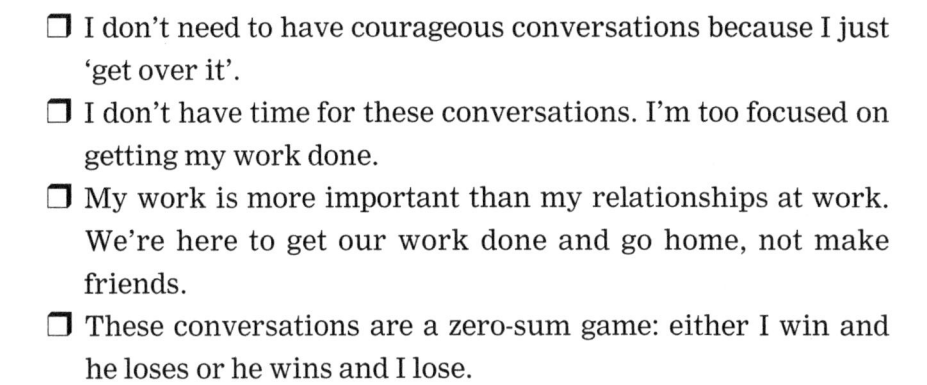

☐ I don't need to have courageous conversations because I just 'get over it'.
☐ I don't have time for these conversations. I'm too focused on getting my work done.
☐ My work is more important than my relationships at work. We're here to get our work done and go home, not make friends.
☐ These conversations are a zero-sum game: either I win and he loses or he wins and I lose.

The book *Crucial Conversations*, by Joseph Grenny, Kerry Patterson, Ron McMillan and Al Switzler, helped me to understand that I had many incorrect perceptions about courageous conversations. It showed me that there are techniques I could implement that would help me to better prepare for – and manage – these conversations. First, examine your feelings about the situation: you have to determine whether your negative feelings are due to what happened or whether something else is bothering you. The last thing you want to do is unleash all of your emotions on someone when the situation with that person only accounts for half of them. The next step is to understand your level of upset, because you don't bring up every slight or annoyance. It's important to pick your battles, use your energy wisely and bring up the situations that really matter. One test I use to see if something is really bothering me is noticing if a situation is still on my mind a few days later. In that case, I have to address it. If I've forgotten about it, I move on, but if I'm still bothered by it, I ask myself: 'Have I calmed down enough to have a rational conversation?' If not, I try to figure out what element of the situation really has upset me. I try to be open to the possibility that there is something that I don't know, that I misunderstood something or that I am taking an assumption about the person or the situation as fact. Many times, our anger is the result of believing that we know what the other person was thinking or intending. I also think about my role in the breakdown. Was there something that I said or did that could have contributed to the tension in the relationship? As hard as it may be, own your part, because we all play a role.

Once I've worked through these thoughts, I prepare for the conversation by asking myself the following:

- ❏ What is my goal for this conversation? Is it an apology, validation, clarity? What will make me feel it was worth my time and energy to have this conversation?
- ❏ What assumptions am I making about the other person's intentions or actions? What don't I know about this person or the situation? What might he or she not know about me or the situation?
- ❏ Is this a zero-sum game for me? What would a scenario look like in which the other person and I can give up something and get something that matters to each of us?
- ❏ What are all the possible directions (negative and positive) in which this conversation could go?
- ❏ How can I focus more on the solution and less on the problem?

Let me expound on the fourth question above. One of the biggest revelations I had about having courageous conversations was managing my own expectations. At McKinsey, we often used the term 'release your agenda'. I would go into a conversation and would be certain of what the other person was going to say and what the final outcome of the conversation would be. As you know, human beings are quite unpredictable creatures, so those conversations often did not go as I had planned and I would get upset. Once I realised that this was a source of great frustration (and sometimes bad behaviour) for me, I decided to spend time before each conversation imagining and reflecting on a range of possible outcomes. I would also accept that any of these scenarios was likely to happen and that there might also be an outcome that I could not anticipate. If I expected positive feedback, I would imagine the opposite, and if I expected an apology, I would imagine the person

Communication is key

not apologising. If I thought I knew exactly what had happened, I imagined the opposite: what if there is information that I was missing? This approach helped me deal with whatever the outcome of the conversation was. The key was to stay open, be present and embrace how the conversation unfolded.

When you are ready to schedule the meeting, tell the person what situation you want to address so that he or she has time to reflect and prepare if they choose to. Send an electronic invitation so that the time is blocked on the calendar, and reserve a quiet place with as few distractions as possible. Once you've thought through the logistics, prepare how you want to frame the conversation. How you open the conversation sets the tone, so spend time thinking about your opening statement. You need to open the conversation in a certain and clear way. Below are a few areas to cover. Once you're in the conversation, go over the first two questions and then check in with the person to make sure you're aligned:

- ❒ Indicate your wish to resolve the issue, and frame it as a common goal, a win-win situation. You may say the following: 'I know we both are committed to making this project a success. Your support and expertise is critical to making that happen, so I want us to work well together. I want both of us to walk away with more clarity about this project and a better understanding of how best to communicate with each other.'
- ❒ Name the situation you want to address: 'Do you remember this meeting/conversation/email?'
- ❒ Describe the facts of the situation: 'Is this how you remember the meeting? If not, what is your recollection?'
- ❒ Share your emotions/feelings about this issue: 'I felt . . .', 'I sensed . . .' or 'My experience was . . .'
- ❒ Clarify what is at stake: is it performance, quality, project success?
- ❒ Identify and explore the role you played in the situation: 'I realise I wasn't as clear as I should have been, which left room for ambiguity and misinterpretation' or 'Was it something that I said or wrote that upset you?'

The most important overall tip is to try to strike a balance between advocacy and inquiry. Advocacy is when you're actively stating your perspective, and inquiry is when you're asking questions to increase understanding and clarity. While you should share your experience of the situation, you should also be open to hearing what the other person has to say. You want to get their perspective, see if there are any facts that you are missing and clear up any assumptions that you have made. The table below offers tips to reflect on and remember during your courageous conversation:

	Inquiry	Advocacy
Lead with	• 'Help me understand …' • 'I get the sense that this is critical to you. What is most important to you? Why is that important to you?' • 'I feel like I'm missing something. What do you feel that is?' • 'What do you need from me?'	• 'I'm assuming that …' • 'Here is what I propose …' • 'Achieving [fill in the blank] is what is critical to me …' • 'Here are the pressures I am under …' • 'Here are a few nuances that you may not be aware of …'
Make suggestions …	• 'Did you try …?' • 'Have you thought about …?' • 'Why don't you say …?'	• 'Yes … And …' • Focus on what you agree with and join them to build a solution. • Provide early signals that you hold a different opinion.
Avoid	• 'Don't you think …?' • 'Isn't it true that …?' • 'Didn't you say …?'	• 'Yes … But …' • Hinting that your way is the only logical one.

Remember that you want to be solution-oriented, not problem-focused. At the end of the day, after you hash out the details of who said what when, where and how, you should focus the majority of the conversation on the way forward. What can you and this other person put in place and commit to that will help lessen the likelihood of another discussion like this one and build your relationship?

Problem-focused questions	Solution-focused questions
• What is the issue?	• What do you want to happen going forward?
• Why does this continue to be a problem?	• What do you need to make your goal a reality?
• What happened?	• What do you already have to make your goal a reality?
• What is the root cause?	• What are some baby steps you could take to create the situation you want?
• Whose fault is it?	• How far have you come already?
• What have you tried to address it?	• What lessons have you learnt?
• Why haven't you resolved it yet?	• How will you apply these lessons going forward?

During the conversation, if you feel that it is getting heated or unproductive, it's okay to press pause and say, 'I think we need to take a break and revisit this conversation at a later time.' Remember, the goal isn't merely to finish: it is to resolve the tension while preserving and building the relationship. It's better to take a break and calm down than it is to say something you might regret.

Once you've finished the conversation, check in periodically with your colleague to see how he or she is feeling. The next step is to forgive – a word you don't often hear in the corporate space. If someone did something to offend you, forgive the person and move on. You still have to work with this person and you would want others to forgive you. But there's also a selfish reason for forgiving others:

holding a grudge affects our health, stresses us out and makes us less productive. When we forgive, we're happier, more creative, present and authentic. If we can build more forgiving workplace cultures, our teams and organisations will be more trusting, collaborative, connected and effective. This is not a one-and-done exercise: you will have to repeat this forgiveness cycle all over again in the future, because we have different values and we're constantly learning about each other. We will inevitably bump heads in the process.

Other key tips to communicate effectively

Practice makes perfect: You can have the best content but if the delivery is poor, your content won't have nearly the impact that it could have. Before you present or have a high-stakes conversation, practise, practise, practise. Practise in front of the mirror. Practise in front of friends. The more you practise, the more familiar you will become with the material and the more fluid and relaxed your presentation or conversation will be. Make sure you're articulating your words and that you're not speaking too fast or too slow. Plan where you will pause for effect or to allow for the audience to digest the material and ask questions.

Top-down communication: In a top-down communication culture, you should think about the two or three key takeaways and communicate them first. This technique can be used in any forum where you are communicating with others (for example, email, presentations, reports). *Note: Even though this is a great way to communicate, it may not work in your organisation. If you work in a bottom-up culture, determine how you can be the most effective bottom-up communicator.* Okay, back to top-down . . . When I am communicating with people, I ask myself: do I believe in what I am trying to say? What is the crux of my message? And what is the 'so what', the key insight? You alone need to shape the narrative, not allowing your audience to come to their own conclusions. This doesn't mean that you are closed to what others have to say, but it *does* mean that you should draw their attention to what you think is most important. What are you *really* asking for? What am I trying to influence this person to believe? If I was confident in what I am saying, what would I say? How would I say it? What would my body language be in that moment? I would be standing up straight, making eye contact and with my shoulders back and a tone of certainty in my voice. If you don't believe what you're saying or asking for, you cannot expect others to believe either.

The other important aspect of effective communication is to outline the WIIFM (What's In It For Me?) and The Ask. Every human being wants to know that what you are saying is going to solve her problem and make her look good. The Ask entails asking the seniors what you need from him or her to make your request a reality. It can be financial resources, an extra pair of hands, time, or their influence. Be clear about what you're trying to say, what you need and how it will help the other person. This will increase your likelihood of getting the support you need.

> We undermine ourselves when we preface sentences with 'This may be stupid, but I wonder, I don't know if you guys will like this, but I was just spitballing,' instead of just saying, '*We should go here*.'" – Refilwe Moloto

Communicating a sense of urgency: Another communication topic that I have received feedback on is the importance of communicating a sense of urgency. Your employees and managers want to see outward signs that show that you're 'in it' with them – 'it' being whatever the crisis of the day is. They want to know that you're down in the arena, ready to do battle alongside them. Communicating a sense of urgency is one way for you to convey that you're willing to share the burden with your manager or team member.

Communicating a sense of urgency that aligns with your personality and temperament is important. I am not a very emotional person, and when others are freaking out, I become calm – someone has to be the voice of reason! Nevertheless, my calm demeanour has often been misinterpreted for a lack of concern or urgency. A couple of ways to communicate that you care is to respond quickly to emails and phone calls. Jot down what the other person is saying, stay engaged and ask thoughtful questions about who, what, why and when as it relates to the crisis. Offer potential solutions if you have any and communicate that you will do whatever you can to help. Or you could even say things like: 'We'll get this sorted out together.' Think about how you could convey your shared sense of urgency in an authentic way.

Overcommunicating: Overcommunicating is a technique that can be applied in any type of organisational culture. When you overcommunicate, you share important information multiple times and in multiple formats to ensure that the key stakeholders internalise your message. As I once heard Funeka Montjane, Standard Bank Chief Executive, Personal and Business Banking, say, 'You might have to repeat your idea multiple times in a meeting to ensure that you are heard.' You might be ignored for any number of reasons (race, gender, age, hierarchy, etc), but don't get discouraged. Keep sharing your ideas and taking up space. In a high-pressure environment, people are preoccupied with their own work, pressures and anxieties, so they might have to see or hear a message several times before they can internalise it. As a professional development manager, I have seen several instances where a bit of overcommunicating would have prevented a severe relationship and team breakdown. For example, if you know that in two months you're going on a long-planned Mauritius holiday, you should communicate that to the team as soon as your leave is approved. If you have a team calendar, put it on the schedule, and if there isn't one, create one. During meetings, you should also mention your upcoming holiday at those meetings, and remind your manager and your teammates at least once a week in the weeks leading up to your departure.

Leading up to the holiday period, do as much as you can to avoid negatively impacting the team. Consider creating a work plan with key tasks, deadlines, status updates and a handover document that outlines any critical documents, instructions, contact details or information that the person filling in for you will need. Create those materials one month before you leave and share them two weeks before you leave. Also make sure that that person is extra-comfortable with the work. Around this time, ask your stakeholders if they have any additional questions, and include those in the handover document. Depending on how accessible you want to be during your holiday, you can also tell the team that you'll be checking email once a day if that is the case. If you execute this plan, you can enjoy your holiday and the team can rest easy. This way of managing your time away shows a tremendous amount of ownership and maturity. You're not just leaving the team high and dry and saying 'good luck': you are still taking ownership, equipping the team to be successful in your absence.

Another technique for overcommunicating on a regular basis is the check-in/check-out method. Always make sure you communicate to your manager the status of projects or assignments. Do this proactively, not reactively. Proactive communication builds trust, alleviates manager anxiety, shows great maturity and in many cases will reduce (or even eliminate) micro-management. If your manager knows your daily priorities, what you're working on, what the status is on your work and what you plan to deliver, there is less for her to worry about and thus less for her to bother you about. This technique can be especially useful if you are not working in the same location as your manager, if your manager has several direct reports or if you and your manager do not get a tremendous amount of face-time during the day or week. The more you can anticipate her questions and communicate based on them, the better.

Remember that it will be up to you to determine the pace of your organisation and the proper frequency for these types of communications. In fast-paced environments, I would recommend a daily check-in/check-out email, but you will have to figure out what works best for you and your manager. The check-in email will provide a short layout of your plans for the week, while the check-out email lists what you've accomplished and what is still outstanding. These should be short bullet-point emails, not a research paper. Before you implement this system, discuss it with your manager to make sure you're covering the items that are most important to her. Ask for feedback from your manager on the frequency of your verbal and written communication to make sure what you're doing is working.

Conclusion
Organising you for impact

I hope that after reading this book you understand (read: know without a shadow of a doubt) that *intelligence isn't enough*. Being smart is great, but your impact at work will never reach its full potential if you don't reflect deeply on yourself, others and your environment. As you reflect on the key takeaways from the book and how to implement them, I want to leave you with three parting steps: your mindset matters; be intentional and organised; and assess, adjust and celebrate.

Step 1: Mindset matters

As I have stressed in every chapter, your mind is your most powerful asset. Your behaviour begins with how you think; your beliefs about the concepts I've offered in this book are no different. If you don't believe them, your behaviour will not reflect them. Real change begins with embracing these concepts or, at the very least, being curious about how you could apply them in your career. If you can't find a way to connect personally with these ideas, don't go any further. Spend some time unpacking the root of your resistance. Is it that you aren't sure you can implement these ideas? Do you feel overwhelmed? Does stepping outside your comfort zone make you uncomfortable? Does my advice feel fake and contrived to you? If so, why? Is there a way for you to reframe your perspective that resonates with who you are?

When you're doing something new, there will always be discomfort. When I first started addressing tension in my workplace relationships, it was extremely uncomfortable. But as I faced more and more of these situations head-on, I became more comfortable. I knew what the downsides were if I didn't have them: more tension, broken relationships, less support and, ultimately, less impact. If I have to choose between the pain of having the conversations and the pain of *not* having them, I will choose to have them. Focus on the long-term benefit over the short-term discomfort.

Step 2: Be intentional and organised

If you're ready to embrace the ideas in this book, now is the time to put them into action. You're going to have to become very intentional about incorporating these behaviours into your daily, weekly and monthly routines. I don't want you to read this book and then let it collect dust on your bookshelf. It should be a career-guidance manual that you refer to often.

With all the information that I've presented, you might be wondering where to start. Just like you would do with any other big project in your life, break the lessons into smaller, manageable parts. To help you implement these ideas, I've shared a six-week template below that you can use to work your way through each chapter. Schedule a repeating appointment in your calendar to reflect on your key takeaways from each chapter.

Chapter	Top area you're building on	Key sub-area(s) you're building on	Key 'aha' moments or questions	Next steps (big or small)	Progress
Preface and Chapter 1	Mindset	Fear	I am afraid of failure. What is driving my fear?	Focus on the learning, not the outcome.	I took a risk and shared a new idea in a meeting.
Chapter 2					
Chapter 3					
Chapter 4					
Chapter 5					
Chapter 6 and Conclusion					

One of the biggest keys to delivering quality results on time is to be organised. Organisation can be the difference between delivering on time and not. When I was a first-year consultant at Arthur Andersen, I almost missed a *very* important client deliverable because I was not keeping track of key information that I needed to gather from the client. I knew what I needed to do, and I had the resources to do it, but my lack of organisation left me in a panic as I scrambled at the last minute for this information.

My organisational skills have improved over the years. In my teens, I was a complete and total disaster. If you are like me, there is hope. You can get better at it, and if you are organised, you should strive to get even better. Being organised will not only help you make time for yourself, but also help you meet your various personal and professional commitments. When I was writing this book, I had to discipline myself to meet the publisher's deadline. I used many of the tips below to accomplish that. From this point forward, your life will only get busier: you might go back to university while working full-time, you might get married and have children, you might have to care for your elderly parent, and you'll probably end up managing a team, or even managing managers who lead teams. Your projects at work will get more complicated, too. This is why you have to keep revisiting your priorities and reconsidering how you spend your time. No extra hours or minutes will be added to your day, so you need to think about how best to spend the time you've got.

Make a concerted effort to organise yourself to give yourself the best possible advantage. Keep in mind that this will not magically happen. Will things pop up that are totally unplanned for? Yes. Will deadlines shift and totally muck up your carefully orchestrated work plan? Absolutely. Because you can't plan everything in advance, let's focus on what you *can* control and influence.

Below are three key areas you should focus on if you want to get more organised: organising information, organising time and energy, and organising tasks.

Organising information

When you start working, you'll probably find that you receive 50 to 100 emails every day. You've probably never had that amount of email before in your life. You will receive invites, information and multiple requests from different people, and each project will have many moving parts – different people you'll have to speak to, and different pieces of information that you'll have to gather, organise, analyse and provide insights on. You want to be seen as someone who is responsive and knows what is going on. So how do you keep up? (Although I present a few tips here, you should also check out books such as Tim Ferriss's *The 4-Hour Workweek* or *Getting Things Done* by David Allen.)

Some people recommend not checking your email before a

certain time in the day, because emails are other people's agendas for you and you need to start off your day by focusing on *your* priorities before you're hijacked by someone else's agenda. Test that approach in your environment. Will it work or will people be flipping out if you don't reply by 8 am to an email that was sent at 7 am? Ask successful people at different levels of your organisation how they manage email. For example, one of my teams had the following rule for emails: respond to any email on the same day if it was received by 6 pm that day. If the email comes after 6 pm, you can answer it the next business day.

Many of my executive assistant friends follow the rule that you should only touch an email once: either file it, action it or put in a folder with other items that you need to action later. Create folders in your email inbox according to topic, client, customer or whether action is required. In my email inbox, for example, I have unique folders for each client. I have an internal company email folder where I keep important messages from company leadership. You can use colour-coded flags as well. In my company's email system, I can highlight an important message with a yellow or red flag, depending on the level of urgency, and I can pin the red-flag emails to the top of my email list. I schedule a repeating appointment in my calendar to clear my emails at least a few times per week. I know that if I don't do that, I won't naturally make time. If my inbox gets out of control, it's easy for me to miss important emails and risk missing deadlines.

For documents, I create a folder for each new year and then, within them, I create more folders according to client name. When I name documents, I usually lead the document with the date on which the document was created. If I collaborate with a client, customer or colleague on the document, I will use version numbers and update those version numbers until the document is finalised. For example, if I created a document on 11 March 2021, the name of the document will be '20210311 Client ABC Leadership Development Plan v1'. If I send it to my colleague and he makes changes, he will save the document as '20210311 Client ABC Leadership Development Plan v2', and so forth. Once we have finalised the document, we rename it '20210311 Client ABC Leadership Development Plan vFINAL'. With this naming convention, we know when the document was edited, which makes it easy for me to track our progress. If you work in an environment where you are constantly moving around and handling hard-copy information, you might want to scan documents and then save the PDF documents in folders on your laptop. This way, you'll always have an electronic copy as a backup.

Organising time and energy
Time is the one resource that you cannot buy. It's one of those resources that are equally distributed to each of us every day. Nevertheless, some people are just better than others at making the most of their time. Determine which priorities will provide the most impact for you (the 80/20 rule). Then figure out the most efficient way to achieve them and organise your schedule to reflect your priorities. Determining what you will say 'yes' and 'no' to are both critically important.

But there is another important element to keep in mind: managing your energy. This is about figuring out your daily, weekly, monthly and yearly energy cycles and scheduling your work and your breaks (as much as within your power) to fit those cycles. If you are a morning person, for example, you might want to schedule your most challenging work for that time of day because that is when you are most alert. I started thinking about how to energise myself during the day as well – grabbing a cup of tea an hour after lunch or taking a quick walk outside. During the course of the year, you can monitor when you start feeling tired and need a holiday. Obviously, sometimes you might not have a choice, but if you do, be aware of your energy cycles, communicate them to your manager and teammates and try to manage your schedule according to those cycles.

But let's go back to the topic of managing time and energy. Here are a few techniques that have helped me over the years:

- **Time yourself:** A technique I learnt from my brother is to use the timer on your phone to focus yourself. This can also help with procrastination. If there is a task that I really don't want to do, I will say to myself: 'Let's just work on it for 30 minutes or an hour.' Sometimes the hardest part is getting started, but once you start, you'll notice that you'll get some momentum and find that you can go on for a little bit longer. The timing helps you see how fast the time flies and how much time we waste. You can also time your breaks. (Yes, breaks are important!) Every hour or 90 minutes, get up and take a five-minute walk outside, grab a glass of water, do some stretches at your desk or meditate. These breaks help to refresh you and increase your productivity.

- **Schedule work time and set boundaries:** Block time on your calendar to complete your work to ensure that it is your top priority. Early on in my career, I used to accept other people's requests and demands of me, and then I would use the time I had left to complete my own tasks. I quickly realised that I needed to start prioritising my work, because only I would be held responsible if I did not complete my work on time and at the expected level of quality. From then on, if I had an urgent meeting with multiple people and the only available time was during my blocked work time, I would be willing to move it. However, I made sure that my work was just as important as what others were asking of me. Block off and protect time in your calendar to think, to check email and to work on different projects. If you have four very important meetings, for instance, try scheduling them back-to-back so that you reduce the 'dead' time between each meeting. A study by researchers Gloria Mark, Daniela Gudith and Ulrich Klocke revealed that when a person is distracted by an interruption that is not related to the task at hand, it takes up to 23 minutes and 15 seconds to be fully focused again on the task they were doing before the interruption.

For example: if you block 1 to 5 pm for your personal work time and schedule your meetings before and after that, you would have a solid block of time to focus, apply your mind, make real progress and take the necessary breaks. You may not always be able to schedule your time in this way, but it is worth asking others if they are flexible. Some days you may end up with two one-hour blocks in between your meetings, but try to influence that as much as you can. And if you can't, be mindful of it and select another day to set aside a dedicated block of work time.

- ☐ **Establish an end to the workday:** When you think the whole day is for work, that is exactly how long it will take you to do your work. This is still a bad habit that I struggle with from my consulting days. If you set a deadline of 6 pm, you'll work much more efficiently. You need time during the week to decompress, spend time with your family and friends, watch your favourite show on TV, read a book, exercise or do absolutely nothing.
- ☐ **Create repeat invitations:** I use repeat invitations as a sure-fire way to ensure that I focus on what matters. If I say that I want to check in with my mentor, sponsor or colleague on a regular basis, or even attend a regular exercise class, I create a repeating invite to remind myself. These check-ins are really important to me; I know I won't naturally set them up without a reminder. You can use your work calendar to set daily, weekly, monthly, quarterly or custom-frequency invitations. Sometimes the date and time might not work for me or the other person, but the repeating invite serves as a reminder to move the meeting and it helps this priority stay on my radar screen.
- ☐ **Calendar evaluation:** At the beginning and end of each week, reflect on your priorities and how you will spend your time. If someone were to look at your calendar without any expla-

nation, would they be able to tell what your priorities are? Does it line up with what you say is important to you?
- ☐ **Determine your energy formula:** In Chapter 6, I shared what a former Life Healthcare senior executive says are the four things he needs to do on a consistent basis to re-energise himself. If there was one theme that emerged from the interviews I conducted for this book, it is that all the interviewees would advise their younger selves to relax, enjoy the moment, don't take yourself so seriously and have more fun. For me, going to the spa for a massage is my hobby, and having days with absolutely nothing scheduled helps me relax and recharge. Do things that don't necessarily have a point but simply because they bring you joy. Everything is going to be okay. What are the work activities that energise you? Coaching and facilitating training classes make me come alive. What works for you? Begin giving some serious thought to what you need to re-energise yourself personally and professionally. It's going to be more critical now than ever.

> The importance of rest and reflection are things that I've really had to learn." – *Obenewa Amponsah*

Organising tasks

When you organise your tasks, it's important to start with the end in mind. What does success look like in the end? Spend time thinking about your plan to achieve success. Often, we want to jump straight to execution mode without thinking it through. Be strategic about how you do your work. You have to work smarter and not just harder. Share your plan with key stakeholders to make sure you're not missing anything.

There are so many tools people can use to organise themselves: good old-fashioned pen and paper, Excel, Microsoft Project (MP) and a plethora of smartphone applications. Test them all out to see which one works best for you. Find a tool that lets you see a visual representation of your project timeline and the sequencing of tasks. This tool should also allow you to indicate whether certain tasks are dependent on other tasks being completed, and it should automatically amend the start and due dates, based on those dependencies.

One of the things I do 30 minutes before I stop working for the day is to think about what needs to happen the next day, by the end of the week, the end of the following week or the end of the month. Before I leave the office on Friday, I write my to-do list for Monday so I can hit the ground running. You can't just plan for the next day: start looking ahead. Are there things that you need to kick off now, tomorrow morning or early next week? Are there things that you should ask people to start working on now while you do other work in the meantime? I usually start by making a list by client and the dates by which the activity needs to start and finish. I build in wiggle room, especially if I am dependent on others for information. Take into consideration unplanned changes and mishaps: it's always better to plan for them in advance. For example, if today is Monday and I need something from a client by Friday, am I going to wait until Thursday to ask them or should I ask the person now, just in case he is swamped and doesn't have time to complete my item right away? You also have to know yourself. I once worked with someone who struggled to meet deadlines, and I asked him why. He said he liked spending a lot of time thinking about the task and not enough time putting it down on paper. If this is true about you, schedule enough time for thinking and, likewise, enough time for doing.

Procrastination

One of the biggest enemies of time management is procrastination. Because I still struggle with perfectionism, I sometimes get overwhelmed when I think about a big task (and the fear of not doing it perfectly) and I 'faff around' (as South Africans would say).

Basically, I procrastinate. That feeling of being overwhelmed keeps me from starting the task. To get myself out of the slump, I tell myself: 'Carice, everything doesn't have to be done today. What is the first step you can take? What can you do right now? Who do you need to talk to? What information do you need to gather?' Once I've broken the big task down into smaller, manageable tasks, I make a list and start.

Like most people, I get easily distracted by the internet and social media. (Once, I think I almost reached the end of the internet when I was avoiding doing a project!) Let's be honest, sometimes the work is just boring and we don't want to do it. Or there might be things you enjoy but you've tired of doing them in the homestretch and you just can't find the motivation to wrap up those last bits. You have to figure out what distracts you and then set up a working situation that eliminates or minimises distractions. For example, when I have an assignment that requires deep concentration, I might work from home. Or, if I go into the office, I will isolate myself in a private room because I get easily distracted with office conversations if I sit in the open plan with my colleagues. I leave my cellphone in another room, far away from me, which makes it less of a distraction.

Over the years I've also learnt that I hate working in silence, so I like to turn on music. However, I realised that playing my favourite songs on my playlist defeats the point, because I will start singing and chair-dancing along! Instead, I play calming classical or jazz music on YouTube. I bring along my lip balm and hand lotion so that I don't have to get up to fetch them, thus getting distracted. Instead of solely focusing on the task that I don't want to do, I think about how much more time I need to finish as compared to how much time I've already spent. I visualise the sense of accomplishment I will feel when it is finally off my plate, or how energised I'll feel when it is done and I can move on to something I really enjoy. I also remind myself that if I want a different life, I will have to maximise my time.

What distracts you? What environment is most conducive to you getting your work done? Do you need silence or a bit of background noise? What emotions are you avoiding when you procrastinate? (Remember, mine is the feeling of insufficiency and of being overwhelmed, due to my perfectionism. Sometimes it's just plain ole boredom!) Once you know what your formula is, write it down somewhere on your phone and on a piece of paper to remind yourself of that winning combination next time you start procrastinating.

Step 3: Assess, adjust, celebrate – rinse and repeat

As you're implementing these ideas, make sure you're setting a monthly or quarterly check-in with yourself to take a step back to assess and adjust your plan. Life happens. Priorities change. Goals shift. Relationships evolve. This is the time to look at what is working and what is not working for you. Last year's strategies and goals may not be relevant anymore. Maybe you were promoted, and what you need to demonstrate or achieve now is different. Are you giving minor details major time and energy? Also remember to celebrate those big – and small – wins. Maybe you mustered up the courage to have a conversation that you had been avoiding. Perhaps you've drummed up the nerve to introduce yourself to a senior leader you've quietly admired from afar. Celebrate that! Acknowledging your progress helps to build your confidence to carry on and apply your new knowledge.

Perhaps you're not exactly where you want to be in your career at the moment. But don't panic: at least you're not where you *used* to be. See your career through the lens of progress, not perfection. Remember that building your career is a lifelong journey. You're going to work with all kinds of people with different personalities and values. You might live in different countries and work in different functions, industries or company cultures. You will unearth different qualities in yourself – good and bad – from different situations. Get used to discomfort. Embrace it. Make peace with it, because it's the way of the world. But remember: the better you know yourself, the more equipped you will be to deal with an ever-changing world. Make the time to invest in *you*. It will be the best investment you will ever make.

Acknowledgements

They say it takes a village to raise a child. Well, the same can be said for writing a book. While my name is on the cover, it took an entire army of people to make my vision a reality.

Had it not been for the sacrifices that my parents, grandparents and great-grandparents – Wayne, Barbara, Albert Sr, Elizabeth, Carrie, James, Lela, Bessie and Donnie – made for my education, I would not have been in a position to work in any of the organisations in which I learnt so many valuable lessons. Their love, hard work, faith, determination and resilience created the foundation for all of the experiences upon which this book is written.

Thank you Fungayi, for always making me laugh, telling me that I'm capable of so much more than I ever imagined and listening to me whine as I went through the arduous process of writing and editing this book.

I really wish everyone had a protector-best friend like my sister Jocelyn. Thank you for being the most ardent cheerleader a girl could ever ask for.

Many thanks to Dr Jennifer Madden for conceptualising the interviews for the book and encouraging me to write it when it was just a passing thought in my head. Special thanks to sound engineer extraordinaire Kahlil Pedizisai for professionally recording the interviews.

Special thanks to the entire team at Jonathan Ball Publishers: Aimee Carelse, who I sent my initial manuscript to; my publisher, Nkanyezi Tshabalala, for your tremendous support during this process; and my editors, Caren van Houwelingen and Alfred LeMaitre, for helping me structure my thoughts and sharpen my ideas.

ACKNOWLEDGEMENTS

One of the elements that makes this book so special is the rich and candid insights shared by so many people across the African diaspora whom I admire and respect. Thank you to all the individuals who gave of their time for interviews and quotes: Tina Taylor, Timothy Maurice Webster, Obenewa Amponsah, Thokozile Lewanika Mpupuni, Dr Puleng Makhoalibe, Neliswa Fente, Damany Gibbs, Fungayi Kapungu, Dr Jennifer Madden, Merafe Moloto, Kagiso Molotsi, Zimasa Qolohle Mabuse, Jocelyne Muhutu-Remy, Alinafe Thupa, Asande Mahlabela, Amy Dove, Nadine Moodie, Tiyani Majoko, Ronald Tamale, Connie Mashaba, Penny Moumakwa, Tiffany Hinton, Shrey Viranna, Acha Leke, Nomfanelo Magwentshu, Aisha Pandor, Stefano Niavas, Ipeleng Mkhari, Refilwe Moloto, Simon Hurry, Rachel Adams, Artis Brown, Gary Watson, Shenece Garner Johns and Celiwe Ross.

I've always loved words, and my passion for writing as a child went dormant for many years until Khanyi Dhlomo gave me an opportunity to be a monthly contributor for *Destiny* magazine. Thank you for giving me a chance to kickstart that dream again. This is my first book, and without the help of my seasoned writer friends I would have had no idea what I was doing. Thank you Janine Jellars, Timothy Maurice Webster and Irene Ndiritu for your help during various stages of my book-publishing process.

During the hard times in my career, there were people who really helped me see these tests as part of my testimony. Thank you to my Pastors Craig L Oliver, André Olivier and Wilma Olivier for helping me to uncover my true identity, believe bigger and grow my faith.

Every woman needs a strong tribe and I definitely have mine. Thank you to my friends Takenya Taylor, Ashley Lee, Nakia Buckner, Kimberly Brown, Lakeshia Hunt, B.J. Wiley Williams and Denise Long, who supported me and provided a sounding board, and sometimes just a good laugh, during all the ups and downs of my career.

I would not have been able to write this book without the

Acknowledgements

colleagues, mentors, sponsors and managers who have supported me, created opportunities and provided the very learnings that I speak of in this book: Martha Greenway, Marisa Greenlee, Chaka Booker, Ingrid Hamman, Agustina Mendez, Margaret Brooks, Lisa Rushing, Greg Whittle, Jackie Fitzgerald, Missy McNabb, Paula Coetzee, Lori Paulk Mintz, Eileen Laudadio, Donna Rachelson, Richardean Few, Lynn Liao, Akeshia Craven, Charlotte Houston, Peggy Hazard, Dr Frances Frei, Margot Zielinska, Tim O'Malley, Barry Callender, the LEAD Atlanta Class of 2010 and The Broad Residency Cohort 6 (special shout-out to my Advisory Group – Jeff Kang, Marnie Pastor and Cordell Carter).

A special shout-out to Rivers Church Team B, Wayne Anderson Jr and my real-life aunties and uncles – Katherine Stover, Albert Owens Jr, King Henry Brown Jr, Geraldine Claxton, Ronnie Claxton, Cherry Williams – and my aunties and uncles in my vivid imagination: Oprah Winfrey, Iyanla van Zant, Dr Robin Smith, Pastor TD Jakes and Dr Phil McGraw, who helped me manage my mindset and unpack and embrace my story.

I've had the honour of being part of the leadership journeys of some fantastic people – the McKinsey Leadership Programme Fellows, Bain & Company consultants, the Seed Academy and Orange Corners entrepreneurs, among others. Thank you all for the valuable lessons you taught me.

Sources

Note: All definitions in the text are taken from *The Merriam-Webster Dictionary*, www.merriam-webster.com.

Articles, blogs, books, in-person events, social media posts and podcasts

'About the Organizational Culture Assessment Instrument (OCAI)'. OCAI Online, December 2019. www.ocai-online.com.

Abrams, Abigail. 'Yes, Impostor Syndrome Is Real. Here's How to Deal With It'. *Time*, 20 June 2018. time.com.

Adams, Rachel. Post made on 16 February 2020. LinkedIn. www.linkedin.com/in/rachel-nyaradzo-adams-177b3817/detail/recent-activity/. Accessed 14 September 2020.

Allen, David. *Getting Things Done: The Art of Stress-Free Productivity*. New York: Viking, 2001.

Aronson, Joshua. 'Stereotype threat'. In-faculty profile, Steinhardt School of Culture, Education and Human Development, New York University, 2020. steinhardt.nyu.edu.

Bolani, Sihle. 'I quit my job after 8 months'. Blog post, Working While Black, 18 June 2019. workingwhileblack.co.za.

Booker, Chaka. 'Can Being Smart Hurt Your Ability To Lead?' *Forbes*, 26 August 2020. www.forbes.com.

'Brené Brown: The 2 most common ways we off-load hurt'. *Super Soul Sunday*, Oprah.com, season 7, episode 622, 4 October 2015. www.oprah.com.

'CliftonStrengthsAssessment'. Gallup.com, 2020. www.gallup.com.

Davis, Dominic-Madori. 'One of the only 4 Black Fortune 500 CEOs just stepped down – here are the 3 that remain'. *Business Insider*, 21 July 2020. www.businessinsider.com.

Dweck, CS. *Mindset: The New Psychology of Success*. 15th ed. New York: Random House, 2006.

Edmondson, Amy. 'Creating psychological safety in the workplace'. *Harvard*

Sources

Business Review IdeaCast, episode 666, *Harvard Business Review*, 22 January 2019. hbr.org.

Ferriss, Timothy. *The 4-Hour Workweek: Escape 9–5, Live Anywhere, and Join the New Rich*. New York: Crown Publishing Group, 2007.

Folkman, Joseph & Jack Zenger. 'What great listeners actually do'. *Harvard Business Review*, 14 July 2016. hbr.org.

Frei, Frances. 'How to build and rebuild trust'. TED.com, April 2018. www.ted.com.

George, Bill & Peter Eagle Sims. *True North: Discover Your Authentic Leadership*. Hoboken, New Jersey: John Wiley & Sons, 2010.

Goleman, Daniel. 'Emotional Intelligence'. www.danielgoleman.info/daniel-goleman-what-predicts-success-its-not-your-iq/, 17 July 2014. www.danielgoleman.info.

Groysberg, Boris, J Yo-Jud Cheng, Jeremiah Lee & Jesse Price. 'The leader's guide to corporate culture'. *Harvard Business Review*, January–February 2018. hbr.org.

Gudith, Daniela, Ulrich Klocke & Gloria Mark. 'The cost of interrupted work: More speed and stress'. Paper presented at the 2008 Conference on Human Factors in Computing Systems, Florence, Italy, 5–10 April, 2008.

Hofstede, Geert. 'The 6-D model of national culture'. No date. geerthofstede.com.

Hurry, Simon. Post made on 2 March 2020. LinkedIn. www.linkedin.com/in/simonbhurry/detail/recent-activity/shares/.

Leonard, Jayne. 'What is learnt helplessness?' *Medical News Today*, 31 May 2019. www.medicalnewstoday.com.

Lu, Denise, Jon Huang, Ashwin Seshagiri, Haeyoun Park & Troy Griggs. 'Faces Of Power: 80% Are White, Even As US Becomes More Diverse'. *The New York Times*, 9 September 2020. www.nytimes.com.

Mahanyele, Phuti. Keynote address at McKinsey Leadership Programme graduation ceremony. The Venue, Johannesburg, South Africa, 15 April 2016.

Marmenout, Katty. 'Organisational Culture Profile'. In Rodney A Reynolds, Robert Woods & Jason D Baker (eds), *Handbook of Research on Electronic Surveys and Measurements*, pp 313–316. Hershey, Pennsylvania: Idea Group Reference/IGI Global, 2007. psycnet.apa.org.

Martin, Sharon. 'What causes perfectionism?' Psych Central, 1 January 2018. blogs.psychcentral.com.

Maxwell, John C. *The Five Levels of Leadership: Proven Steps to Maximise your Potential*. Center Street, 2011.

'MBTI Basics'. The Myers & Briggs Foundation, 2020. www.myersbriggs.org.

McLeod, Saul. 'Freud and the unconscious mind'. Simply Psychology, published 2009, updated 2015. www.simplypsychology.org.

Monico, Nicolle. 'The 12 Steps of Alcoholics Anonymous (AA)'. American Addiction Centers: Alcohol.org, 24 July 2020. www.alcohol.org.

Montjane, Funeka. McKinsey Leadership Programme Speaker Series. McKinsey & Company office, Johannesburg, South Africa, 28 August 2015.

'Pareto Principle (80/20 Rule) & Pareto Analysis Guide'. Juran, 12 March 2019. www.juran.com.

Patterson, Kerry, Joseph Grenny, Ron McMillan & Al Switzler. *Crucial Conversations: Tools for Talking When Stakes Are High*. New York: McGraw-Hill, 2012.

Riopel, Leslie. 'Goleman and other key names in emotional intelligence research'. Positive Psychology.com, 1 September 2020. positivepsychology.com.

Sandberg, Sheryl & Adam Grant. *Option B: Facing Adversity, Building Resilience, and Finding Joy*. Knopf, 2017.

Sepah, Cameron. 'Your company's culture is who you hire, fire and promote: Part 1, The Performance-Values Matrix'. LinkedIn post, 1 February 2017. www.linkedin.com.

'Sheryl Sandberg opens up the about the death of her husband'. *Good Morning America*, ABC News, 24 April 2017. abcnews.go.com.

'Sponsorship: Defining the Relationship'. *Harvard Business Review Women at Work* podcast, series 4, episode 3. *Harvard Business Review*, 29 October 2019. hbr.org.

Stein, Judith. 'Using the stages of team development'. MIT Human Resources, 2020. hr.mit.edu.

Stone, Michael. 'Forgiveness in the workplace'. *Industrial and Commercial Training*, 34(7) (2002): 278–286.

Stroessner, Steve & Catherine Good. 'Stereotype threat: An overview'. No date. diversity.arizona.edu.

'The 70-20-10 Rule for Leadership Development'. Center for Creative Leadership, 2020. www.ccl.org.

Wang, Nancy. 'Don't ask for mentors, ask for sponsors'. *Forbes*, 2 September 2019. www.forbes.com.

Winfrey, Oprah. 'Oprah Winfrey on Career, Life, and Leadership'. Stanford Graduate School of Business, YouTube, 28 April 2014. www.youtube.com.

Interviews

Artis Brown, via Zoom, 13 June 2020
Aisha Pandor, 18 July 2018
Nomfanelo Magwentshu, 16 July 2018
Acha Leke, 11 July 2018
Jocelyne Muhutu-Remy, 11 July 2018
Stefano Niavas, 10 July 2018

Sources

Tiffany Hinton, 17 June 2018
Connie Mashaba, 14 June 2018
Kagiso Molotsi, 14 June 2018
Damany Gibbs, 13 June 2018
Fungayi Kapungu, 13 June 2018
Dr Jennifer Madden, 13 June 2018
Dr Puleng Makhoalibe, 11 June 2018
Ipeleng Mkhari, 18 June 2018
Refilwe Moloto, 18 June 2018
Penny Moumakwa, 18 June 2018
Obenewa Amponsah, 6 June 2018
Zimasa Qolohle Mabuse, 6 June 2018
Thokozile Lewanika Mpupuni, 6 June 2018
Ronald Tamale, 6 June 2018
Timothy Maurice Webster, 6 June 2018
Tina Taylor, telephone, 1 June 2018
Shenece Garner Johns, email correspondence, 30 August to 1 September 2020

Index

Page numbers in italics indicate figures and tables.

action and action plans 31, 77, *120*, 185, 188, 210–211, 223, 230–232
Adams, John Quincy 47
Adams, Rachel Nyaradzo 63
advocacy 252, *252*
Advocate 211
agenda 112, *113*, 224, 250, 263
Alchemy Inspiration 57, 168, 243
Allan Gray 10
Amponsah, Obenewa 18, 87, 93, 139, 149, 267
anger 135–136, 148, 192, 216, 234–235, 248, 249
Aon Hewitt 176
apology 62, 66, *127*, 136, *198*, 223, 232–233, 250–251
appreciation 47, 72, 76, 123, *127*, 144, 148, 183, 219
Aronson, Joshua 97
Arthur Andersen 48–49, 70, 176, 202, 261
The Ask 255
assessment 56, 164–173, 229, 239, 244, 270–271 *see also* Assessment Instrument *under* Organisational Culture; CliftonStrengths Assessment
assumptions 71, 120, *153*, 153–155, *154*, *155*, 173, 250
authenticity 118, *140*, 158, *158*, 159, *184*, 194–200, *198 see also* branding and differentiation *under* personal authority 21, 166–168, 172, 175, 196, 235, 248
avoidance 198, 229, 243, 248, *252*, 257, 269, 270
awareness 22, 47, 55, 56–57, 184, 187, 191, 216

baggage, emotional 55, 68–72, 123–124
Bain & Company South Africa 10, 182, 195
balance 23–24, 56, 90, 73, 104, 107, 147, 171, 173, *198*, 234, 246, 252
behavioural iceberg model 152–155, *153*, *154*, *155*
beliefs 41, 49, 55, 85, 86–89, 110, 153, 160, 164, 170, 183, 220–221, 244 *see also* impostor syndrome; mindset; psychological safety; values
bias in the workplace 11, 25, 40–45, 118, 163, 180, 183
Birmingham, Alabama 70
Black
  people 11, 13, 44, 70–71, 94, 98, 99, 167, 170–172, 187, 240
  professionals 12, 98, 115, 201
blame 11, 53, 68, 77, 232, 235
body language 114, 123, 130, 148, 218, 236, 242, 243, 255

Index

Booker, Chaka 150
boundaries 117, 121, *127*, 223, 246–247, 265–266
breaks 9, 43, 89, 93, 248, 253, 264, 265, 266 *see also* holidays
Brown, Artis 74, 99, 137, 148, 152, 217
Brown, Brené 149
business 13, 17–18, 25, 109, 114, 117, 118, 124, 168, 177, 181–183, 192
    schools 21, 28, 66, 80, 83, 88–89, 95, 145, 158 *see also* Harvard Business School; London Business School

Caldwell, David F 174
calendars 33, 131, 143, 244–245, 265, 266–267
Cameron, Kim S 174
career development 17–22, 26–30, 37, 38, 39, 49–50, 52–54, 58, 70, 196, 270–271
Carnegie Mellon University 139
Center for Creative Leadership 16
Chatman, Jennifer 174
Cheng, J Yo-Jud 174
Chicago Public Schools 80
choice *20*, 21–22, 26–30, 129, 148, 156, 203
Chow, Professor Rosalind 139
Clance, Pauline 91
Clan Culture 174
CliftonStrengths Assessment 100, 127, 158
coaching 25, 37, 52–53, 92, 105–106, 222, 223, 235–237, 246, 247, 267 *see also* Mentor; mentors
collaborative environment 69, 216, 228, 230, 254 *see also* environment *under* corporate
comfort zone, stepping outside one's 65, 117, 121, 214, 259

communication 13, 24, 113, *126*, 178–179, 181, 191, 216–258
comparison 95–96 *see also* Self-Confidence vs Arrogance Comparison chart
compassion 89–90, 99, 101, 155
Competing Values Framework 174
conflict management *125*, 132–137, 219–220, 247–254
connection 22, 26, 74, 112, 146–152, 163, 190, 213
Connector 211
consultants 80, 124, 152–156, 178, 197, 207–208, 234, 261
control 20, *20*, 54, 94, 218, 235, 262, 263
conversations
    courageous 221–224, 248–253
    personal dynamic 222, 223, 246–254
    productive 12, 134, 142–143
    tips to improving 222–239
conversations, professional
    delivery 222, 224–233
    development 222, 223, 233–239
corporate
    culture 69, 80, 167, 171
    employees 11, 13
    environment 11, 13, 31, 41, 51, 62, 72, 81, 91, 98, 110, 166, 180, 217 *see also* collaborative environment
    landmines, avoiding 73
    setting 75, 128
    space 9, 11, 13, 23, 72, 163, 165, 240, 253
courage 49, 85, 130, 132, 221–224, 247, 248–249, 252, 270 *see also* authenticity
CQ *see* cultural intelligence
credibility 41, 50, 138, *140*, 141, 166, 178, 182, 195, 200, 201, 220
Crucial Conversations (Grenny, Patterson, McMillan and Switzler) 249

INDEX

cultural intelligence 160–185
customers and customer service 13, 17–18, 45, 46, 109, 161, 162, 175, 182, 192, 215, 236

Dash, Stacey 135
deadlines 62, 166, 225, 226–229, 231, 257, 261–262, 263, 268
decision-makers and decision-making 12, 27, 29, 66, 86, 94, *113*, 126, 138, *140*, 171, 211, 231, 232
Deloitte Consulting 10, 48, 84, 145, 176, 177, 179
DeLong, Thomas 159
difference 101, 127, 144–146, 162, 163, 219–220, 240, 261, 270–271
differentiation 15, 30, 39, 75, 122, 161, 191, 194, 199–200
Dweck, Carol 75–76

Edmondson, Amy 220
email 111, *126*, 131, 139, 228, 258, 262–264, 265
emotional
　intelligence (EQ) 15, 24, 146–152, 157, 160
　inventory 101–102, 152
　investment 26
　offloading and outbursts 137, 149
　unpacking 150
empathy 118, 124, 157
empowerment 20, 28, 30, 53, 54, 189
energy 112, *125*, *126*, 148, 158, *125*, *126*, 264–267
Enron 48
EQ *see* intelligence *under* emotional
Ernst & Young 48
Excel 75, 80, 81, 92, 182, 197, 225, 237, 238, 242, 267

expectations 10, *19*, 31, 38, 44, 59, 83, 111, *113*, 128, 178, 242

failure 64–67, 93, *140*, 196, *261 see also* resilience
family 9, 11, 72, 95, 168, 171, 194–195
fault *20*, 100, 105, *253*
fear 28, 64–68, 91, *153*, 153–155, *154*, *155 see also* courage
feedback 26, 37, 38–39, 57, 61, 77, 102, 123–124, *126*, 168, 192–194, 207–208, 210, 211, 233–235, 239–245
feelings 25, 147–149, *153*, 153–155, *154*, *155*, 251
Five Levels of Leadership, The (Maxwell) 47
Folkman, Joseph 123
Forbes 196, 210
Ford, Henry 86–87, 105
Ford Motor Company 86
'forming-storming-norming-performing' stages of group development 219–220
Frei, Frances 118
Freud, Sigmund 152, 153
Fulton County Schools Board (Atlanta, Georgia) 176–177

gaps, perceiving and closing 10, 13, *19*, 30, 77, 121, 123, 127, 132, 133, 210–211
gender roles 170–171, 172
generations 10, 12, 13, 83, 90, 157, 165, 168
George, Bill 151
Gibbs, Damany 103
goals 18, 27, 29, 31, 33, 36, 45, 66, 86, 111, 122, *125*, 142, 209, 244, 253
Goldman Sachs 141, 202
Goleman, Daniel 15
Google 10

Index

gratitude, practice of 106
Grenny, Joseph 249
Groysberg, Boris 174
Gudith, Daniela 265

habits 47, 162, 164, 221
Harris, Carla 199
Harvard Business School 10, 33, 80, 84, 86, 89, 91, 94, 118, 136, 144, 151, 156, 159, 174, 199
HBR Women at Work 141
hearing 97, 122, 133, 167, 240, 241, 252
help, asking for 73, 154–156, 169, 214, 225–226
Hierarchy Culture 174
Hinton, Tiffany 204–205
Hofstede, Geert 164
holidays 42, 256–257, 264 *see also* breaks
Hunt, Vivian 204–205
Hurry, Simon 240

Ibarra, Herminia 211
ideas 87, 178, 181, 256
identity 41, 59, 61, 161, 189, 208, 209
ikigai 82
Imes, Suzanne 91
impostor syndrome 55, 91–93
individualism 164
individualistic vs collectivistic cultures 171, 173
influence 54, 73, *126*, 230–231
information 69, 179, 262–264
inquiry 252, *252*
insecurities 25, 63, 128, 149
instructions 49, 223, 228, 230, 257
Integrated Culture Framework 174–175
intentions and intentionality 106–107, 250, 260–270
internal net worth 55, 58–63

internet 9–10, 22, 95, 269
interviews 15, 32, 44, 74, 91, 194–195, 267
introverts 188, 190, 213–214, 246

Jenner, Kendall 161
jobs, new 15, 67, 103, 115 *see also* new hires
Jobs, Steve 87
Johns, Shenece Garner 180, 183

Kapungu, Fungayi 144, 152
Klocke, Ulrich 265
knowledge 11, 22, 23, 24, 41, 103, 122, 130, 138, 145, 213, 236, 270

language 45, 74, 114, 121, *127*, 166, 221, 224, *232, 233, 234*
body 114, 123, 130, 148, 218, 236, 242, 243, 255
lateness, habitual 165–166
leaders and leadership 10, 16, 29, 39, 40, 41, 47–50, 63, 75, 124, 143–146, 151, 152, 193, 197, 236, 245
development 12, 91, 95, 134–135, 158, 233
learning 16, 22, 52, 66–67, 79, 103, 105, 136–137, 156
Lee, Jeremiah 174
Leke, Acha 34, 36, 68
Life Healthcare 246, 267
lifestyle 32, 82, 104, 213–214
limitations 86–89, 99, 151
listening 122–124
logic 118, 150, 197
London Business School 211

Mabuse, Zimasa Qolohle 28, 79, 129, 196
Madden, Dr Jennifer 30, 40, 102
Magwentshu, Nomfanelo 90–91, 116, 117, 162, 176, 200

Mahanyele, Phuti 29
Maier, Steven 98
Makhoalibe, Dr Puleng 57, 168, 243
managers 25–26, 42, 52, 109, 116–117, 121, *126*, 127–131, 135–137, 207, 214, 224–232, 234–235, 245, 246, 256, 257–258
managing up 130–131
Mandela, Nelson 203
Mark, Gloria 265
Market Culture 174
marketing 18, 21, 27, 161, 191, 192
Martin, Sharon 61
Mashaba, Connie 161, 192
maturity 149, 168, 233, 257
Maxwell, John 47
Mayer, John D 147
MBTI *see* Myers-Briggs Type Indicator
McKinsey & Company 10, 12, 13, 34, 36, 52–53, 67, 68, 75, 80, 90–91, 92, 95, 110, 116, 117, 118, 154, 158, 162, 167, 176, 177, 178–179, 186, 189–190, 193–194, 200, 204–205, 207, 208, 234, 250
McMillan, Ron 249
meditation and spirituality 103–104
mentality 55, 72–75, *76*, 80, 85, 99 *see also* mindset
Mentor 211
mentoring 25, 26, 38, 72, 79, 108, 115, 191, 214
mentors 19, 37, 38, 77, 79, 137–146, *140*, 160, 245
milestones 36, 44, 60, 83, 84, 111, *113*
mindset 20, *20*, 24, 44, 46, 51–107, *76*, *78*, 115, 137, 248, 259–260 *see also* story
Mindset: The New Psychology of Success (Dweck) 75–76
mistakes 13, 37, 51, 52, 62, 67, 171–172, 197, 198–199, 232–233
Mkhari, Ipeleng 46, 52, 90

Moloto, Refilwe 71–72, 255
Molotsi, Kagiso 64, 172
Montjane, Funeka 256
Morgan Stanley 199
Moumakwa, Penny 89, 170–171
Mpupuni, Thokozile Lewanika 44, 72–73, 110, 115, 119, 163, 165, 200, 220, 229, 232
Muhutu-Remy, Jocelyne 32, 35, 118, 124
Myers-Briggs Type Indicator (MBTI) 96, 158

myths 84, 190
Naspers South Africa 29
needs 58, 106, 120, 152, *153*, 153–155, *154*, *155*, 165, 192, 217
networking, professional 13, 72, 115–116, 118, 142, 213, 214
new hires 74, 91–93, 108, 116, 175–176, 178, 180, 236, 247–248
Niavas, Stefano 39, 54, 67, 137

Obama, President Barack 172
obstacles 35, 36, 54, 100, 111, 131, 145
offences, dealing with 132, *132*, 133, 134, 198
opinions 35, 89, 197, 207, 215, 232, *252*
opportunities 12, 30, 44, 52, 58, 62, 68, 145, 170, 213, 214, 237–239
Opportunity-Giver 211
optimism 104, 105
Option B: Facing Adversity, Building Resilience, and Finding Joy (Sandberg) 106
O'Reilly III, Charles A 174
Organisational Culture
  Assessment Instrument 174
  Profile 174
organisations and organisational cul-

ture 12, 23, 24, 39–40, 164, 171, 173–180, 206–213, 259–271
orientation 165, 174
outcomes 223, 250–251
overcommunicating 256–258
ownership 20, 34–41, 50, 58, 75, 76, 77, 106, 225, 226, 234, 257

Pandor, Aisha 146
Pareto Principle 20
participation 38–39, 40, 75, 178
partners 52, 176, 178, 193, 202, 204
patterns 191, 208 *see also* mindset
Patterson, Kerry 249
perceptions 59–60, 75, 194, 197, 199–200, 210, 215, 216, 229, 249 *see also* mindset
perfectionism 55, 61–63, 268, 270
performance 11, 30, 31, 36, 37, 38, 41, 52–53, 58, 59, 109, 117, 152–154, 196, 199, 236, 245
  rating 27, 52, 53, 67, 77, 79, 138
  review 38, 51, 52, 115, 194, 201–202, 245
permanence 104, 105
personal
  boundaries or constraints *127*, 223, 246–247
  branding and differentiation 18, 24, 30, 62, 75, 186–215, *188*, *198*, *212*, 216
  lives, divulging details of 68–69
Personal and Organisational Culture Alignment Plan *184*, 187, *188*
personalisation 104–105
personality 35, 56, 70, 96, 158–159, 161, 195, 213–214, 248, 256 *see also* Clifton-Strengths Assessment; Myers-Briggs Type Indicator
perspective 53, 81, 101, 138, 139, 165–166, 167, 194, *198*, 218, 219, 221, 223, 230, 231, 236, 237, 241, 252, 259

planning 16, 30–32, 35, 68, 93–94, 254, 262, 268
plan of action 53, 172, 183–185, *184*, 188, *188*, 192, 207, 210, *212*, 244, 245, 257, 258, 267, 270
PlayNicely 240
power 73, 203, 235, 248, 264 *see also* empowerment
PowerPoint presentation 74, 80, 81, 92, 139, 176, 177, 182, 197, 207–208, 237
practice 113–119, *120*, 136, 145, 173, 254
preparation 93, 117, 151, 233
presence 194, 210, 214
pressure 62, 70, 75, 85, 111, 167, 171, 177, 191, *252*, 256
Price, Jesse 174
PriceWaterhouseCoopers 48
Princeton 88
priorities and prioritisation 33, 35, 226–228, *227*, 264, 265–267
problem solving and management 35, 66, 67, 73, 80, 81, 97, 112, 167, 182, 253, *253*
procrastination 265, 268–270
professional
  delivery conversations 222, 224–233
  development 10, 11, 52, 59, 102–103, 216, 222, 223, 233–245, 256
  dress code 201–202, 205
professionalism 13, 172, 204, 229
progress 211, 245, *261*, 264, 266, 270
projects *19*, 111, *113*, 124, *125*, 131, 238–240
psychological safety 220
purpose 18, 26–30, 34, 61, 95–96, *140*, 175, 217, 227, 248
putting your head down 16, 72, 73, 74

qualifications 9, 10, 13, 15, 44, 58, 60, 110, 137, 171, 214

INDEX

questions and questioning 21–22, *140*, 145, 153, 159, 166–168, 196, 215, 235, 237, 242, 243, 250, 251–253, *253*
Quinn, Robert E 174

Rachelson, Donna 30, 186, 192, 193
racial discrimination and segregation 41, 70–71, 169, 171
racism in the workplace 11, 38, 39, 40–45
reflection *19*, 100, 134, 259, 267
Relationship Conversation Starters 131
relationships 16–18, 22–23, 25–28, 43, 45, 61, 70, 73, 74, 108, 109, *113*, 116, *120*, 127, 138, 140, 142, 146, 210–211 *see also* leaders and leadership
reports and reporting 36, *125–126*, 181, 182, 183, 225, 234, 237, 239, 240, 257
research 21, 35, 191, 199, 210, *212*, 230, 258
resilience 52, 67, 68, 99, 100, 105, 106, 157
resources 18, 111, *113*, *140*, 190, 225, 255, 261, 264 *see also* coaching; therapy
respect 128–129, 193, 206, 215, 231, 232
response 39, 134, 135, 152, 217, 221
responsibility *20*, 37, 45, 105, *113*, 236, 237, 241, 242, 243
rest 104, 122, 257, 267
risks and risk-taking 65, 67, *140*, 171–172, 174, 196, *198*, 220, *261*
roles 39, 47, 92, *113*, 170, 172–173, 178, 211, 219, 251
Rowling, JK 65
Rumi 55

sacrifices 27, 33–34, 115, 180, 203, 239, 247
Salovey, Peter 147
sameness 122
Sandberg, Sheryl 106

scenarios 26, 67–68, 86, 115, 167, 222–249, 250–251
schedule 264, 265–266, 267, 268
Schultz, Howard 209
Seales, Amanda 135
Secret List of Offences (SLOO) 132, *132*
self-
awareness 55, 56–57, 216
doubt 58–63
investment 100–107
talk 55, 89–91, 101
worth 60–63, 99
Self-Confidence vs Arrogance Comparison chart 187, *188*
Seligman, Martin 98, 104
seniors 92, 167, 197, 199, 203, 233, 246
sense of self 87, 90, 151, *198*
Sepah, Cameron 173
setbacks 51–52, 90, 102, 105
sexism 40, 43, 97
70-20-10 guidelines for learning 16
Shanduka Group 29
sharing *126*, *198*, 199, 213, 214, 218–219, 234, 245, 251, 256
shortcuts 191
skills 13, 15, *19*, 74, 80, 92, 93, 118, 122, 209, 216, 236, 248
SLOO *see* Secret List of Offences
social media 22, 95, 122, 194, 210, 213, 214, 269
solutions 35, 40, *66*, *76*, 228, 232, 250, *252*, 253, *253*, 256
speaking up 62, 65, 67, 166–168
sponsors *19*, 138–139, *140*, 141, 143, 145, 146, 185, 199, 238, 244, 245, 266
sponsorship 70, 72, 141, 144, 145
stakeholders 111, 119, 132, 247, 256, 257, 267
Standard Bank 256

Index

standards 48, 55, 61, 75, 80, 81, 189, 229
Stanford Business School 66
Starbucks 209
Steele, Claude 97
stereotypes 41, 42–43, 69, 169
stereotype threat 55, 97–98
'storming' phase 219–220
story 10, 57, 100, 103, *125*, 133, 145, 152–158, 209
Strategiser 211
strategising 13, 18, 51, 73, 74, 182–183, 214
strengths 100, *125*, 127, 176, 234, 242, 244
structure 64, 96–97, *126*, 138, 174, 182, 194
success 15, 29–30, 31, 32–34, 41, 58, 72, 74, 91–94, 110, 115, 165–172, 178, 239, 267
suggestions 65–66, *252*
Switzler, Al 249

Tamale, Ronald 30, 83, 146–147, 181–182, 202, 240
tasks *19*, 29, 36, 44, *113*, 224, 228, 235, 257, 267–269
Taylor, Tina 38, 61, 64, 141–142, 143, 166, 197, 206, 213, 245
teamwork and teammates 52, 65–66, 70, 73, 97, 116, 121, 149, 174, 217, 220, 232, 238, 256–257
tension 111, 112, 120, 127, 130, 132, 160, 247–254, 260
therapy 105–106
thought patterns and processes 54–56, *153*, 153–155, *154*, *155*
time and timeliness 18, 20, 74, 83–86, 111, 158, 165–166, 207, 225–229, 235, 261–268
trade-offs 33–34

training 16, 23–24
triggers 25, *126*, 149–150
trust 113–114, 118–119, 129, 145, 149, 179
truth 56–57, 130, 190
Tuckman, Bruce 219
Turner, Nat 135
12-step programme (Wilson) 56

uncertainty avoidance 164
United States 34, 47, 88, 97, 98, 161–162, 170, 171, 190
universities and colleges 11, 16, 88, 92, 94 *see also names of specific universities and colleges*
University of Alabama 70
University of California, San Francisco 173
University of Michigan 174
urgency, communicating sense of 255–256

values 32, 49, 58, 59, 60–61, 113–114, 115, 119, *125*, 127, 196
victims and victors *20*, 53
vision 28, 29, 47, 48, 82–83
voice 74–75, 90–91, 93, 171

Wallace, Governor George 70
weaknesses 48, 56–57, 100, 169, 210, 233
Webster, Timothy Maurice 25, 55–56, 122, 156, 157, 191, 203, 208
'What Great Listeners Actually Do' (Zenger and Folkman) 123
'what if' exercise 67
Wilson, Bill 56
Winfrey, Oprah 65, 66, 81, 237
words 177, 199, 220

work
   environment 12, 14, 16, 20, 40, 79–80, 92–93, 96, 97, 206, 213–214 *see also* cultural intelligence; organisations and organisational environment
   ethic 74, 109, 128, 229
   frustrations 9, 96, 110
   impact at 20, 24, *24*, 45–46, *46*, 50, 114, 182, 200–206, 259–271
   nature of 22–23
   relationships 11, 12, 16, 24, 25–26, 61, 71–72, 74, 108–159, *113*, *120*, 162, 170, 247–254

Yale 88

Zenger, Jack 123

CPSIA information can be obtained
at www.ICGtesting.com
Printed in the USA
BVHW041606160321
602658BV00013B/719